Your Psychology
Project

Your Psychology Project

The Essential Guide

Jennifer Evans

SAGE Publications
Los Angeles • London • New Delhi • Singapore

First published 2007

SAGE Publications Ltd
1 Oliver's Yard
55 City Road
London EC1Y 1SP

SAGE Publications Inc.
2455 Teller Road
Thousand Oaks, California 91320

SAGE Publications India Pvt Ltd
B 1/I 1 Mohan Cooperative Industrial Area
Mathura Road, New Delhi 110 044
India

SAGE Publications Asia-Pacific Pte Ltd
33 Pekin Street #02-01
Far East Square
Singapore 048763

British Library Cataloguing in Publication data
A catalogue record for this book is available from the British Library

Library of Congress Control Number: 2006939947

ISBN 978-1-4129-2231-9
ISBN 978-1-4129-2232-6 (pbk)

Typeset by C&M Digitals (P) Ltd., Chennai, India
Printed on paper from sustainable resources
Printed in Great Britain by The Cromwell Press Ltd, Trowbridge, Wiltshire

This book is dedicated to Matthew

BRIEF CONTENTS

CONTENTS

PREFACE

This book aims to give undergraduate psychology students clear guidelines in writing their psychology project, from both quantitative and qualitative paradigms. Students often complain of the need for practical examples in order to master the skill of writing a project successfully. This book aims to very clearly map out the requirements of a project in psychology, and to illustrate ways to meet these aims.

Many of my students come for their first supervision meetings with one major question: does their research question meet the requirements of a good project; is it good enough? In my experience, students are often unable to make the connections with the theoretical application of the requirements of a good project, for example addressing a significant psychological phenomenon, and making clear the relevance to the advancement of psychological knowledge, or offering reasonable interpretations of the research results with reference to the existing psychological literature. Students often find this requirement difficult to address; they find it abstract and do not know where to begin. In theory they understand these concepts, but are unable to apply them to their project idea. This book demonstrates, with the use of practical examples, how this can be accomplished.

This book also aims to equip students with the knowledge, skills and abilities to carry out and write up their projects. The book in essence acts as a survival manual or guide, and covers all areas of a psychology project, from conception of an idea, to writing up the final draft. This book not only guides students through examples illustrating how to do things right, but also how to do the right things. Psychology is often referred to as primary training in thought, in how to think critically about concepts and constructs, but also in how to think creatively and innovatively. It is through this capacity to be innovative that the psychology knowledge base advances.

This text focuses on the fundamental aspect of a successful project, which is the role of the research question. The research question or hypothesis governs the appropriateness of the method of inquiry, and hence the appropriate analytical procedures, that will be utilised to answer the research question posed. Students often fail to see this pertinent relationship at the early stages of the project, which can cause difficulties later on in the process. The book will also deal with the thoughts involved in thinking through the whole research process, in order to create a seamless piece of work.

The final year project is often referred to as a thesis or dissertation; this is generally due to the fact that students carrying out a quantitative research project are required to make an argument and then try and prove it. For a long time, this was the norm, as quantitative research dominated psychology. However, with the changing nature of research within psychology, the term 'thesis' (or 'dissertation') no longer covers the range of research projects that undergraduate psychology students undertake in their final year. For example, qualitative research of an exploratory nature does not make assumptions and arguments from the onset; rather theory is generated following data collection. Therefore the term 'project' is more descriptive of the range of research that undergraduate students undertake in their final year as part of their degree.

Suggestions for further reading

To detail every method of inquiry that could be used for your psychology project is beyond the scope of this book. The essentials and main ideas behind different types of research for your project are presented. Suggestions for further reading are given at the end of each chapter so that you can delve further into specific areas that are important for your own project.

The book does not go through the basics of setting up new project files in NVivo or data files in SPSS. This text makes the assumption that, as final year students, you already have a working knowledge of these applications, but don't worry if you haven't – you will be directed towards relevant further reading.

ACKNOWLEDGEMENTS

A big thank you to the editorial and production staff at Sage Publications Ltd in London. In particular I would like to thank Michael Carmichael, Emily Jenner and Claire Reeve.

A thank you is also owed to all my students who have, over the years, asked some very interesting questions about their psychology projects. I am very grateful to the past students who offered some very useful advice for students about to embark on their psychology project. In particular I would like to thank Shane Barry, Joanna Elomari, Danielle Lyons, John O'Donaghue, Lyndsey Phelan, Nereko Lekuona, Sinead O'Loughlin, Jillian Woods and Jiaying Zhao. I would like to thank Shane Barry and Sinead O'Loughlin for the use of examples from their research projects which are used throughout. I would like to thank Ian Tyndal for constructively reviewing some of the chapters.

Finally I would like to thank my parents Myles and Dolores, and my husband Matthew, whose support is always unconditional. I would also like to thank my grandparents for financially supporting me when I first started my own primary degree in psychology. And a special thank you to Polly, for sitting by my feet during the write-up of this text; I owe her hundreds of walks.

UNIT 1

SETTING YOURSELF UP FOR SUCCESS

Introduction

Generally, students of psychology are required to undertake a project in the final year of their degree. This is often a daunting task, using existing knowledge gained throughout the degree usually with minimal supervision. Therefore the successful completion of the psychology project is often the most challenging academic requirement a student will face during their undergraduate degree. The process involves creativity and innovation, critical thinking, persistence, discipline, independence, and also feelings of uneasiness and insecurity. The good news is that it is possible to approach your final year psychology project with an attitude of confidence, and positive, forward thinking as opposed to anxiety and apprehension.

It is comforting to learn that those students who are most successful in completing their psychology projects are those who have set themselves up for success. These are the students who have put the appropriate structures in place, to aid them during the research process. *Unit 1: Setting Yourself Up for Success* makes it possible for every student to learn how to carefully plan, and lay down, solid and realistic foundations to facilitate successful completion of their research project.

Chapter 1 of this essential guide, *The Psychology Project as a Means of Acquiring Knowledge*, begins by broadly dealing with psychology as a scientific discipline and demonstrates that the essence of science is described as a way of thinking, the systematic logic used in asking and answering questions, and producing more knowledge. The role of the research project is therefore a means of inquiry; through formulating questions and finding answers to them, students add to the knowledge base.

Chapter 2 entitled *Ethics for Research in Psychology* deals with the crucial issue of ethics in psychological research, in the planning, execution and reporting of both quantitative and qualitative research. The chapter also highlights the codes of ethics, laid down by a number of major professional bodies, to act as a shared moral framework for making ethical decisions.

Chapter 3, *Choosing a Topic and the Research Proposal*, deals with the practicalities of evaluating topics from your potential list of topics, in order to choose the most appropriate one. The chapter also focuses on how to formulate a good research question, and the role of creativity and innovation. The functional importance of the research proposal is also highlighted, which is often neglected by undergraduate students.

Chapter 4, *A Connected and Convincing Argument*, deals with the appropriate style for writing your research project, and describes the importance of your project delivering a convincing and connected argument with an inherent logical structure, in order to produce a seamless piece of work. The importance of clear communication and effective writing is highlighted, and some tips for scientific writing are provided.

Chapter 5, *Self-Management*, deals with the important skills and meta-competencies that can be developed by students in order to successfully endure the research process, from the conception of an original idea to the final write-up of the psychology project. These foundation chapters demonstrate that completing your project is very much a personal endeavour involving the whole person. Chapter 5 addresses important aspects of self-regulation, as a way of scheduling, being organised, timetabled and self-managed. The importance of goal setting, and the role of short-term wins are highlighted as successful motivational strategies. Building on the theme of self-regulation, different time-management techniques, and strategies for overcoming procrastination are demonstrated. Emphasis is also placed on the role of self-management as a very effective mechanism for managing the stress or anxiety of the undergraduate psychology project, for example setting realistic short-term goals and priorities to help reduce anxiety and create a sense of control and accomplishment. Ways to overcome writer's block are also included, and the importance of tailoring a system of strategies that meets individual needs will be highlighted throughout.

Chapter 6, *Maximising Supervision*, deals with this often-neglected area. Students often under-estimate the valuable resource that supervision is. This chapter deals with how to maximise the benefits of supervision, by focusing on the establishment of the student–supervisor relationship, and on practical approaches to maximising feedback.

Chapter 7, *How to Handle the Research Literature*, deals with ways of handling the research literature, from sources of the literature to evaluating it. The role of the research literature for psychology as a science, and the importance of reading academic journals as opposed to popular journals that may not adhere to scientific rigour are highlighted. Students are often intimidated by the vastness of the research literature in psychology and the related social sciences, so some of the major sources of the academic literature are provided, in order to give the student some visibility in the literature fog. The main journals in psychology are also dealt with, along with the major electronic databases that are available. Some tips are also given for using the search engines of the major electronic databases. Finally, the chapter illustrates useful ways to organise the literature you have reviewed, in order to use time as effectively as possible.

Chapter 8, *How to Write a Good Introduction*, deals with the introduction chapter of your psychology project. It highlights how writing the literature review comprises science and art. This section also deals with practical issues, such as what to include, and how long the literature review should be. It is demonstrated that length should not be used as a substitute for tight organisation and clear writing. Advice from Sternberg (2003) regarding the importance of reliability, validity and internal consistency in the literature review is also given. The chapter also presents five useful strategies to highlight the importance of your study, and focuses on the importance of making your hypotheses very explicit at the end of the introduction.

Chapter 9, *Sampling Considerations*, this brief chapter deals with the important issue of sampling for your research project. Sampling issues are important for both quantitative and qualitative methods of inquiry, but they are considered at different times during the research process. For example, in qualitative research they are generally most important during the simultaneous data analysis and data-collection phase, while in quantitative research they are most important during the planning and design stage of the research process. Some popular probability and non-probability techniques are also illustrated.

Chapter 10, entitled *Sourcing Materials and Measures for Psychological Research*, provides useful information on how to source both published and unpublished tests and measures, and therefore to save valuable time for the undergraduate researcher of psychology. The chapter also deals with the very important issue of ethics for test users. Issues of reliability and validity are also dealt with in an attempt to aid the undergraduate student in becoming an objective and knowledgeable consumer of the vast number of psychological materials and measures that are available.

1

THE PSYCHOLOGY PROJECT AS A MEANS
OF ACQUIRING KNOWLEDGE

Objectives

On reading this chapter you should:

- understand how psychology operates as a scientific discipline;
- understand the role of the undergraduate psychology project as a means of acquiring knowledge; and
- be aware of the usefulness of viewing qualitative and quantitative research situations as opposite ends of a continuum, as opposed to two distinctly separate approaches to inquiry.

Overview

Section 1.1 deals broadly with how psychology operates as a scientific discipline, and demonstrates how science can be viewed as a way of thinking (which involves asking and answering questions) and to produce more knowledge. Section 1.2 goes on to consider the psychology project as a means of acquiring knowledge. Section 1.3 deals with acquiring knowledge in psychology both quantitatively and qualitatively – it is proposed that it is useful to view the two approaches as research situations on opposite ends of a continuum, as opposed to two distinct approaches to research and inquiry within psychology. Finally Section 1.4 gives a brief overview of the importance of your research question in choosing a quantitative or qualitative method of inquiry.

1.1   What is the Purpose of Science for Psychology?

Often when people think of the word 'science', the first image that comes to mind is one of test tubes, computers and people in white laboratory coats. Some sciences, such as physics and chemistry, deal with the physical and material world, for example with chemicals and electricity. These natural sciences or hard sciences are generally the basis of new technology, and therefore receive a lot of publicity.

The social and behavioural sciences, such as psychology, sociology and anthropology, involve the study of people, including their beliefs, attitudes and behaviours. People do not always associate these disciplines with the word science, and are sometimes referred to as 'soft sciences'. The reference to soft does not mean that these disciplines lack scientific rigour or that they are sloppy or limp; it refers to their subject matter. Human behaviour and social life are far more fluid and transient than the tangible composites of chemistry and physics. However, the natural sciences are not made more scientific than psychology by virtue of their laboratory equipment. It is important to note that although many processes of inquiry produce scientific tools and products, it is the process of inquiry or way of thinking that encapsulates the essence of science.

The essence of science is this way of thinking. Science therefore encompasses a process of formulating specific questions, and finding answers to these questions, in order to gain a better understanding of phenomenon. These gains in our understanding produce and increase our knowledge base. This is reiterated by Chalmers' (1990) statement that science aims to produce knowledge of the world. Therefore, scientific research in psychology involves posing a question and then initiating a systematic process to obtain valid answers to that question. This process is carried out utilising the scientific method, which serves the basis for scientific inquiry. The overall goal of psychology as a science is to understand behaviour and phenomenon. Using the scientific method, understanding comprises four important goals of being able to *describe*, *predict*, *understand* and *control* behaviour or phenomena.

1.2   The Psychology Project as a Means of Acquiring Knowledge

The psychology project is an integral component of the undergraduate student's curriculum. Psychology departments continue this long tradition of inquiry, through the requirement of the final year project. The role of the research project is therefore a means of inquiry; through formulating questions and finding answers to them, students add to their knowledge base. Figure 1.1 depicts the cyclical recursive nature of the research process, and reflects the thinking process whereby new information results in new knowledge and understanding.

Through this process of inquiry, the primary purpose of the undergraduate psychology project is to provide the student with practice in asking and answering questions. In carrying out your project, you gain valuable experience and training in planning, conducting, analysing and presenting an independent

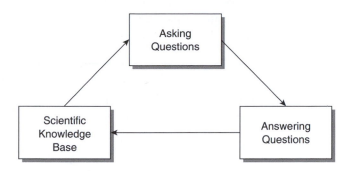

Figure 1.1   The scientific process of inquiry

research project. More specifically, you will develop the necessary skills involved in conducting library research, academic writing, designing research, collecting, analysing and interpreting data. Also, on a more general level, you will learn about the conventions and requirements of psychological research, which will equip you for post-graduate research, and for communication within the scientific field of psychology.

1.3   Quantitative and Qualitative Methods of Inquiry

A method is a systematic approach to a piece of research. Psychologists use a wide range of methods of inquiry. There are a number of ways in which the methods used by psychologists are classified, the most common being between quantitative and qualitative methods. Camic, Rhodes and Yardley (2004) note that it is time to abandon the view that what separates quantitative and qualitative approaches is whether to count or not to count, measure or not measure, sample or not sample. This view is supported by Shweder (1996, p. 179) because all social science research counts and measures in some way or another, the true difference is what to count and measure, and what one discovers.

It can therefore prove useful to view the quantitative and qualitative approaches to research in psychology as situations on opposite ends of a continuum representing the field of psychological research. Figure 1.2 illustrates that at one polar end of the continuum, there is pure quantitative research, apparent by clearly defined variables, theories and hypotheses. On the opposite end of the continuum is pure qualitative research in psychology, which relies on the subjective interpretation of cases and events. The qualitative and quantitative research undertaken by undergraduate students generally falls away from the polar ends of such a continuum. Quantitative research aims at having external as well as internal validity. Students also recognise the implications of very sterile laboratory conditions which are not transferable to real life settings, while qualitative research aims at making some contribution to

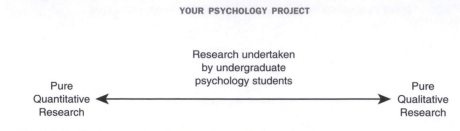

Figure 1.2   Continuum of qualitative and quantitative research

theory and application in general as opposed to developing a new theory for each case.

In between these two polar extremes, therefore, are numerous different approaches to research. With this in mind it is easier to see how both approaches may share some common ground with regard to psychology as a science. Qualitative research that investigates cases, which may be utterances, narratives, attitudes, phenomenon, events, etc., are comparable to quantitative research that investigates variables and constructs. This derivation arises from the idea that cases have the same analysable features as variables, and hence a shared scientific foundation exists. For example, cases can have varying characteristics, just like characteristics of a variable can vary. Therefore it is possible to investigate similarities and differences among such cases.

The debate as to whether quantitative and qualitative research methods can be complementary is ongoing. Although the two styles share basic principles of science, the two approaches differ in significant ways. Each has its strengths and weaknesses. I agree with King (1994) that the best research often combines features of both approaches, in order to build a more complete picture of the phenomenon. For example, there may be two stages in the same piece of research, with a qualitative approach yielding initial ideas which can then by investigated via a quantitative approach. This also coincides with Todd (2003) who has also noted that although the two approaches have traditionally been seen as competing paradigms, in recent years researchers have begun to argue that the divide is artificial. That the distinction between quantitative and qualitative can be a false one is obvious when they are viewed as two approaches to studying the same phenomena. However, the problem arises when they provide different answers (Clark-Carter, 2004). Nonetheless, the distinction can be a convenient device for classifying methods.

1.4   How to Choose the Appropriate Method of Inquiry: Quantitative or Qualitative?

Your choice of method of inquiry for your psychology project will largely rely on your research aims and your research question. The role of the research question will be dealt with in more detail in later chapters; however, it is beneficial at this point to briefly deal with the issue. For example, if you have developed a research question that addresses causes of behaviour, it will be appropriate to carry out an experimental research project in order to answer your research question. On the other hand, if your aims are to describe a phenomena from the participant's own frame of reference, then qualitative methods would usually be appropriate.

Imagine your goal is to refine an area within psychology that has already been thoroughly researched, in this situation you might want to use a tightly controlled experimental design to investigate a cause and effect. However, if you are researching a new area within psychology, you might decide on a more exploratory qualitative method. Also, if you are interested in people's behaviour, but not in their beliefs and intentions, an experiment might be appropriate. Or if you want to know the meaning that the behaviour has for the participant, then you may want to employ a qualitative method of inquiry.

Undergraduate students often use quantitative methods of inquiry, such as the true experiments, quasi-experiments, correlational and differential research. Some common qualitative methods of inquiry are semi-structured interviews, grounded theory and interpretative phenomenological analysis.

Summary

The essence of science is the systematic logic used in asking and answering questions, and producing more knowledge. The role of the research project is therefore a means of inquiry: through formulating questions and finding answers to them, students add to their knowledge base. It is useful to view quantitative and qualitative approaches to research as situations on opposite ends of a continuum, as opposed to two distinct approaches to research and inquiry in psychology. Whether you use a qualitative or quantitative method of inquiry for your project will largely depend on your research aims and your research question.

Further Reading

Camic, P., Rhodes, J. and Yardley, L. (eds) (2004) *Qualitative Research in Psychology: Expanding Perspectives in Methodology and Design.* Washington: APA.

Chalmers, A. (1990) *Science & its Fabrication.* Buckingham: Open University Press.

Ragin, C. (1987) *The Comparative Method: Moving Beyond Qualitative & Quantitative Strategies.* Berkeley and London: University of California Press.

Todd, Z., Nerlich, B., McKeown, S. and Clarke, D. (eds) (2004) *Mixing Methods in Psychology.* Hove and New York: Psychology Press, Taylor & Francis.

2

ETHICS FOR
RESEARCH IN PSYCHOLOGY

Objectives

On reading this chapter you should:

- be aware of the major functions of ethics codes, and why they play such a crucial role in psychological research;
- be familiar with the four common overarching principles, which the major standards are based around;
- understand the interdependence of ethics and the research process;
- be able to make the necessary ethical decisions involved in the planning of your research project, in the status and welfare of your participants, and in the interpretation of your data; and
- also be aware of the noteworthy issues involved in ethics for qualitative research.

Overview

Chapter 2 deals with the crucial issue of ethical consideration for research in psychology, and more specifically for you, the undergraduate psychology student, about to embark on your first piece of independent research. It is important to realise that one of the major judgement errors made by undergraduate psychology students is that they fail to realise the importance and relevance of ethical principles to their research project. The vital role played by ethics in the planning, execution and reporting of quantitative and qualitative research cannot be overstated. Instead of seeing psychological science and ethics as separate, a superior understanding recognises their essential interdependence. As will become apparent, ethical issues must be addressed at all stages of the research process. The topic of ethics is therefore presented in this section (Setting Yourself up for Success) to highlight its importance.

Two major purposes for codes of ethics have been cited in the literature (Pettifor, 2004). Codes of ethics promote best practice by providing aspirational principles that encourage reflection and decision-making within a moral framework, and also act to regulate professional behaviour, through monitoring and through disciplinary action against those who violate prescriptive and enforceable standards of conduct (Sinclair, 1987; Lindsay, 1996; Pettifor, 1996; Fisher, 2003; Pack-Brown and Williams, 2003). It is crucial that you are aware that the goal of ethics is to encourage ethical thinking (Pack-Brown, 2003) for your research project as opposed to mere rule-following. Rules tend to proliferate as a function of the virtual impossibility of covering every conceivable situation (Stark, 1998) that the undergraduate psychology researcher may encounter. Furthermore, lists of rules often encourage an unthinking cookbook approach to ethical conduct that can lead to misapplication of the rules (Stark, 1998). Ethics, therefore, lend moral structure to your decision-making throughout the research project: from the planning of your study, your treatment of participants, to the interpretation of your results.

Section 2.1 highlights the codes of ethics laid down by a number of professional bodies. The Draft Universal Declaration (2005) and the Meta-Code of the EFPA (1995) provide a shared moral framework, organising ethical standards around four overarching principles, which is shown to act as a very useful template for professional organisations to adapt their code around.

Section 2.2 then considers ethical issues in planning your study, in the status and welfare of participants, and in the interpretation of research. It is also important to note that although these guidelines exist and are actively enforced by each organisation, there is no national or international legislation to enforce them. It is therefore up to individual universities and colleges to enforce these ethical principles, which is usually done in the form of ethic review committees or boards, and it is up to you, the psychology student, to uphold them. Finally Section 2.3 pays special attention to some ethical issues arising from qualitative research.

2.1   Shared Moral Framework

Clearly, ethics is the study of good and bad, and of the general nature of morals in different societies (Sartorius, 1999, p. 3). Pendersen (1995) proposed universalism of ethics codes, universal values based on common humanity, respect for the diversity of beliefs, and standards based on differences in culture, religion and political systems. Similarly Gauthier (2003) proposes that psychologists have the right to useful ethical guidance for their professional and research behaviour, and that all individuals have the right to effective protection from the misuse of psychology. This coincides with the International Union of Psychological Science (IUPsyS) who, in 2002, mandated a working group to prepare a Draft Universal Declaration of Ethical Principles for Psychologists (Pettifor 2004), which was presented in June 2005. This pragmatic scheme involved the IUPsyS, the International Association of Applied Psychology (IAAP) and also the International Association of Cross-Cultural Psychology (IACCP).

The Draft Universal Declaration (2005) describes ethical principles and values for the international psychology community. It provides a shared moral framework, organising all ethical standards around four overarching principles, which are clearly the embodiment of guidelines based on values and principles, within what is technically a code. The Meta-Code of the EFPA (1995) is based around four similar principles, developed to act as a very useful template for other organisations to adapt their code around. Many professional bodies have structured their code of ethics around these templates, as illustrated in Table 2.1: the Canadian Code of Ethics for Psychologists (CPA, 2000), the Code of Ethics: For Psychologists Working in Aotearoa/New Zealand (New Zealand Psychological Society, 2002), the Ethical Principles of Psychologists and Code of Conduct (APA, 2002) and Code of Professional Ethics (PSI, 2003). The British Psychological Society is currently revising The Ethical Principles for Conducting Research with Human Participants (BPS, 1978; q.v.), which share many similarities with the common codes.

2.2   Ethical Considerations in Psychological Research

It is important to understand the interdependence of ethics and the research process. Ethical considerations during the research process can be categorised into three major areas as seen in Figure 2.1.

Planning the study

When planning a research project, the codes of ethics mentioned above deal with the researcher's basic problem of balancing the need to discover new principles of behaviour with the need to protect participants. Research ethics can no longer be viewed as a set of rules to be applied, but rather as a way of reasoning about constructing a relationship with participants (York University Task Force on Ethical Issues in Research, 1992).

There are a number of things for you, the undergraduate psychology student, to consider before embarking on your research project. In planning your study it is vital to consider its ethical acceptability under the relevant ethics codes. If an ethical issue is unclear, it is important to resolve the issue with your supervisor, or your institutions ethics review board. The important role of the research proposal is highlighted. As will be drawn out in the following chapter, the process of writing the proposal will aid you in making intelligent and ethical research decisions, and also in flagging any potential ethical concerns for your supervisor.

You should ask yourself about the worthiness of your proposed project, and whether it will contribute to psychology in some meaningful way. It is appreciated that poor science is unethical. Rosenthal (1994) proposes considering

Table 2.1   Combination of major codes of ethics

Universal Declaration of Ethical Principles for Psychologists (2005)	
Principle I	Respect for the Dignity of All Human Beings
Principle II	Competent Caring for the Well-Being of Others
Principle III	Integrity
Principle IV	Professional and Scientific Responsibilities to Society
European Federation of Psychologists Association (EFPA) Meta-Code of Ethics (1995)	
Principle 2.1	Respect for a Person's Rights and Dignity
Principle 2.2	Competence
Principle 2.3	Responsibility
Principle 2.4	Integrity
Canadian Code of Ethics for Psychologists 3rd edn (2002)	
Principle I	Respect for the Dignity of Persons
Principle II	Responsible Caring
Principle III	Integrity in Relationships
Principle IV	Responsibility to Society
Code of Ethics: For Psychologists Working in Aotearoa/ New Zealand (2002)	
Principle 1	Respect for the Dignity of Persons and Peoples
Principle 2	Responsible Caring
Principle 3	Integrity in Relationships
Principle 4	Social Justice and Responsibility to Society
Ethical Principles of Psychologists and Code of Conduct (APA, 2002)	
Principle A	Beneficence and Non-maleficence
Principle B	Fidelity and Responsibility
Principle C	Integrity
Principle D	Justice
Principle E	Respect for People's Rights and Dignity
Code of Professional Ethics (PSI, 2003)	
Principle 1	Respect for the Rights and Dignity of the Person
Principle 2	Competence
Principle 3	Responsibility
Principle 4	Integrity
Ethical Principles for Conducting Research with Human Participants (BPS, 1978; q.v.)	
Principle 1	Introduction
Principle 2	General
Principle 3	Consent
Principle 4	Deception
Principle 5	Debriefing
Principle 6	Withdrawal from the investigation
Principle 7	Confidentiality
Principle 8	Protection of Participants
Principle 9	Observational Research
Principle 10	Giving Advice

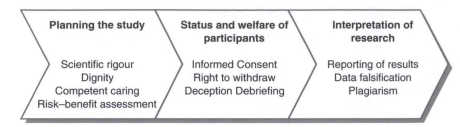

Figure 2.1   Three major stages for ethical considerations

the quality of research as a factor in ethical decisions, 'everything else being equal, research that is of a higher scientific quality is more ethically defensible' (p. 127). It is unethical to ask people to participate in your study if it has little or no likelihood, because of poor conceptualisation and design, of producing meaningful results or furthering scientific knowledge. Your research project must be planned so that the chance of misleading results is minimised. It is important to realise that if your project has flawed methodology, your results will be of no value and the time of the participants will have been wasted.

Planned steps must always be taken to protect and ensure the dignity and welfare of all your participants. Inadequate attention to respect for person, beneficence and justice can affect the scientific viability and validity of your research. Part of the planning stage also involves determining the degree of risk to be encountered by participants. Under the principle of competent caring, you are required to demonstrate an active concern for the well-being of your participants. This can be achieved by minimising the invasiveness of your study. Rosnow and Rosenthal (1997) developed a risk–benefit model to assist the researcher. The basic dilemma is to weigh the scientific value of the study being planned against the degree of intrusion on those contributing data.

This model demonstrated in figure 2.2. is useful for judging whether your research proposal will be passed or rejected. A study falling at A would not be approved as the risks are high and the benefits are low, whereas a study falling at D would be approved because the risks are low but the benefits are high. Obviously this is the ideal situation for your psychology project. Studies that fall along the B–C axis can be difficult to determine whether they would be approved or not, and you should stay clear of any ideas for your research that fall along this axis. For example, although a study that falls at C has low risk, the benefits of carrying out the piece of research are also low; therefore it is unlikely to yield any benefit and would probably not be approved. A study that falls at B has high benefits but also has high risks. The undergraduate psychology student is advised to avoid these research situations, as you may not have the experience to minimise the risks and maximise the benefits that an experienced researcher can.

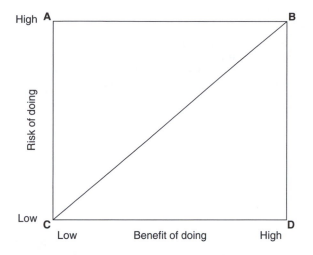

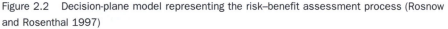

Figure 2.2   Decision-plane model representing the risk–benefit assessment process (Rosnow and Rosenthal 1997)

Status and welfare of participants

Informed consent and withdrawal

It is very important to ensure that all the participants that take part in your study are volunteers. As noted by Jonas (1969), only the authenticity of volunteering overcomes the depersonalising effect of being treated as a token or sample in an experiment. A major ethical consideration concerns the status of your participants, focusing on the issues of informed consent, deception and the right of participants to withdraw from your study at any time. You are required to make it crystal clear to your volunteers that even after they have consented to participate in your study, they can leave at any time. You are also required to inform your participants of any objectives of your study which might affect their willingness to participate.

Participants should give informed consent formally, after they have been informed of the nature of your study, and are invited to sign a consent form (see Figure 2.3).

It has been argued that true informed consent is impossible in qualitative research (Eisner, 1991) – the researcher often follows up new and promising leads, which cannot be anticipated in advance. For qualitative research of this nature, it is important that you inform your participants of this trend in the data-collection process. At least then they will be aware that this could happen. Your participants may think that you have deceived them if a partic-ular issue comes about, and they weren't informed of it.

15

An Investigation of the Self-Reference Effect

The purpose of this study to determine how accurately people can remember information related to themselves. If you participate, you will be required to complete a computerised task involving word lists and questions. The task will take approximately 10 minutes to complete. The exact hypothesis that is being investigated will be explained to you at the conclusion of your participation. If you have any questions or concerns about your
participation or about the study, you may contact me at _____

I have read the description of the investigation of the Self-Reference Effect, and I voluntarily agree to participate. I understand that I can withdraw from the study at any time, without penalty, and that my participation and the record of my performance will be kept strictly confidential.

When the entire investigation has been completed (tick the relevant box)

Would ☐ Would not ☐
like a brief summary of the overall results.

Signature of Participant   Date
_____   _____

Figure 2.3   An example of a consent form

Also note that if you plan to use children, i.e. anyone under the age of 18, as your participants it is very important to get not only *their* consent, but also the consent of a parent/guardian. You should also make sure that you are up to speed with guidelines and acts relating to using children in research.

Deception

During your research you should continually ask yourself about your relationship with the participants. Are you telling the truth? Has a climate of trust developed? The principle of integrity promotes the value of truthfulness and accurate communication, therefore, the intentional deception of participants over the purpose and general nature of your project should be avoided whenever possible. Also the experience of deception can cause many adverse effects, which violates the principle of care.

However, there are a number of psychological processes that are modifiable by participants if they knew that these processes were being studied. In such cases the statement of the research hypotheses in advance of consent and collection of the data would confound the research, by affecting the construct validity of the variables under investigation. There is universal recognition within the codes of ethics that a distinction can be made between withholding some of the details of the hypotheses under investigation and deliberately misleading participants of the purpose of the research. In this situation it is imperative that you discuss and get the go-ahead from your supervisor.

Confidentiality

The principle of respect for the dignity of all human beings involves upholding the value of privacy of participants, and the value of confidentiality of the personal information they disclose. Ensuring confidentiality has a potential scientific benefit of improving the internal validity of your study if it leads participants to be more honest and open when responding (Blanck, 1992).

If your study could potentially cause your participants some form of social embarrassment, you should keep their responses anonymous. In this circumstance, it is important to ask participants to refrain from using their names or any other identifying information. It is important that you do not include a space for a signature on the consent form. However, this level of anonymity is not always possible. In such cases, you can keep participants' responses confidential by simply removing any identifying information from their records once you have used them, and replace with a code. If you will need to test participants on more that one occasion, random numbers can be assigned to participants at the beginning of your experimentation.

Debriefing

As the principle of competent caring suggests, you are ethically obligated to seek ways to benefit participants even after your research is completed. An effective way of meeting this standard is to provide the participants of your study with a post-experimental session known as debriefing. It is imperative that you do not view your participants as a means to an end, as mere pawns or objects of which to collect data on or from. You must respect their unique worth and inherent dignity. Remember that once your data has been collected, your responsibility towards your participants does not end there.

Once your project is finished, or when you have analysed and interpreted your results, you should offer your participants a debriefing session. The amount of time spent debriefing depends on the complexity of your study, but generally, a properly conducted debriefing session can take longer than your experimentation. During this session, you should answer any questions your participants have regarding any aspect of your project. It is also important that you are explicit about their role in your study, and explain your research question and the main findings. Smith and Richardson (1983) found that participants who were thoroughly debriefed evaluated the research more positively. The importance of leaving your participants with a good feeling about their participation cannot be over-emphasised. As already mentioned, they have invested their time and energy into your project.

The debriefing process can also be useful for your discussion section, as it helps you learn how participants viewed the procedures in your study. It can provide leads for future research and help identify problems in current protocols (Blanck et al., 1992). This point will be dealt with again in later chapters.

Interpretation of research

The ethical principles of integrity and professional and scientific responsibility involve upholding the values of truthfulness, honesty and accuracy. Failure to conduct research in an ethical manner undermines the entire scientific process, impedes the advancement of knowledge and ultimately erodes the public's respect for scientific and academic communities (Shaughnessy, Zechmeister & Zechmeister, 2003).

Reporting of results and data falsification

You are ethically obligated to be scrupulously accurate in managing your data. The integrity of your data is of pivotal importance to the advancement of the knowledge base for psychology as a science. Science is founded on knowledge derived from investigations, therefore, if the data are false, it creates very negative implications for science. Data falsification can take numerous forms, the most extreme of which is when the researcher fails to collect any data and manufactures it. Another form involves altering or omitting some of the data collected, in order for the results to fit a preconceived biased trend. A final form of data falsification involves guessing or creating missing data, in order to generate a complete data set. In all the cases cited above, each involves deliberate deception, which has already been discussed as violating the ethical principles such as integrity.

Freedom of information

Remember that any information related to an identifiable person constitutes personal data processing. It should comply with data protection principles of fair processing of data and security of data. You should familiarise yourself with the relevant freedom of information acts; for example, the Data Protection Act 1998 includes the European Union, UK, Canada, Australia and New Zealand, while the Safe Harbor Framework is used in the United States and was approved by the EU in 2000.

Plagiarism

It is also your responsibility as a researcher to abide by the principle of intellectual property and to avoid plagiarism. Plagiarism refers to the copying or close paraphrasing of someone else's work, and is considered a violation of the principle of integrity. Accusations of plagiarism can ruin your academic career, and possibly prevent you from being awarded your psychology degree. Plagiarism can often result from the failure to double-check a source, or from the failure to use quotations when relevant. Failure to acknowledge secondary sources can also result in plagiarism. It is important that you always cite a secondary source as such; it is unethical to report information or points of view in a way that implies that you read the original work. Remember that secondary sources involve an interpretation, which may or may not be correct.

2.3   A Note on Ethics in Qualitative Research

Although the ethical issues addressed in the previous section apply to both quantitative and qualitative processes of inquiry, a special note is made regarding qualitative methods. New emerging qualitative methods of inquiry are presenting a new backdrop of ethical issues, and their use requires reconsideration of how to utilise conventional ethical principles and standards (Haverkamp, 2005). Similar to quantitative research, Morrow (2005) proposes trustworthiness as a core criterion for quality and rigour in qualitative research. As will be discussed later in the text, qualitative research demonstrates an emphasis on the distinctiveness and individuality of human experience rather than on investigating universal theories of human behaviour.

As already noted, researchers are obligated to abide by the principle of respect for the dignity of all human beings, which involves upholding the value of participants' privacy, and the value of confidentiality of the personal information they disclose. However, qualitative research can often involve extensive quotations from participants, which can make it very difficult to disguise participants' identity, constituting a potential violation of research confidentiality (Haverkamp, 2005). In such cases, it is important that participants are aware of this, *prior* to giving their consent to participate.

Another obvious difference between the two types of research is the role played by the participants. In qualitative research, both the researcher and participants are far more engaged in the emergent research process. Participants are often required to disclose information that is potentially emotional; therefore the researcher must uphold the principle of competent caring, by demonstrating an active concern for the well-being of participants.

A final caution is made regarding the interpretation of qualitative data. During the interpretation process, the qualitative researcher has a much broader scope for making sense of the data collected, based on their intuitions, creativity and personal experience. Kvale (1996) refers to this interpretative process as 'personal subjectivity'. Remember that the integrity of data is of pivotal importance to the advancement of the knowledge base for psychology as a science.

Summary

The Draft Universal Declaration (2005) describes ethical principles and values for the international community. When planning your research project, planned steps must be taken to ensure the dignity and welfare of all your participants, while also ensuring that your research is designed to a high level of scientific rigour. It is very important to ensure that all your participants have given their informed consent and are aware of their right to withdraw at any point. The principle of respect for dignity involves upholding the values of confidentiality and privacy. According to the principle of competent caring, you are obligated to debrief your participants. The failure to conduct research in an ethical manner undermines the entire scientific process and impedes the advancement of knowledge; therefore it is imperative that you are scrupulously accurate in managing and reporting your data. You must also avoid plagiarism of any kind, as it is considered a violation of the principle of integrity.

Further Reading

APA (American Psychological Association) (2002) Ethical principles of psychologists and code of conduct. *American Psychologist*, 57: 1060–73.

Barnyard, P. and Flanagan, C. (2005) *Ethical Issues and Guidelines in Psychology*. London: Routledge.

Fisher, C. (2003) *Decoding the Ethics Code: A Practical Guide for Psychologists*. Thousand Oaks, CA: Sage.

Havercamp, B. E. (2005) Ethical perspectives on qualitative research in applied psychology. *Journal of Counselling Psychology*, 52(2): 146–55.

Pettifor, J. (2004) Professional ethics across national boundaries. *European Psychologist*, 9(4): 264–72.

Rosnow, R. L. and Rosenthal, R (1997) *People Studying People: Artifacts and Ethics in Behavioral Research*. New York: W. H. Freeman & Company.

3

CHOOSING A TOPIC AND THE RESEARCH PROPOSAL

Objectives

On reading this chapter you should:

- understand the importance of choosing a research topic that lends itself to a 'do-able' project;
- be able to evaluate potential topics;
- be able to formulate a valid research question (and hypothesis);
- understand the importance of creativity, and its relationship to innovation in formulating your research question;
- understand the integral role played by the research question;
- understand the vital role of the research proposal;
- be aware of the common pitfalls to be avoided in writing a successful proposal; and
- be able to write a logical and persuasive research proposal.

Overview

Chapter 3 deals with the practical issues of choosing an appropriate topic for your research project, and with the all important task of developing a research proposal. Section 3.1 deals with the practicalities of evaluating topics from your potential list, in order to choose the most appropriate for your project. Section 3.2 focuses on how to formulate a good research question. The role of the research question and different types of questions are dealt with in Section 3.3. Section 3.4 highlights the functional importance of the research proposal, which is often neglected by undergraduate students. The proposal acts as an exercise in thought, a reference point for supervision, and also as a motivational device. Section 3.5 deconstructs the proposal into its major components in order to make the development of the proposal more manageable. Section 3.6 presents the issue of the writing style of the proposal. Section 3.7 looks at some common pitfalls in developing a good proposal, while Section 3.8 provides a checklist for developing your research question and proposal.

3.1   Choosing a Topic

Often students adopt idealistic goals for their psychology project, due to the competition for good grades and for postgraduate places. You may want to make a significant contribution to the psychological literature, or you may want to publish your work; these are both very important and useful goals, but they should not override the importance of a 'do-able' project.

Often students want to research very broad, all-encompassing topics. Such broad topics involve more time and effort than most undergraduate psychology students can afford. However, topics that are too narrow should also be avoided as it is very difficult to generalise such results. You must strike a balance; your topic should be narrow enough to focus your project but not too narrow that the results have no generalisability. Also, your topic should be broad enough to generalise but not to the extent that you cannot manage the area and your project.

Simple strategies for evaluating potential research topics

It is quite common for undergraduate psychology students to develop a list of potential research topics. The difficulty arises when students must choose a topic from their list, and develop a research proposal. Often students ask me if they can submit two or three proposals, with the hope that I will inform them of the best idea and therefore make the decision for them. Supervisors are generally not in a position to do this, as it is unethical for anyone but the student to make this decision – this decision-making is, in itself, part of the research process. The following are three very essential questions that you can ask yourself regarding your potential research topics, as illustrated in Figure 3.1.

1. Does the topic elicit interest and curiosity in you?

The first decision you should make regards how you actually feel about the topics on your list, and whether you could stick with the topic through to the completion of a research project. It is very important that the topic you choose is of interest to you and that it also elicits curiosity within you. Your interest and curiosity should manifest themselves by adding to your enthusiasm about your project, and therefore have the potential to act as a powerful motivational device.

2. Is the topic worthwhile?

It is very important that you pick a topic that is worthwhile. As already noted in Chapter 2, poor science is unethical. It is unethical to ask people to participate

Figure 3.1   Three simple strategies for evaluating a potential research topic

in your study if it has little or no likelihood, because of poor conceptualisation and design, of producing meaningful results or furthering scientific knowledge.

If your topic is not worthwhile, not only is it unethical, but you are also failing to satisfy the requirements of meaningful results with theoretical and practical implications. Hence, you will fail to meet the full requirements for an undergraduate project in psychology, and you will ultimately lose precious marks. If the examiner of your project reads your project and thinks 'Well, so what?', then you have not met the full requirements of your psychology project. It is important to note that it is your responsibility to come up with valid topics that are worthwhile. Your supervisor's role is to guide you through the research process, not to generate topics for you.

3. Is the topic do-able?

As recently noted, it is of paramount importance that the topic for your project is feasible. You must make critical decisions regarding whether you will be capable of collecting primary data to answer your potential research question. For example, students are often interested in topics related to psychopathologies, such as schizophrenia or multiple personality disorders; however, at undergraduate level, it is not appropriate or permissible to gather information from such a sample, due to the code of competent caring for example.

A topic that Irish students are often interested in is the prison service. They may want to investigate inmates' quality of life, or they may be interested in the prison staff. At undergraduate level, students have great difficulty in gaining access to such sensitive samples, regardless of the aims of their study. Some students, due to family connections, etc., go through the process of getting permission to get into such places, and can spend numerous weeks waiting for a response, which is usually 'no'. Precious time is lost, which would have been saved by making critical decisions as mentioned above.

It is also important to decide whether you would have enough time to gather the information and carry out your analyses. Undergraduate students, for example, often do not have the time or resources to invest in participant observation studies, and should settle for some other method of inquiry that suits their research goals. Once you have narrowed down your list of topics, the next step in setting down the foundations for a successful psychology project is to develop your research question.

3.2 How to Formulate a Good Research Question

Idea generating

As already noted, all research begins with an idea, which can be the most difficult stage of the research process. Leonard and Swap (1999) define creativity as a process of developing and expressing novel ideas that are likely to be useful. Creativity is very important in considering the process of generating hypotheses for your psychology project, because generating your research question, like generating knowledge, is a creative act (Vicari & Troilo, 2000).

Generating a new idea is the beginning, not the end, of the creative process. Novelty for its own sake may result in nothing more than an intellectual exercise. Creativity is therefore an essential part of innovativeness, the starting point of a process which when skilfully managed brings an idea into innovation, (Leonard & Swap, 1999). Creativity is the process of imaginative thinking (*input*), which produces new ideas (for example the research question and hypothesis) while innovations are the *output*, in this case the completed psychology project.

Popper (1959) notes that there is no logical path leading to new ideas – they can only be reached by 'emfuhlung', i.e. creative intuition. However, it is important to note that creativity is more than just dreaming up grand ideas, insights and problems; the solutions to these problems must be original and feasible. This again highlights the importance of a do-able project in developing a research question where the solution is in fact feasible.

Leonard and Swap (1999) propose five steps that capture the essential features of the creative process, as seen in Figure 3.2.

It should come as no surprise that creativity comes from a well-prepared mind and so *Stage 1* of the process is preparation. There also needs to be an opportunity for innovation to occur, which is *Stage 2* of the creative process. The generating of your research question is a prime example of a need to exercise creativity. *Stage 3* involves the importance of generating as many initial ideas as possible. Creative ideas can begin with vague thoughts, and initial ideas can emerge in both scientific and non-scientific ways. In this early idea-getting phase, one should not be too critical of initial ideas because premature criticism might destroy an emerging good idea. The old saying rings through here – you shouldn't throw the baby out with the bathwater.

Cryer (2000) proposes numerous useful ways of generating options at this early phase in the creative process, as illustrated in Table 3.1 below.

Stage 4 of the process involves incubation: Leonard and Swap (1999) recognise the need for time out from struggling with an idea or issue. *Stage 5* involves selecting an idea from your generated list. Early ideas need to be nourished, thought about and taken seriously. Curiosity, interest and enthusiasm are critical ingredients. Once an area of interest is identified, it is useful to dive right in by reading articles and relevant books in the area.

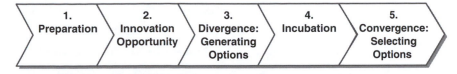

Figure 3.2   The creative process in five steps (Leonard and Swap, 1999)

Table 3.1   Strategies for generating creative ideas (Cryer, 2000)

1. Talking things over
2. Keeping an open mind
3. Brainstorming
4. Negative brainstorming
5. Viewing the problem from imaginative perspectives
6. Concentrating on anomalies
7. Focusing on byproducts
8. Viewing the problem from the perspective of another discipline

Using the research literature to generate ideas

As already noted, ideas for your research project often come out of the research literature. At this early stage in the research process, students are often intimidated by the vast amount of information available, and sometimes find themselves lost amidst the literature fog. There are a number of ways to approach the research literature; you could select a small number of topics within psychology which are of interest to you, and investigate them in depth. For example, a researcher may have an interest in children's reasoning but no particular idea for a research project. The interest, however, is enough to point the researcher to an area within which more defined ideas can be developed. For the new researcher in particular, interest in the area to be studied is critical in helping to sustain the hard work to follow. Remember the point about curiosity helping to generate ideas and sustain effort.

Another strategy is to acquaint yourself with research at the cutting edge of psychological knowledge. This can be achieved by keeping yourself up to date with top journals dedicated to your area of interest. For example, if your area of research is memory, it would be important to check each new issue of *The Journal of Experimental Psychology: Learning, Memory and Cognition*. A final strategy is to start with general readings such as the *Annual Review of Psychology*, and progress to more specific journal articles. Research questions can also develop from finding gaps in the literature, by attempting to refute or prove an existing theory, through everyday observations of behaviour, or from the need to solve a practical problem, as illustrated in Figure 3.3.

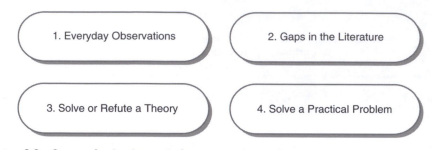

Figure 3.3   Sources for development of your research question

3.3   Clarifying and Refining your Research Question

The next stage involves clarifying and refining your ideas into research questions, as vague ideas are insufficient in psychology as a science. This process usually involves examining the research literature, in an attempt to learn how other researchers have conceptualised, measured and tested the concepts that are of interest to you and related to your ideas. While reviewing the literature, you will continue to work on your ideas, clarifying, defining and refining them, until you have produced one or more clearly posed questions based on a well-developed knowledge of previous research and theory, as well as on your own ideas and speculations.

The research question plays a vital role throughout the research process. It is vital that you present a clear statement of the specific purposes of your study. The research question simply formulates this specific purpose as a question. In writing the introduction section of your research project, your review of the literature must be defined by your research question which acts as the guiding concept.

Careful conceptualisation and phrasing of the research question is of paramount importance, because everything done in the remainder of the research process is aimed at answering your research question. The question that you develop might involve highly specific and precisely defined hypotheses typical of quantitative research. Or it might be phrased in a much more general manner typical of qualitative research. To a large extent, the research question that is posed will dictate the way you conduct the rest of the research process. This crucial aspect cannot be stressed enough: remember that throughout the grading of undergraduate projects, one fundamental issue is addressed when reading each section of the research: was that appropriate for the research question being asked? Students often fail to see this cardinal relationship at the early stages of the project, which can cause difficulties later on in the process.

1. Existence Questions

Example: Is there such a thing as the unconscious?

2. Descriptive and Classification Questions

Example: What are the personality characteristics of parents who slap their children?

3. Comparative Questions

Example: Are males better at mental rotation than females?

4. Composition Questions

Example: What are the factors that make up intelligence?

5. Relationship Questions

Example: Is body image related to self-esteem?

6. Causality Questions

Example: What are the effects of exercise on reaction time?

Figure 3.4   Different types of research questions (Meltzoff, 1999)

Different types of research questions

During this early stage of the research process, one works from the general to the specific using rational and abstract processes to systematically develop ideas towards valid research questions. In successfully asking questions, a very important requirement must be met. The question must be answerable with data; without this crucial caveat of testability, research questions are nothing more than a speculation.

Meltzoff (1999) illustrates that there are a number of different types of research questions that call for different methods of inquiry in seeking answers. Figure 3.4 illustrates these different types of research questions.

Evaluating your research question

One of the biggest difficulties for undergraduate students, at this stage of the research process, is that they are unsure whether their idea and research question are good enough, and whether they meet the requirements of originality and significance. If you have been having such feelings of doubt and uncertainty, you are certainly not alone. Originality can be achieved in a number of ways. First of all your research question can be original, or you may design your methodology in an original fashion, and finally your solution or answer to your research question may be original. Originality also arises from solving gaps in the literature, or by finding evidence for or against an existing theory using a novel or new method of inquiry. Originality can also arise from solving a practical problem in a new way, or a practical problem that did not have a solution.

Significance refers to whether your idea and research question are worthwhile. As already noted, in order to be worthwhile your research question should yield valid and meaningful results or findings, which will add to the existing knowledge base in psychology. The thought processes involved in developing your research proposal can aid in determining whether your research question is original and significant.

3.4   The Role of the Research Proposal

Your research proposal describes what your proposed research is about, what it is trying to achieve, how you will go about achieving it, what you find out and why it is worth finding out (Punch, 2001). Often undergraduate students under-estimate the importance of the research proposal, and fail to see the vital functions that it serves. This section highlights the functional importance of the research proposal, as seen in Figure 3.5.

An exercise in thought

The research proposal serves a number of useful functions. The most pertinent is that it helps you to think through each step of your research project. By writing the proposal you essentially have the opportunity to try out ideas, be creative and explore alternatives, without recruiting a single participant. If you

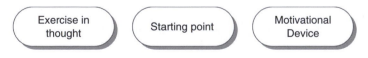

Figure 3.5   Functional importance of the research proposal

have a few ideas for your psychology project, you can write up a proposal for each one, and compare and evaluate them, to help you choose the most viable idea. This useful writing process also helps you make intelligent and ethical research decisions.

Starting point for supervision

The research proposal can serve as a very effective reference place for your supervision. The proposal also allows your supervisor to think through your research plan so that they can give advice that will improve your study. On the other hand if your supervisor is unsure of your research focus, or of the relevance of your research question, a well-written proposal allows them to make a more concrete informed decision regarding its approval. Remember that a well-written research proposal could convince your supervisor that your research is worthwhile, and that you have the competence to carry it out.

Motivational device

The research proposal can also help you stay on the right track, and act as a powerful motivational device. The undergraduate research project is a timely endeavour – once you have embarked on this journey, it is possible to loose track or become disheartened. Returning to the proposal can remind you of the potential contribution your project could make to psychology as a science, and to the practical applications that could ensue. Chapter 5 deals with motivation and your psychology project in more detail.

3.5   The Research Proposal Deconstructed

Undergraduate students often find the development of an effective research proposal for quantitative and qualitative projects an exasperating and difficult experience. This section deconstructs the proposal into its major components, as seen in Figure 3.6, in order to make the development of the proposal more manageable and practical.

1. Statement of the research problem

It is vital that your present a clear statement of the specific purposes of your study. It is important that you also explain, very clearly, why your research question is worth answering. What do you hope to learn from it? What will this new knowledge add to the existing field? What new perspective will you bring to the topic? For quantitative research you must also very explicitly

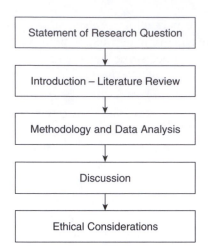

Figure 3.6   Components of the research proposal for both quantitative and qualitative research (Note: not all universities require a discussion section)

state your hypothesis(es). This is the tentative prediction of the answer to your research question. Sometimes students assume that their hypotheses are obvious, and do not state them. This is a major mistake, which should be avoided at all costs. No matter how obvious your hypotheses appear, it is imperative that you state them. Clear hypotheses are very important, as the rest of the quantitative research process is geared towards establishing confirmation of them.

2. Introduction – literature review

The literature review is generally incorporated into the introduction. The main purpose of this section is to provide the necessary background or context for your research problem. The framing of the research question is the most crucial aspect of the research proposal. If you frame your research question in the context of a general long-winded literature review, the significance of your research question could ultimately be lost and appear inconsequential or uninspiring. However, if you frame your research question within the framework of a very focused and current research area, its importance will be markedly apparent.

The literature review demonstrates your knowledge and understanding of the theoretical implications of your research question. It demonstrates your ability to critically evaluate relevant research, and illustrates your ability to integrate and synthesise information. Try to outline conflicting research in the area that your project will try to resolve. Most importantly, the literature review convinces your supervisor that your proposed research project will make a substantial contribution to psychology as a science. For the reasons mentioned, even qualitative proposals require a literature review; however, you need to strike a balance between adequate knowledge to focus your study, and immersing too much in the literature that your study becomes too contaminated with prior expectations. This idea is dealt with in more detail in Chapter 8.

3. Methodology

Your methodology is very important because it illustrates how you plan to answer your research question. It acts as a work plan and describes how you will complete your project. It is crucial that you include sufficient information for your supervisor to ascertain if your methodology is sound and demonstrates scientific rigour. Quantitative and qualitative methodologies do not lend themselves to the same description and will therefore be dealt with separately in more detail in Units 2 and 3 of the text.

Quantitative methodology

Design – What are your independent variable(s) and dependent variable(s)? It is very important that these are operationally defined, using precise and concise language. Also mention how you propose to measure them. What type of design do you propose to answer your research question(s)?

Participants – How will you choose your sample? Do you foresee any difficulties accessing this sample? Are there any limitations to using such a sample?

Materials – Describe the type of equipment and materials you plan to use.

Procedure – Explain, in as much detail as you can, how you propose to conduct your research.

Statistical considerations – Although you have no results as yet, it is important that you demonstrate an understanding of the statistical analyses that will answer your research question. It is imperative that you suggest procedures that are appropriate considering the type of design you propose to utilise and the type of data that you will collect. For example, if you are comparing two different groups, and have proposed an independent groups design, then, if it is interval/ratio data, an independent t-test would be appropriate, but if the data was categorical, then a χ^2 would be appropriate to answer the research question.

Qualitative Methodology

Silverman (2003) notes the importance of the theoretical underpinnings of the methodology chosen, and the contingent nature of the data chosen in qualitative research. Your research paradigm, for example grounded theory, should be included in your proposal. Explain the assumptions of your research paradigm.

Qualitative methodology should deal with a description of the cases chosen, the procedures for data collection and analysis in terms of their suitability to the theoretical framework applied and how they satisfy criteria of reliability and validity (Silverman, 2003). It is important to realise that in qualitative research, data collection and data analysis often occur simultaneously.

4. Discussion of potential findings

It is important to note that not all universities require a discussion section in the research proposal. It is advisable that you check the polices of your university to ascertain whether this section is necessary. In my view, it is beneficial that you discuss the potential impact of your proposed research project. This can be communicated in a few sentences, the goal of which is to demonstrate to your supervisor that you believe in your project.

5. Ethical considerations

As already noted in Chapter 2, planned steps must always be taken to protect and ensure the dignity and welfare of all your participants, and that inadequate attention for respect and beneficence can affect the scientific viability and validity of your proposed research. It is also crucial that you demonstrate an active concern for the well-being of your participants, by minimising potential harms and maximising the benefits of participating in your study. It is very important that all participants are volunteers, and have given informed consent to take part. It is also important to map out how you will uphold these ethical obligations.

3.6   A Note on Writing Style

It is important to keep in mind that your proposal is an argument. An effective research proposal, therefore, should be clear and precise, be persuasive and convincing, and demonstrate the broad implications of the research (Silverman, 2003). One of the benefits of viewing your proposal as an argument is that such a structure pushes you to stress your thesis or line of thought. This structure also requires that your arguments and statements are consistent with each other. One of the main aims of the popular writing and publication formats is clarity of communication. This very much parallels with the principle of parsimony, which is applied to science in general. Cryer

(2000) proposes that the research proposal should use language and terminology that is understandable to an intelligent lay person as well as to a subject matter expert.

Silverman (2003) warns that you should never be content with a proposal which reads like a stream of undigested theories or concepts. It is crucial that you use precise and concise language that a non-specialist can understand. By explaining all relevant concepts and variables, you will have demonstrated the ability to write and think clearly and critically. Remember that your research proposal is your supervisor's best way of getting a sense of your thinking, and it illustrates that your research project itself will be organised in the same logical way. Morse (1994a) highlights the importance of a well-thought-out proposal in noting that a sloppily prepared proposal sends the message that the actual research itself may also be sloppy. It is very important that you are convincing of the practical importance of your research project, and that you develop a sufficient contextual basis for your research problem.

3.7 Common Pitfalls

Students often have difficulty in writing a research proposal that gains the support of their supervisor and their university's ethics review board. The following are some common mistakes made in proposal writing.

1. Vague presentation of your research problem.
2. Framing your research problem within a long-winded literature review.
3. Failure to demonstrate the significance of your research proposal.
4. Vague methodology and proposed handling of your results.
5. Inadequate consideration of ethics for psychological research.
6. Poor writing style which lacks clarity and precision.

3.8 Checklist

- Does your research question address an original and significant psychological phenomenon? 'An original contribution to knowledge' does not mean that it must explore a new problem; it can also result from a novel reassessment of a familiar question.
- Is your research question clear?
- Can your research question be answered by data?
- Have you developed a clear, persuasive and comprehensive research proposal that will guide you through the research process?
- Is your research question consistent with each aspect of your proposal?
- Does your proposal explain the logic behind your proposed investigation as opposed to merely describing it?

Summary

There are some simple strategies for evaluating potential research topics, for example deciding whether a topic elicits your interest and curiosity, whether the topic is worthwhile to investigate and whether it is feasible. Creativity and innovation are important in generating a valid research question. Creativity can be viewed as the process of imaginative thinking (*input*) which produces new ideas, while innovations, in this context your research question and your psychology project, are the *output*. The research literature is also important in generating ideas. The careful conceptualisation and phrasing of the research question is critical, as everything done in the remainder of the research process is aimed at answering that question.

The research proposal acts as a useful exercise in thought, allowing you to think critically through each aspect of the research proposal and to make necessary ethical decisions. The research proposal also serves as a very effective starting point for supervision, and also acts as a powerful motivational device. Both qualitative and quantitative research proposals can be broken down into the statement of the research question, the introduction-literature review, methodology and data analysis, discussion and ethical considerations. There are a number of mistakes often made by undergraduate students, from hazy presentation of the research problem, to poor writing style. A clear, precise and persuasive writing style is critical in demonstrating the practical and theoretical significance of your project, and in demonstrating your ability to think and plan in a logical, rigorous manner.

Further Reading

Cryer, P. (2000) *The Research Student's Guide to Success*. Buckingham: Open University Press. (Aimed at post-graduate level. Details useful creative strategies.)

Punch, K. F. (2001) *Developing Effective Research Proposals*. London: Sage Publications.

Silverman, D. (2003) *Doing Qualitative Research: A Practical Handbook*. London: Sage Publications.

4

A CONNECTED AND CONVINCING
ARGUMENT

Objectives

On reading this chapter you should:

- understand the importance of a flowing project with a logical and convincing argument;
- understand the basic rules of precise and concise writing;
- be able to use the tips for scientific writing; and
- be aware of the implicit assumptions between you and the reader of your project.

Overview

Although it is expected that as a final-year psychology student, you will have mastered the intricacies of research design and methodology, it is not as likely that you will have mastered the appropriate style for writing your research project. Section 4.1 describes the importance of your project delivering a connected and convincing argument with an inherent logical structure, in order to produce a seamless piece of work. Section 4.2 describes the importance of clear communication and effective writing, and details three roads to clear communication: economy of expression, precision and adherence to grammatical rules (APA, 2001). This is expanded on in Section 4.3, which offers some useful tips for scientific writing, such as the composition of a paragraph, the use of transitional devices, the proper tense and the correct person and voice. Finally, Section 4.4 deals with the implicit assumptions that exist between you, the author and the reader.

4.1 A Connected and Convincing Argument

The goal of scientific writing is effective communication. As already noted knowledge is a social creation, and writing is one of the main ways in which knowledge is shared and communicated (Gilbert, 1996). There is much to communicate in a research project, yet word-count restrictions demand that your project is precise and concise. Guidelines are therefore necessary to aid communication while minimising the space used. Organisation is key to a good quality project: most universities recommend that the body of a research project be organised into four major parts – the introduction, the method, results and discussion.

Creating a good structure can be the most difficult part of writing. If the structure is right then the rest can follow fairly easily; remember that no amount of clever language can compensate for a weak structure and bad organisation. Structure is important so the reader of your project can stay on track with your argument and the underlying aim of your research. The reader should know where they have just been, where they are and where they are heading. Therefore at any given time when reading your project, the reader should know what they have just read, what they are presently reading and what they are about to read. A strong structure also allows readers to know where to look for particular information. It can also act as a quality check for you, as it is very likely that you will include all the important and essential information to make your argument. Sternberg (2003) notes that it is crucial that your arguments are valid and consistent, highlighting the importance of the reliability, validity and internal consistency of your project. Overall your project must be a connected, convincing argument, and imposing a strong structure should ensure that your arguments and statements are consistent with each other.

4.2   Clear Communication and Effective Writing

As you already know, it is not enough to have good ideas, you must present them in a way that people will receive them. Effective communication and writing is important to meet this goal. One of the main aims of report writing is clarity of communication. This aim is met by keeping the report as concise as possible. This is very much in parallel with the principle of parsimony, which is applied to science in general. Also remember that bad grammar, style and poor spelling can destroy all your hard work, and can influence how your project will be evaluated.

The American Psychological Association cites three roads to clear communication:

1. Economy of expression

The first avenue refers simply to saying only what needs to be said. One should use short words and short sentences, as this makes your project easier for readers to understand, again utilising the principle of parsimony. However, if something is complicated, do not sacrifice accuracy for the sake of brevity.

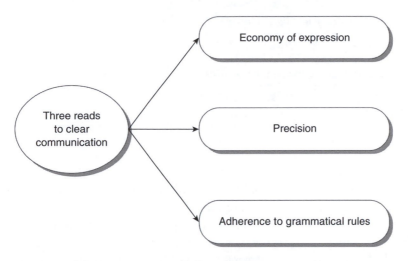

Figure 4.1   Three roads to clear communication (APA, 2001)

2. Precision

It is crucial that you choose the right word for what you want to say, and that you use the appropriate technical terminology when appropriate.

3. Adherence to grammatical rules

If one fails to adhere to grammatical rules, this interferes with clear writing, hence distracting the reader and thus causing ambiguity.

On a much broader level, failure to communicate research in a clear manner can have detrimental effects on psychology as a science – it affects the construct validity of concepts used.

4.3   Some Tips for Scientific Writing

This section deals with some tips for effective and efficient scientific writing, as illustrated in Table 4.1.

1. The paragraph

The basic unit of writing is the paragraph. Rarely will a sentence in your psychology project stand alone. When you introduce an idea, you should develop the point that you are making. Often students can fall down by introducing an

Table 4.1   Tips for scientific writing

1. The paragraph
2. Transitional devices
3. The proper tense, correct person and voice
4. Numbers in the text
5. Abbreviations
6. Over reliance on specific terminology

idea and then leaving it in mid-air; this often occurs in the discussion section. Each paragraph you write should begin with a central concept or idea, which is then developed and finally summarised.

A good paragraph has two main characteristics, first of all it should be unified, in that each sentence within the paragraph contributes to the same basic concept. Secondly, the sentences in a paragraph should flow logically and of course naturally. The ideas presented in each sentence should relate to those contained in the sentences before and after. There are a number of techniques that can be used to improve the flow of your project, which will be dealt with next.

2. Transitional devices

One key to improving the flow of your project is to use transitional devices. Transitional words or devices are useful in tying one sentence to another, and connecting different ideas. Common types of transitional devices are shown in Table 4.2 below.

3. The proper tense, correct person and voice

Writing in the correct tense for your project can be quite confusing, most of your project is written in the past tense, while some statements are written in the present tense. In fact, the concluding sentence of your abstract can be in the present tense, for example 'the practical implications of the results are discussed thereof'.

Your project should mainly be written in the past tense because most of what you are describing and reporting has already been done. The literature that your refer to has already been written and, when you are writing up your project, your study has already been conducted. Therefore discussions of past research, your procedure and statements of your results should all be in the past tense.

As already noted, certain statements may be written in the present tense. For example, you can use the present tense for statements which have continuing applicability, and definitions of well-defined theory can be stated in the present tense. When you refer to a table or figure in your text, you can refer to

Table 4.2 Examples of transitional devices

Transitional device	Example
Repeating words or phrases	Lewin proposed that there is nothing as practical as a good theory. Many theorists have been influenced by Lewin's work.
Making comparisons	Similarly/on the other hand/yet/in contrast
Expand your point	In addition/furthermore/also
Use pronouns	Piaget's work set the foundations for much of development psychology. He also...
Give examples	For example/to illustrate/to demonstrate
Summarise	In summary in short/to sum up
Derive conclusions	As a result thus/as a consequence/therefore

them in the present tense, as cc statements of general applicability in the conclusions of your abstract and in the discussion, as already noted. What is apparent is that the future tense should always be avoided.

It is generally accepted, in scientific writing, that you write in the third person and the passive voice. However, it is important to note that this rule generally applies to scientific writing of a quantitative or experimental nature, where the aim is to de-emphasise the personal nature of the study. There is disagreement about the traditional use of the passive voice because it can be viewed as taking responsibility away from the researcher. For example, saying 'an independent t-test was carried out' suggests that the person responsible for carrying out the statistical test is unknown, and this is not the case – it is reasonable to assume that the researcher carried it out.

In qualitative research, it is considered appropriate to use the first person, 'I', as opposed to the third person as in quantitative research. The reason for this is because you have acted as the research tool in that your findings have been generated from the material that you have produced (for example the transcripts developed from an interview) and you have used your own creativity to develop meanings and relationships between the categories that emerged. Remember that in qualitative research it is not appropriate to describe your study as an experiment as you have not manipulated any variables; instead refer to it as a study. Also avoid using the term 'hypothesis', it is important that you stick to using 'the research question' or aim of your study.

4. Numbers in the text

Due to the nature of psychological research, you will have statistics included in the text of your project. Numbers below 10 should be expressed in words, while all numbers from 10 and above should be expressed as a number.

5. Abbreviations

It is advised that you do not overuse abbreviations in your project. Some terms have a universal meaning and can be used to make the reading of your project easier; for example 'IQ' can be used instead of 'Intelligence Quotient'. If you are unsure of whether a term has universal familiarity within psychology, either ask your supervisor or avoid the abbreviation.

6. Over-reliance on specific terms

Students often rely too much on specific terms, for example the word 'which'. Gordon Allport, in his epistle to project writers, notes the over-reliance on this word, and refers to a project that is oversaturated with the word 'which' as a masterpiece of cacophony or disharmony.

4.4   Implicit Assumptions

To meet the goal of precise but concise communication, you, as author and the reader of your project, can both make certain implicit assumptions. The reader can assume that the author understands statistics and research methods, and that you have described any unusual or unexpected events. Therefore a number of things can be left unsaid in a research report, because the reader can assume that commonly accepted procedures were used and that the details of the procedures are unimportant. For example, there is no need to state the null hypothesis (Ho) – stating it would be redundant. The author also assumes that the reader understands statistics and research methods, and should therefore refrain from teaching the reader statistics:

Illustrative example 4.1

Do not teach statistics to the reader.
Do not say 'a dependent t-test was performed *because*...'
But you can say 'a dependent t-test was appropriate to test the hypothesis...'

As the author, it is important to focus on information that the reader cannot get elsewhere – your own thoughts and actions as a researcher, your conclusions, suggested practical implications and directions for future research, etc. It is also critical, as the author, to describe clearly and concisely all of the important mental and physical activities you performed in creating,

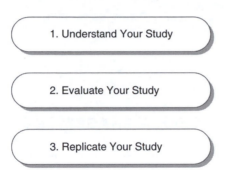

Figure 4.2   Overall goal of the information included in your study

conducting and interpreting the study. Your overall goal is to provide readers with the necessary information to understand, evaluate and replicate your study as seen in figure 4.2.

Summary

Overall your project must be a connected, convincing argument. One of the main aims of report writing is clarity of communication. This aim is met by keeping the report as concise as possible. This is very much in parallel with the principle of parsimony, which is applied to science in general. There are a number of ways to aid scientific writing, for example adherence to rules for writing paragraphs, using transitional devices, using the proper tense, and using the correct person and voice. There are a number of implicit assumptions between you, as the author, and the reader, for example the rules of hypothesis testing.

Further Reading

Sternberg, R.J. (2003) *The psychologist's companion: a guide to scientific writing for students and researchers*. (4th edn). New York: Cambridge University Press.

5

SELF-MANAGEMENT

Objectives

On reading this chapter you should:

- understand the importance of goal setting, and be able to set your own project goals and be able to achieve them;
- be able to develop a holistic time-management schedule that meets your individual needs in successfully completing your psychology project;
- be able to develop the meta-competency of self-management in creating a sense of control and a positive attitude towards your research project; and
- be able to utilise ways to help overcome or avoid procrastination.

Overview

Successfully completing your psychology project is contingent on persistence. Section 5.1 highlights useful ways to self-manage, in terms of developing skills of planning, monitoring, evaluating and reinforcing, which are involved in self-regulation. Students often adopt idealistic goals, due to the competition for good grades and post-graduate places. You may want to make a significant contribution to the psychological literature, and you may also want to publish your work; these are both very important and useful goals, but they should not override the importance of a do-able project. Motivational strategies that focus on clear, practical and realistic goals are vital. A strategy for goal setting based on the SMART framework (i.e. goals that are Specific, Measurable, Action-oriented, Realistic, and Time-based) is exemplified for this end. The role of short-term wins are also demonstrated, as a strategy for maintaining high motivational levels.

Section 5.2 deals with time management, building on the theme of being self-regulated and well organised. Different time-management techniques are demonstrated, for example prioritising, breaking tasks into smaller more manageable tasks and using all available time. Following this, Section 5.3 looks at some useful strategies to help avoid or overcome procrastination. These involve deconstructing the task at hand into smaller more manageable units, and carrying out related tasks as a way of easing yourself into the target task. Section 5.4 presents some useful ways of overcoming writer's block, by breaking crystallised thought patterns. Section 5.5 then emphasises the role of self-management as a very effective mechanism for promoting a positive attitude towards your psychology project, by creating a sense of control and accomplishment. Finally, Section 5.6 provides a checklist for setting goals and managing your time towards the successful completion of your project.

5.1   Motivational Strategies

The undergraduate psychology project involves a lengthy process, in which the student must remain motivated towards successful completion. The concept of motivation refers to internal factors that impel action and to external factors that can act as inducements to action (Locke and Latham, 2004). There are three aspects of action that motivation can affect: direction (choice), intensity (effort) and duration (persistence). This coincides with accepted definitions of motivation, as the contemporary (immediate) influence on the *direction*, *vigour* and *persistence* of action (Atkinson, 1964). Therefore, motivation affects not only the acquisition of your skills and abilities but also to what extent you utilise your skills and abilities (Locke and Latham, 2004).

Using the goal-setting framework of self-regulation, the basic premise is that behaviour is motivated by internal intentions, objectives or goals (Locke and Latham, 1990), which you are in control of. Locke and Henne (1986) proposed four ways in which goals affect behaviour: they direct attention and action to behaviours that the person believes will achieve the goal; they mobilise effort in that the person tries harder; they increase persistence, resulting in more time spent on behaviours necessary for goal attainment; and they can motivate the search for effective strategies to attain them. Clearly goals can be viewed as proximal constructs, tied closely to specific behaviours (Kanfer and Ackerman, 1989). For example, you might have the goal of reading an article in an hour; this goal is tied closely to particular behaviours relevant for performance.

In the context of the psychology project, self-regulation refers to your ability to monitor, control and direct crucial aspects of the research process for yourself. This framework of self-regulation enables you, the student, to be in control and to manage the process. This sense of ownership in itself produces motivation for successful completion of your psychology project. Kanfer and Ackerman (1989) propose that self-regulatory processes are critical determinants of performance and, hence, of the development of competencies necessary for the successful completion of your psychology project. Self-regulation subsumes three interdependent activities as shown in Figure 5.1.

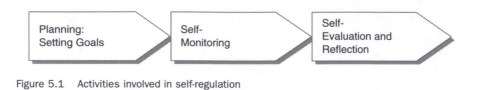

Figure 5.1   Activities involved in self-regulation

Activity 1 – Planning: Setting goals

The first activity involved in self-regulation is planning. It is very important to write down your goals. The simple act of writing something down raises your level of commitment. Writing your goals down involves getting ideas out of your head and into reality, and transforms your goals into a concrete plan of action that you intend to follow. As a result, written plans can provide tangible reminders of the bigger picture and help keep you focused.

Clearly, at this organisational stage, goals are the tools to help you define where you want to commit your time and energy; to realise what you want to achieve; and to provide you with the necessary direction to do so. Luckily, setting goals is a learned skill, which can be developed using the SMART framework (see Figure 5.2) – a very effective mnemonic structure for setting goals.

1. Set Specific goals

With regard to specific, you should set goals that are clear and free from ambiguity. Your goals should also have tightly defined outcomes, such as evaluating an article. Therefore, by setting specific goals, you crystallise and really secure what the goal is about in your mind, which increases the likelihood that it will be achieved. Remember also that it is far easier to put off something that is vague, for example doing some reading, as opposed to something specific, like reading and evaluating an article.

2. Set Measurable goals

It is also important that you set tangible goals that you can measure and accomplish. By introducing an element of measurement into your goal, you will be much more aware and informed of your progress towards it, as it facilitates much stronger and reliable feedback. By making your goals measurable, you are also increasing goal specificity, as mentioned above.

3. Set Action-oriented goals

Write down your goals as active statements, starting with the word 'To' for example 'to evaluate, to read, etc.'. This will act to translate your goals into

$S \rightarrow$ Specific

$M \rightarrow$ Measurable

$A \rightarrow$ Action-oriented

$R \rightarrow$ Realistc

$T \rightarrow$ Time-based

Figure 5.2   SMART mnemonic framework

specific targets that require your action to accomplish them. Unless you are willing to expend effort towards achieving your goals, all you are really doing is stating your desires, which is a different process to goal setting.

Activity 2 – Self-monitoring

The next stage involves monitoring your progress towards your goals. Successful self-monitoring involves focusing on behaviours that have functional significance for goal attainment (Kanfer & Ackerman, 1989), as established at the planning stage.

4. Set Realistic goals

It is imperative to note, however, that attention to your performance is not synonymous with accurate assessment of your abilities. It is possible to make flawed judgements of competence that may lead to insufficient allocation of effort and, consequently, inadequate performance (Kanfer, 1987; Bandura, 1988). With this caution in mind, it is important to highlight the practical importance of realistic attributions of competence and ability, and do-able, reachable goals.

5. Set Time-based goals

It is vital that you set realistic time frames for your work. When you set target dates for completion, this sets a structure that enables you to develop strategies for completion, and also creates a sense of urgency. Therefore, instead of merely talking about what you plan to do, having a time period helps spur you into action because you start to think about when things need to happen.

Identify obstacles to your goals

There will often be obstacles in the path toward any goal; what is important is how you overcome them. It is important at this stage to identify potential

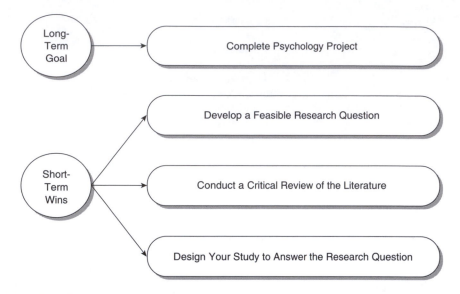

Figure 5.3   Examples of a long-term goal and short-term wins

obstacles that may preclude your goal attainments. It is best to think of obstacles in advance, rather than to wait for them to pop up when you are too busy to figure out what to do about them. For every obstacle you can think of, write down an action that will help you move past it. Two examples are given below:

Example of obstacle: Delay of an article from an interlibrary loan.
Solution: Go back and review your literature review to date while waiting.

Example of obstacle: You miss a deadline that you have set.
Solution: Add an extra hour to your schedule for a week to catch up.

The role of 'short-term wins'

The completion of your psychology project is the ultimate long-term goal, but it can prove difficult to keep your motivational levels high throughout this whole process. The implementation of 'short-term wins' (Kotter, 1996) are useful, both as a motivating factor and as a mechanism for tracking the progress towards the longer-term goals, as seen in Figure 5.3.

Activity 3 – Self-evaluation and reflection

Self-evaluation involves a comparison of your current performance with your desired goal state. This requires a realistic assessment of the outcome of performance, by checking your progress against the ideal or standard that you originally set. Target dates also help you evaluate where you are in relation to successfully accomplishing your goals, acting as a feedback or self-regulatory mechanism, and as a means to measure your performance. The final stage involves self-reflection, on the success or failure of your goal attainment.

If you do not reach your goal by the specified time, set a new deadline, do not leave it to chance. Write down a new deadline, and work towards reaching your goal. When you are setting your goals, you may not anticipate all the obstacles that you encounter, or you may find the opposite, that a goal was easier than you expected and you can move onto more difficult goals. Likewise, as your journey through your psychology project progresses, you may find that your goals will need to be updated from time to time. The advice here is to modify your goals as necessary; remember that the activity of setting goals is a means to an end, which is reaching your ultimate goal: the successful completion of your psychology project.

Therefore the process of self-regulation, with its strong focus on goal setting, motivates you, the undergraduate psychology student, to achieve your goals. It also helps build your confidence based on measured achievement of goals, and also the perception of progress is critical for your continued motivation and perseverance.

5.2   Time Management

Time management is a series of methods that can help improve the quality, success and momentum of your psychology project. It is important to note that no two people have precisely the same idea of what constitutes effective time management. While there is no one-size-fits-all plan for managing time, there are basic principles (see Table 5.1) that can be applied to your project; the key is to be flexible and to have a plan.

1. Plan ahead

Planning is the fundamental building block of time management and is worth all the time you can put into it. An old cliché puts this importance into context: 'if you fail to plan, you plan to fail'. But it isn't enough simply to create a great plan or schedule. You must be able to implement it, i.e. put the schedule into practice. In order for this to happen, you must be accurate about the day-to-day realities of your college work and other responsibilities, and allow for the usual interruptions, crises and delays. Like a new pair of jeans, your schedule should fit comfortably, with a little room to spare in case they shrink in the wash, not to mention expanding waistlines.

Table 5.1   Eight time-management techniques

1.   Plan ahead
2.   Holistic approach
3.   Over-estimate time schedules
4.   Keep a diary
5.   Break down tasks
6.   Keep track of progress
7.   Prioritise
8.   Do hardest tasks during optimal concentration

2. Holistic approach

The best time-management plans involve the whole person; they encompass the whole of your life, rather than just your academic responsibilities. It is imperative, therefore, to schedule in blocks of time for family, friends, your social life and exercise, as opposed to assigning them 'whatever time is left'. This will help prevent those feelings of 'my life is on hold while I complete my project', and will help promote a more positive attitude and mind set.

3. Over-estimate time schedules

A very effective time-scheduling technique that you can apply is to somewhat over-estimate the time you think a task will take in order to ensure on-time delivery even in the face of unforeseen delays, for example if you forget to save a day's work on your computer, or if an inter-library loan is delayed. This can act as a positive reinforcement and as a short-term win.

4. Keep a diary

From week to week, keep a diary of how you actually spend your time. You may find that you have more time to use than you initially anticipated. This type of diary will then serve as a very useful aid when writing up your method-ology, especially the procedure section, which needs to be very specific, accurate and detailed.

5. Break big tasks into smaller manageable chunks

It's very easy to put off tasks of huge magnitude. By breaking a big task into manageable tasks, and setting a timetable for doing each task, you can accomplish this daunting task with a lot less hassle and anxiety than by trying to do it all at once. For example, suppose you have 100 cases to input into your statistical package for analysis, by dividing the cases into groups of 20, this already appears more manageable.

6. Keep track of your progress

Every project requires its own schedule. If you have set realistic target dates, your progress should match your plan. If unforeseen developments place you behind your anticipated dates, you can either set a revised completion date, or take steps to accelerate your progress and make up the lost time. For example, if you add an extra hour to each scheduled slot for a week or so, you should find yourself back up to speed.

7. Prioritise

Priority lists can act as useful checklists for work done and work still to do. It is possible to maintain several lists at once: a high priority checklist for urgent or very important tasks, and a medium-priority checklist for less urgent or moderately important tasks.

8. Do the hardest tasks during optimal concentration

To be as economic with your time as possible, try to do your hardest tasks – those requiring maximum concentration and peak efficiency – at those times of the day when your attention and energy levels are highest. If you can coordinate those times with periods in which you have fewer interruptions than usual, all the better. Likewise, try to schedule your routine, low-level tasks for times of the day when you find it hard to concentrate. The key is to pinpoint your hours of peak performance, and schedule your work accordingly.

5.3   Avoiding Procrastination

As already noted, the success of completing your research project can largely depend upon how effectively you use your time. Here are two useful strategies that you can apply when you find yourself practising procrastination, which is one of the biggest robbers of time.

1. Deconstruct the task

If a major task appears off-putting, as already mentioned, break it down into the smallest unit. For example, researching the literature: if you keep putting off this mammoth task, break it down into manageable tasks, such as reading two articles at a time, and then summarising their main points. Clearly this is more do-able.

2. Carry out related tasks

If you are having difficulty beginning a task, try carrying out a related task, as a way of easing yourself into the dreaded task. For example, if you just can't get your head around the discussion section of your project, arrange to meet a fellow student, and discuss your apprehensions and fears. This can help you resolve the issues that are holding you back, and motivate you to get working again.

5.4   Ways to Overcome Writer's Block

Students often need to overcome writer's block, a mental block that is familiar to us all, which needs to be broken in order to continue writing. Everything may have been going perfectly well until you come to one paragraph or a section of your project and you get stuck. You write something down, you know it's not quite right, but you just can't think of a better way to say it. You try to change the paragraph but the result is essentially the same. Your thinking has become channelled or crystallised, and you cannot break out of that particular thought pattern to write differently. A common response to this problem is to take a break, work on something different for a while, and come back to the difficult section later. With the passage of time, the neural pathway becomes less pronounced and it becomes easier to make new connections.

Another solution is to talk about the problem out loud. Ask yourself questions such as: What is the point of this paragraph? What am I trying to communicate? Answer yourself out loud as though talking to someone else. Speaking out loud can help break the block. Research suggests (Bishop, 1994) that the reason this happens is because written and spoken language are processed in different parts of the brain and activate different neurons.

5.5   Promoting a Positive Attitude

Completion of your project can be an overwhelming experience. Unfortunately, feelings of stress and anxiety are common while completing your research project. Feelings of anxiety can arise from bad time management and procrastination, and hence failure to meet deadlines, which can themselves cause more anxiety and stress. As already noted, applying time-management techniques such as deconstructing major tasks into smaller, less discouraging units, setting short-term wins and doing the hardest task during optimal concentration levels, can lower anxiety as useful self-management strategies, which create a tangible sense of control and accomplishment. Over-estimating the time you think tasks will take creates feelings of delight and competency, which give you confidence to complete your project.

5.6   Checklist

- Have you set goals that are Specific, Measurable, Action-oriented, Realistic and Time-based?
- Have you identified obstacles to your goals?
- Have you come up with ways to overcome these obstacles?
- Have you added in short-term goals to keep you focused on the longer-term goals?
- Have you developed a strategy for using the time-management techniques that will suit your schedule for completing your psychology project?

Summary

Motivational strategies, such as the goal-setting framework of self-regulation (involving planning, monitoring, evaluating and reflection) and the mnemonic SMART framework of goal setting, are useful for promoting and maintaining high motivational levels throughout the psychology project. Developing a holistic time-management schedule also facilitates successful completion of your project, while procrastination is a major pitfall that can be effectively avoided.

Students often need to overcome writer's block in order to continue writing by breaking crystallised thought patterns, by changing your medium of thought from writing to talking out loud. It is possible to create a balanced positive attitude conducive to successful completion of your project, by developing meta-competencies of self-management and self-regulation, which help promote feelings of accomplishment, value and autonomy.

Further Reading

Cryer, P. (2000) *The Research Student's Guide to Success*. UK: Open University Press.

6

MAXIMISING SUPERVISION

Objectives

On reading this chapter you should:

- understand the issues involved in establishing a positive and professional student–supervisor relationship; and
- be able to employ strategies to maximise the benefits of supervision in order to improve the quality of your research project.

Overview

This brief yet crucial chapter focuses on a very useful but under-utilised source that is available to the undergraduate student – supervision. Students often under-estimate the valuable resource that supervision is. In my experience, students who fall down when it comes to the grading of their project are very often the ones that did not utilise their supervision adequately and hence have made major errors that could have been easily avoided through the guidance of their supervisor. This chapter therefore deals with how to maximise the benefits of supervision. Section 6.1 deals with the establishment of the student–supervisor relationship. Students are often unsure about what to expect from supervision, and their perceptions of the student–supervisor relationship are often incorrect, which can ultimately lead to disappointment. There are a number of ways that such misconceptions and disappointment can be avoided. Developing a positive professional relationship with your supervisor based on mutual expectations will increase the quality of your undergraduate research. When you enter into a student–supervisor relationship, you will naturally have certain expectations of your supervisor, who in turn will have expectations of you, the student. Conflict can potentially arise if expectations are unclear or ultimately incongruent. Therefore, early discussion of expectations can establish and maintain a positive professional relationship, which can act as an explicit contract to guide the relationship. Finally, Section 6.2 deals with practical approaches to maximising feedback, which can enhance the quality of your psychology project.

Figure 6.1   Ways to maximise the student–supervisor relationship

6.1   Establishing the Student–Supervisor Relationship

The establishment and maintenance of a good relationship between supervisor and student is founded on mutual respect and open communication. There are a number of issues which, if discussed at the beginning of your supervision, will avoid misunderstandings in the future. There are a number of ways to maximise the student–supervisor relationship, as seen in Figure 6.1.

Guidance

An initial aspect of the relationship warranting discussion is the amount of input your supervisor will give on the direction of your research project, and the scope and type of guidance which will be given at undergraduate level. You can realistically expect that your supervisor will provide expert advice, or quality assurance. Your supervisor, having experience in supervising and examining undergraduate projects, will understand the standard your project should meet. Some supervisors read written work and give feedback, while others do not. This depends on the supervisor's style of supervision. It is therefore advisable to check with your supervisor whether they will read your work or not.

Supervision meetings

The establishment of regular meeting times is important. It is the responsibility of the student to attend supervisory meetings, be well prepared and have a clear agenda for the meeting. If your supervisor accepts written work, it is also beneficial to establish turnaround times for work you submit for appraisal. This type of time scheduling and communication are essential for ensuring that your supervisor will be able to give you the feedback you need in the time that you require. It is imperative to remember that your supervisor will have many other commitments; therefore, do not wait until the last minute to submit work for appraisal. It is your responsibility to make satisfactory progress following the feedback and advice you receive from your supervisor. It is also important that you discuss with and obtain the approval of your supervisor regarding any change in the direction or focus of your project.

Informal communication

Whatever schedule is established for formal supervision, it may be necessary to communicate between meetings. Hence, it is useful to discuss whether such communication can take place, via email or by phone, and to establish an appropriate turnaround time for these informal messages.

Written work

As already noted, it is important that you check your university's policies on submitting written work. If it is acceptable to submit written work, it is beneficial to understand your supervisor's expectations of such written work. Discuss whether your supervisor expects your work all at once or in sections, and at what intervals should you submit work. Ascertain whether your supervisor only appraises completed polished work or whether they will accept drafts of work in progress. It is also helpful to establish whether your supervisor would prefer to receive documents in hard copy or electronically via email.

6.2   Practical Approaches to Maximising Feedback

Receiving feedback, and reacting constructively to it, can really enhance the quality of your psychology project. It is therefore useful to be able to apply some techniques that can maximise the potential benefits of supervisory feedback (see Figure 6.2).

1. Always be prepared

It is imperative that you attend each supervisory meeting with a progress report, outlining what you have done since your last meeting. Such a strategy allows your supervisor an insight into your approach to your project. For example, if you have been focusing on the design of your study, before you have established the research question and hypotheses, this would become

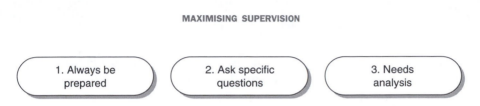

Figure 6.2   Practical approaches to maximising feedback

evident from the progress report and your supervisor could advise a different strategy more conducive to generating the research question first. The progress report also encourages you to put some needed structure on your thoughts, ideas and actions, which will promote critical thinking, but also keeps you focused on what you have done, and what you still plan to do. It is beneficial to keep copies of these reports for when you begin to write the methodology. It is also crucial to generate a list of questions and issues that you want to discuss at each meeting.

2. Ask specific questions

The more specific the question you ask, the more specific the feedback will be. For example, if you submit your literature review for appraisal and ask your supervisor whether it is ok, you are not going to receive the same quality of feedback as asking whether your literature flowed from the general to the specific in a logical order.

3. Conduct brief needs analyses on work for review

When submitting written work for review, it is vital that you are clear on the type of feedback that you require. Conducting a brief needs analysis can help focus the difficulties you have encountered. For example, as you read your results section, you may be unsure whether you have dealt with your descriptives in enough detail, or you may be unsure whether you have carried out sufficient explorative data analysis. Similarly, you may be unsure as to whether you carried out the relevant statistical analyses. Clearly these difficulties have different focuses – highlighting these to your supervisor will give them a clear indication of your needs and difficulties.

Summary

The establishment and preservation of a successful relationship between student and supervisor is founded on mutual respect and open communication. Early in the relationship, it is important to agree on the scope and type of guidance you will receive. By always being prepared, by asking specific questions, and by conducting brief needs analyses, you can take full advantage of your supervisor's expertise and knowledge, therefore taking full advantage of feedback and appraisal.

Further Reading

Cryer, P. (2000) *The Research Student's Guide to Success*. Buckingham: Open University Press. (Aimed at post-graduate level, but deals comprehensively with the issue of supervision.)

7

HOW TO HANDLE THE RESEARCH LITERATURE

Objectives

On reading this chapter you should:

- understand the role played by the research literature for psychology as a science;
- know where to search for literature;
- be aware of some of the major journals in psychology;
- be familiar with the major electronic databases of both full-text articles and abstracts;
- be familiar with how to search using the major electronic databases;
- be able to evaluate the quality of internet-based information;
- know how to review and critically evaluate the research literature;
- be able to organise the literature that you have evaluated; and
- understand that a literature search should be conducted multiple times throughout the research process.

Overview

This chapter deals with the practicalities of dealing with the research literature effectively. Section 7.1 outlines the role of the research literature for psychology as a science, and the importance of reading academic journals as opposed to popular journals that may not adhere to scientific rigour. Students are often intimidated by the vastness of the research literature in psychology and the related social sciences; therefore Section 7.2 outlines some of the major sources of academic literature, in order to give the student some visibility in the literature fog. This section deals with the main journals in psychology, and also describes the major electronic databases that are available and tips for using their search engines.

Section 7.3 gives caution to internet-based information. Section 7.4 describes how to critically review the research literature, through a question-guided process. Finally Section 7.5 illustrates useful ways to organise the literature you have reviewed, in order to use time as effectively as possible.

7.3   The Role of the Research Literature

Science is a community activity in which researchers and scientists try to correct one another's errors by sceptically evaluating each study. Also, scientific facts are built upon replication of finding. In order to critically evaluate and to build evidence for a hypothesis through replication, researchers share the results of their studies by publishing them and thus contributing to the research literature.

Previous research is a critical source of learning about a specific psychological area. Published research provides a background into the issues that pertain to your research question so that your hypothesis and research question fit with existing constructs and, ultimately, with the results of previous studies. The research literature also suggests numerous ideas for interesting studies and describes established procedures that can be incorporated into your research design. It is useful to define the target population early in the design process thus enabling you to develop a more precise research question as well as directing your attention to the most relevant portions of the literature.

The literature review needs to have some academic respectability, therefore the research literature does not refer to popular books and newspapers. It is important to focus on journals for the most current and valid developments in a particular area of research. However, professional journals vary in the quality of the research that they present; for example, some research journals are refereed, meaning that each article undergoes peer review by several psychologists (editorial board) who are experts in the relevant areas. Other journals do not have this structure in place, and the author of the article simply pays the publication costs.

TIP

Check the section that details the journal's editorial policies.
Look for journals published by professional organisations of psychologists such as the APA or the BPS, for example the *Journal of Applied Psychology* or the *British Journal of Psychology.*

It is very important to realise that a literature search should be carried out numerous times throughout the research process. Often students think that it is sufficient to carry out one literature search at the beginning of the process, in order to find a working topic and to develop research questions and hypotheses. This is not the case: you should also carry out a literature search to check for agreement of your constructs, and maybe to develop a new methodology to test them. During your data analysis and interpretation stages, you will go back to the literature to check for concurrence or disagreement with your findings.

7.2   Where to Search for Literature

There are many different sources of research literature in psychology. Textbooks are very useful starting points for introducing yourself to your topic of interest. Textbooks usually rely on secondary analysis of data from well-known work in particular areas. They also give the author's interpretations of findings. It is necessary to read original articles and review researchers' methodologies and results yourself. If your university/college does not hold a journal that you are interested in, it is possible to get an inter-library loan for the articles you need from your library.

The number of psychology journals available is extremely vast. Table 7.1 lists some of the common journals published by the American Psychological Association and the British Psychological Society. It is important to note that this is not an exhaustive list; the purpose here is to give you some starting points for your literature search.

Due to advances in information technology, most colleges and universities subscribe to electronic databases of psychological journals. Figure 7.1 shows the best known and comprehensive. Again it is important to flag that this is not an exhaustive list.

PsycARTICLES™

PsycARTICLES™ is a definitive database of full-text articles from journals published by the American Psychological Association, the APA Educational Publishing Foundations, the Canadian Psychological Association and Hogrefe & Huber. The database contains all material from the print journals except for advertisements and editorial board lists. The database boasts over 30,000 full-text articles covering general psychology and specialised, basic, applied, clinical, and theoretical research in psychology. Publications include the *Journal of Applied Psychology, Developmental Psychology, Psychological Review* and *Psychology and Aging,* from 1985 to the present. Each retrieved record has a link to the corresponding full-text article, which is almost always available in PDF and HTML format. Each record also has a link to the Table of Contents (TOC) for the issue in which the article was published.

Table 7.1   Some of the main psychology journals

Journals published by the American Psychological Association (APA)
American Psychologist
Developmental Psychology
Emotion
European Psychologist
Journal of Applied Psychology
Journal of Consulting and Clinical Psychology
Journal of Counselling Psychology
Journal of Experimental Psychology: Applied
Journal of Experimental Psychology: General
Journal of Experimental Psychology: Human Perception and Performance
Journal of Experimental Psychology: Learning, Memory and Cognition
Journal of Personality and Social Psychology
Psychological Bulletin
Psychological Review

Journals published by the British Psychological Society (BPS)
British Journal of Clinical Psychology
British Journal of Developmental Psychology
British Journal of Educational Psychology
British Journal of Health Psychology
British Journal of Mathematical and Statistical Psychology
British Journal of Psychology
British Journal of Social Psychology
Journal of Occupational and Organisational Psychology

Journal published by Intelligent Synthesis of the Scientific Literature Non Profit Publishers of Annual Review™ Series
Annual Review of Psychology

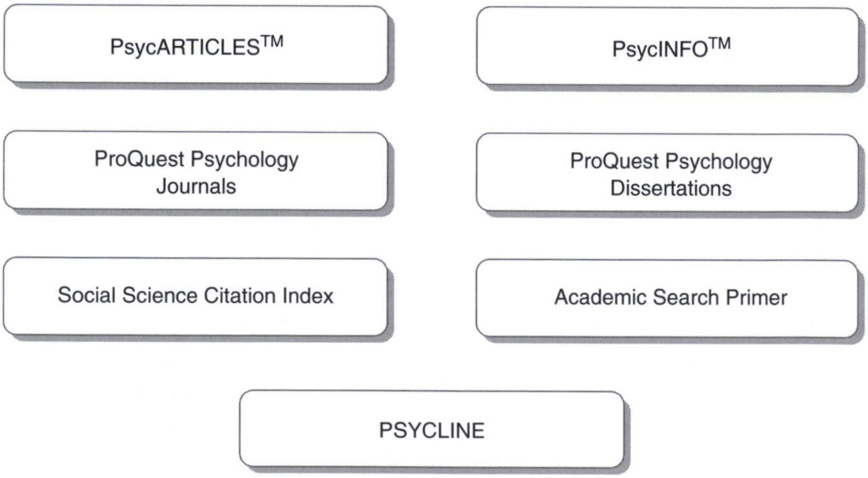

Figure 7.1   Popular electronic databases for psychology

PsycINFO™

PsycINFO™ from the American Psychological Association (APA) is an abstract database of psychological literature from 1840 to the present. It is the most comprehensive database of its kind, containing over 1,700 key titles in the fields of psychology, psychiatry and related disciplines, and an easy-to-browse thesaurus of the APA vocabulary. A facility called PsycINFO™ Plus Text combines this authoritative resource with ProQuest Psychology Journals to provide the key full-text articles that researchers need.

ProQuest Psychology Journals

Based on the PsycINFO™ index, ProQuest Psychology Journals offers information for almost 450 leading psychology and related publications, with over 330 of these in full text, from 1992. ProQuest also includes publications from the British Psychological Society, such as the *British Journal of Psychology*.

ProQuest Psychology Dissertations

ProQuest Psychology Dissertations offers 42,000 doctoral dissertations in psychology published since 1997. Linking to Psychology Dissertations for PsycINFO™, a facility only available from the ProQuest version of the database, creates a powerful, unique combination of resources.

Social Science Citation Index

The Social Science Citation Index provides indexing and abstracting in social sciences from 1999 to present. It is useful in tracing a line of research through citations of a particular article.

Academic Search Primer

The Academic Search Primer database offers indexing and abstracts for over 3,200 academic, social sciences, humanities, general science, education and multi-cultural journals, of which over 1,800 are full-text from January 1985.

PSYCLINE

There is also a very useful journal locator called PSYCLINE, which indexes over 2,000 online psychology and social science journals. This useful site links you to journal home pages and journal information on the web, and can be used to locate online journal articles, contact publishers, browse table of

Table 7.2   Key search procedures for PsycARTICLES™, PsycINFO™ and ProQuest Psychology Journals

PsycARTICLES™	PsycINFO™	ProQuest Psychology Journals
Quick Search Use when you are going to combine several search terms to narrow down your search. If the terms you use are too broad, you will get too many results.	Keyword This is a good place to start. Use AND/OR to make your searches more precise. AND will narrow your search, while OR will broaden it.	Basic Search Use when you are searching for one term.
Field-Restricted Search When you know two or three things about the article or articles that you are looking for; date range, author, journal title, population or age group, key concepts, etc.	Thesaurus Search Use the thesaurus to find terms related to your topic. You can broaden or narrow your searches this way. The + sign means that this term is broken down into narrower terms.	Advanced Search Use when you are searching for several terms simultaneously. Combine using AND.
Full Text Use this search if you know that the article you want contains a certain phrase or citation. Otherwise you will get too many results.	Browse Indexes Use if you are looking for something by a specific author, in a specific journal, studies done in a specific location or in a specific population.	Topic Search Use if you are looking for a specific topic.
Search by Journal Use this search if you know the journal that the article appeared in and a keyword or date.	Hot Topics Provides overviews of current topics in the news.	Publication Search Use this search if you know the journal that the article appeared in and a keyword or date.
Browsing by Journal Click on Browse Table of Contents on the start page. Use this search when you want to find out what has been published in a particular journal recently. Use when you know the journal that has the article you want but are not sure about the date, and when you want to get ideas for research topics.		

contents and abstracts. It also covers English, German, French, Dutch and Spanish language journals.

Different databases use different search procedures and students often have difficulty with getting to grips with the various systems. Table 7.2, therefore, outlines the key procedures for using PsycARTICLES™, PsycINFO™ and ProQuest Psychology Journals.

7.3   A Note on Internet-Based Information

As already noted, the literature review needs to have academic respectability. It is important to realise that practically anyone can post information on the internet without checks on its reliability and accuracy. This inevitably leads to misinformation, propaganda and disinformation on the internet (Sternberg, 2003). Students must always carefully evaluate material found on the internet. It is important to consider when the information on the website was written, and when it was last revised. You should also make a decision on whether the person responsible for presenting the information has the necessary qualifications. If information regarding who is responsible is not presented, stay clear of using this information. It is also important that you evaluate whether the information is reliable and valid.

7.4   How to Critically Review the Research Literature

Once you have chosen a topic, you then have to find out more about the area. Students often find that the more they read, the more confused they become. There are numerous directions to pursue, and so many interesting articles to read. It is very easy to lose sight of your focus, and to continue reading and reading. When reading an article in psychology, you should always have an objective or have particular questions in mind, this facilitates your critical thinking skills through a focused lens as opposed to reading aimlessly. This focused reading is also a very economic time-saving strategy, and can help prevent procrastination as you have very clear goals in mind, which can be broken down into smaller tasks if needed. It is important to understand the very important distinction between critically analysing and criticising past research or journal articles. Over-reliance on criticism should be avoided. Daft (1985) explains his views on criticism of the research literature as follows: 'Previous work is always vulnerable. Criticizing is easy, and of little value; it is important to explain how research builds upon previous findings rather than to claim previous research is inadequate and incomplete' (p. 198). The same rationale was applied by Maslow (1943) when he warned that it is far easier to criticise than to remedy. McGrath (1982) recommends keeping in mind that all research is flawed, and that you should respect the work of those who have worked hard to create the foundation of research for your project.

Meltzoff (1999) defines critical thinking as a skill that one has in thinking about an issue, analysing it, looking at it from all angles and deciding whether there is sufficient evidence of good-enough quality to warrant making a reasoned judgement that is as free of personal bias as possible. The undergraduate psychology student must become a critical consumer of research. Consequently,

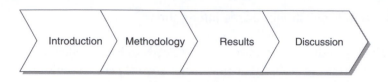

Figure 7.2   Four major sections to consider when reviewing a journal article for your project

critical thinking about research requires a reasonable level of content knowledge about the scientific method. According to the scientific method, 'theory' should describe behaviour, serve as the basis for making predictions about behaviour and provide a tentative explanation for the phenomenon. If you are unsure of the goals of the scientific method, or you have simply forgotten them, it is advisable, at this stage in the research process, to go back and revisit them in any comprehensive research methods text.

The critical thinking process can be viewed as a question-guided process. Undergraduate students often have difficulty in asking the appropriate questions. The following paragraphs detail the questions that you should answer when reading the articles that you have collated for your literature review. During the evaluative and critical thinking process, you will become more in touch with what goals and requirements your own research project should meet. Also, once you are in this frame of mind, it is much easier to write up your own project. These issues can be grouped under the four major sections of the research process: the introduction, methodology, results and discussion (see Figure 7.2). Not all the questions listed will be relevant to each article you review, and remember that the list is not an exhaustive one – you may well come up with other questions as you advance through the process.

Introduction

When reading the introduction and literature review of an article, it is useful to answer the following questions:

- Has the author formulated a logical research question?
- Has the research question been clearly presented and its significance clearly established?
- Was the author's research orientation quantitative, for example experimental, or qualitative, for example interpretative?
- Could it have been approached more effectively from another perspective?
- What is the author's theoretical framework, e.g. cognitive or developmental?
- Has the author evaluated the relevant literature, and have they given a true unbiased account?

Methodology

In reviewing the methodology sections, it is important to address the appropriateness of the basic components, through answering the following questions:

- Was the design adequate to answer the research question?
- Is the independent variable appropriate given the nature of the research question being asked?
- Were the levels of the independent variable appropriate?
- Were the variables of interest operationally defined?
- How accurate and valid were the measurements?
- Were the controls appropriate?
- Could you replicate the study based on the procedure given?
- Are the participants properly selected?
- Was the sample representative?

Results

In evaluating the results section, the following questions might be addressed:

- Were the analyses run appropriate to answer the research question?
- Were the assumptions for the use of the statistical tests met?
- Was adequate descriptive data provided including means and standard deviations, in order to gain an understanding of the data?
- Were the inferential or qualitative analyses clear and logical?
- Were there errors in the calculation or presentation of results?
- Were the tables and figures clearly labelled and presented?
- Were the conclusions validly based upon the data and analysis?

Discussion

Finally, in reviewing the discussion, you might answer the following questions:

- Was there an objective basis to the reasoning, or is the author proving what he or she already believes?
- How does the author structure the argument?
- Can you deconstruct the flow of the argument to establish whether it breaks down logically?
- In what ways does the article contribute to our understanding of the problem under investigation?
- What are the practical applications?
- What are the strengths and limitations of the study?
- What would you do to improve or redesign the study?
- How does the article relate to the specific research question that you are developing?
- Were the generalisations valid?

General

- Do the references match the citations in the text?
- Are the ethical standards adhered to throughout the study?

7.5   Organising the Literature that you have Reviewed

There are a number of ways that you can organise or structure the literature that you have reviewed. The two common approaches are to organise in an author-centric or a concept-centric fashion. To organise your studies by author in the former approach, although common, should be avoided, because it fails to synthesise the literature. The later approach is far more beneficial, and will be dealt with next.

To help organise the literature that you have reviewed in the concept-centric approach, group together the studies that appear to have something in common, for example sharing the same theoretical position. Then organise these groups into files that deal with different emphases as demonstrated in Figure 7.3. Taking the time to develop a logical approach to grouping and presenting the key concepts that you have uncovered that are relevant to your research question and hypotheses will really improve the quality of the literature-review section of your introduction, but will also facilitate your overall argument or thesis of your project.

Once you have organised your files, the objective is to make sense of each file. Sense making is facilitated when your review of the literature is logically

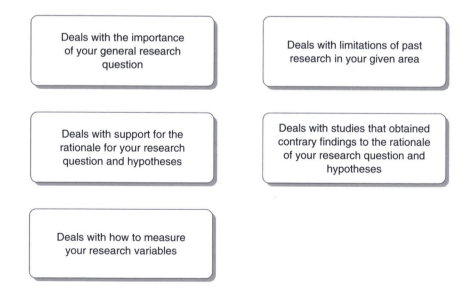

Figure 7.3   Example of files of literature with different conceptual emphases

organised around your research topics central ideas and concepts. This can be achieved by writing a sentence summary to represent the essential point of each file, for example by focusing on what each file has in common. These sentence summaries can act as the topics for each paragraph or point that you want to make. The research in each file can then act as the evidence or justification for the arguments that you are posing through the summary sentences. It is useful to display the relationships, connections and counter-arguments that you developed between the files on a big wall chart to keep you focused on what you want to write. Remember that the organisation of your reviewed literature succeeds when it aids others in making sense of the accumulated knowledge in your area of research.

Summary

Psychology as a science places an important role on the research literature, as a critical source of learning about a specific psychological area, and as a source of inspiration for undergraduate psychology projects. Students have a wealth of resources available to them for researching the psychological literature, including library collections of journals, textbooks, and electronic databases of full-text journals and abstracts. When critically reviewing an article, it is useful to implement a question-guided approach. It is also useful to organise the literature that you have reviewed in order to develop further insights before you start to write your introduction, which will be dealt with in the next chapter.

Further Reading

Hart, C. (2002) *Doing a Literature Review: Releasing the Social Science Research Imagination*. London: Sage Publications.

Meltzoff, J. (1999) *Critical Thinking about Research: Psychology and Related Fields*. Washington, DC: APA.

8

HOW TO WRITE A GOOD
INTRODUCTION

Objectives

On reading this chapter you should:

- understand how writing the introduction combines scientific and artistic writing, in evaluating past research and seeing new links and connections within the literature;
- understand the train of thought involved in writing the introduction from the general to the specific;
- understand the importance of starting your introduction with a strong statement;
- be able to highlight the importance of your study using the strategies highlighted in this chapter;
- understand the importance, for qualitative research, of striking a balance between reading enough literature to formulate a good research question, and reading too much which would bias your judgement of what to expect from your study;
- understand the importance of explicitly stating your hypothesis(es)/research question at the end of your introduction; and
- be aware of the common pitfalls to be avoided.

Overview

Chapter 8 deals with the introduction chapter of your psychology project. The introduction chapter reviews the relevant literature and presents the rationale for your project. The literature review is generally incorporated into the introduction. The main purpose of this section is to provide the necessary background or context for your research problem. Section 8.1 focuses on writing a good introduction and literature review. The purpose of the literature review is to present the reasoning or justification behind your project, and present a critical examination of the existing research that is significant to the research you are carrying out. It allows you to introduce and define the area you wish to study, explaining why it is interesting or important. It is highlighted how writing the literature review comprises science and art. This section also deals with practical issues such as what to include, and how long the literature review should be. It is demonstrated that length should not be used as a substitute for tight organisation and clear writing. Advice from Sternberg (2003) regarding the importance of reliability, validity and internal consistency in the literature review is also given.

Section 8.2 presents five useful strategies to highlight the importance of your study. Following this, Section 8.3 focuses on the importance of making your research question and hypotheses very explicit at the end of the introduction. Section 8.4 deals with the common pitfalls involved in this stage of the model of the research process, and Section 8.5.

8.1   Writing a Good Introduction

The purpose of the literature review component of your introduction is to present the reasoning or justification behind your project, and present a critical examination of the existing research that is significant to the research that you are carrying out. It allows you to introduce and define the area you wish to study, explaining why it is interesting or important. There are a number of ways to establish the importance of your study, which will be dealt with later in the chapter. The literature review demonstrates your knowledge, and understanding of the theoretical implications of your research question. It demonstrates your ability to critically evaluate relevant research, and illustrates your ability to integrate and synthesise information. The cognitive activities involved are rational and abstract processes that manipulate and systematically develop ideas towards the goal of refining them into researchable questions through deductive reasoning. The train of thought here develops and moves from the general to the specific, as it clearly begins with an overview of the research in the area, and ends with the specific aims of your research project.

As already noted in Chapter 7 students often make the mistake of viewing the literature review as a summary. Writing an adequate literature review involves evaluating the available evidence and theories, while also noting gaps in the literature, in order to create a synthesis that points readers in the direction of what appears to be true and accurate about the topic under investigation. Although you indeed need to summarise relevant research, it is also vital that you evaluate this work, and show the relationships between different studies, and how it relates to your research project. Therefore, you should not simply give a concise description of the articles that you are reviewing, you should select what parts of the research to discuss, for example the methodology, and show how it relates to other methodologies that have been used. Remember to use the strategies outlined in Sections 7.4 and 7.5 for this purpose. You should then show how it relates to your project, i.e. what is the relationship to your methodology. Always bear in mind that the literature review should provide the context for your research by investigating what has already

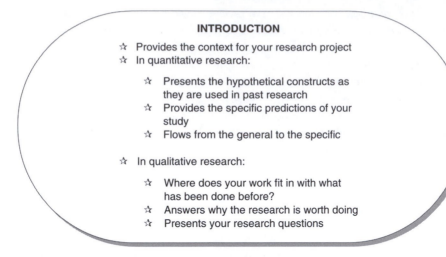

Figure 8.1   The major functions of the introduction

been carried out in the area. Clearly it is not supposed to be just a summary of other researchers' work.

Preparing an appropriate literature review is far from being a mechanical process; rather it comprises both science and art. The scientific aspect comes into play, in that scientific articles must be reviewed and evaluated. As seen in the previous chapter, knowledge and understanding of the scientific method are crucial in making valid evaluations. Creative and subjective processes come into play in making sense of the body of literature, which may require subjective judgements in determining which sources to emphasise, how to combine various sources and how to account for gaps in knowledge on a topic so that a cohesive syntheses of the literature occurs. Creative thinking also involves a process of recognising meaningful connections between apparently unrelated ideas and seeing these connections as key to the development of your study. Previously remote elements of thought suddenly become associated in a new and useful combination. When these links are made, the coin drops and previously unrelated information and ideas are brought together in new meaningful ways.

What to include?

A major difficulty students often face is deciding on what research to include in the literature review. It is advisable to review several older classic works in the area as well as more current research. Critically analysing rather than merely summarising articles, by analysing the strengths and weaknesses, will demonstrate that you have thought critically about what you have read. Remember that you should only include relevant information. If you include irrelevant information, you are not only violating the goals of precise and concise research, but you are also suggesting to the reader that you did not understand what was relevant or irrelevant.

How long should it be?

One of the most common questions that students ask regarding the introduction is: how long should it be? There is no definitive answer to this question. Students often think that the more they write, the better, but this is not the case. Length should not be used as a substitute for tight organisation and clear writing, it is important that you continue the same logic of concise and precise writing; throughout your research project. Some areas within psychology have significantly more research than others, for example cognitive psychology has a vast knowledge base in areas such as memory and learning, whereas more novel or new areas of research do not have such extensive knowledge bases developed, and therefore have less literature to review.

Sternberg (2003) advises, that sometimes a student may write more because they have more to say, and this is perfectly acceptable, providing that they do not stray from the guiding principle of the research question. On the other hand, students sometimes write more because it took several pages to say what could have been said in several sentences. This is not appropriate, as it deviates from the scientific attributes of precision and the concise writing of ideas.

Reliability, validity and internal consistency in the literature review

Sternberg (2003) notes that it is very important that your arguments are valid and consistent with the literature that you have reviewed. In establishing this dimension of your literature review, it is imperative to check that you have explained any inconsistencies, and that you have adequately substantiated each of your arguments. It is also imperative that you have reviewed reliable research – this point goes back to the importance of academic respectability. Sternberg (2003) also points to the importance of internal consistency. It is important that your arguments are consistent with each other, and that they are consistent with your general point of view, which is again guided by the research question.

Do you need to write a literature review in qualitative research?

Wolcott (1990) argues that students mistakenly assume a need to defend qualitative research, and proposes that after a century of qualitative research, there is no longer a need to provide an exhaustive literature review. He also notes the importance of integrating relevant literature as you need it, not in a distinct chapter but in the course of your analysis. Initially this may seem strange; however, this idea of integration reflects the iterative nature of qualitative research.

Reviewing the literature for qualitative-research projects often takes a number of stages, due to its iterative nature. Decisions must be made about the extent to which you should become familiar with the existing literature prior to initiating your study. Although recommendations vary, there is a general consensus toward minimal familiarity with the literature in the early stages of conceptualising your study, developing your research question and data collection (Fassinger, 2005). It is crucial that you strike a balance between enough knowledge to focus the sampling of data collection effectively and yet not so much immersion in existing perspectives that the investigation becomes circumscribed by pre-ordained constructs and prior expectations (Cutcliffe, 2000; Henwood and Pidgeon, 2003).

Therefore, the answer is still yes, you need to include an introduction and review of the literature chapter in your qualitative research psychology project. Your introduction and literature review chapter, however, will be shorter in length than in quantitative methods, but the length of the data-collection and data-analysis sections will be longer.

8.2 Strategies to Highlight the Importance of Your Study

Table 8.1 Strategies to highlight the importance of your study

1. Pervasiveness
2. Significance
3. Precedence
4. Corrects weakness
5. Builds and extends

1. Pervasiveness

There are a number of ways to establish the importance of your study. One way that this can be achieved is to illustrate that the concept is a common part of everyday life, by giving examples or by providing statistical evidence. The following example demonstrates the pervasiveness of motivation and leadership.

Example 8.1   Demonstrating pervasiveness

Motivation and leadership are the two fundamental areas that organisational researchers and practising managers look to in order to understand behaviour inside organisations.

2. Significance

Presenting a real-life example of your concept in action, in order to illustrate how the concept has significant implications for real life, is another way to demonstrate the importance of your study. Example 8.2 demonstrates the practical problems that might be solved by understanding the concept.

Example 8.2   From O'Loughlin, 2005

Different pranayama techniques are believed to have different effects on the mind and body. To calm the mind and reduce stress, to focus the mind and increase awareness, and to create a sense of balance and well-being (Iyengar, 1976; Rama, Ballentine & Hymes, 1979).

---

3. Precedence

Another strategy is to demonstrate that the concept has captured the interest of other researchers:

Example 8.3   From Barry, 2004

The emphasis on research to date has been to investigate why some subjects such as maths and science are more difficult to learn than others (e.g. Sweller, 1988, 1994; Sweller & Chandler, 1994; Paas, 1992).

---

4. Corrects a previous weakness

Showing that your study corrects a weakness in previous research is another way of effectively demonstrating the importance of your study, as seen in Example 8.4:

Example 8.4   From Woods, 2004

With regard to eyewitness memory for emotional events, the internal context at encoding and retrieval are often very different. ... The present study attempted to address many of the problematic issues associated with previous research on eyewitness memory, by investigating the effects of mood regulation through writing, on the accuracy of memory for emotional events.

---

5. Builds on and extends

A final strategy is to show that your study builds on and extends the work of previous researchers:

Example 8.5   From folio 90s

The purpose of this study was to investigate a predictive model of sources of motivation for understanding leaders' use of influence behaviours, and builds and extends on Barbuto & Scholls' (1999) study.

8.3   Stating Your Research Question and Hypothesis

As already noted, the purpose of the introduction is to demonstrate that you have read the relevant research and that you thoroughly understand your research question. Once you have articulated the reasoning behind your research project, you will present your research question and hypotheses (if relevant). For quantitative research, even though your readers may have guessed your hypotheses, you should leave nothing to chance. You must very explicitly state your hypothesis(es) – the tentative prediction of the answer of your research question. Sometimes students assume that their hypotheses are obvious, and do not state them. This is a major mistake, which should be avoided at all costs. No matter how obvious your hypotheses appear, it is imperative that you state them. Clear hypotheses are very important, as the rest of the research process is geared towards establishing confirmation of them.

The statement of your research question tells the reader the intent of your study and sets the stage for what is to follow. When you state your hypothesis, be very sensitive to whether you will be testing it with an experiment or a correlational study. Remember that only with an experimental study is it appropriate to use the word 'cause'. Making hypotheses explicit in the introduction are demonstrated in Examples 8.6 and 8.7 below.

Example 8.6   From O'Loughlin, 2005

The present study aimed to assess if 30 minutes of unilateral forced nostril breathing influenced performance on lateralised cognitive tests and if experience with breathing techniques enhanced the effects of unilateral deep nostril breathing on test performance. The four hypotheses were:

(Continued)

Hypothesis 1:   That unilateral forced right nostril breathing will significantly increase scores on tests of verbal ability.

Hypothesis 2:   That the increase in verbal performance following unilateral forced right nostril breathing will be more significant in yoga participants than in non-yoga participants.

Hypothesis 3:   Unilateral forced left nostril breathing will significantly increase scores on tests of spatial ability.

Hypothesis 4:   The increase in spatial performance following unilateral forced left nostril breathing will be more significant in yoga participants than in non-yoga participants.

Example 8.7   From Barry, 2005

The present study aimed to investigate the effects of spatial ability on the learning of complex science instructional material.

Hypothesis 1:   In group 1 (low spatial ability) mean completion times of participants who follow diagram-based instructions will be significantly faster than participants who follow text-based instructions on the molecule construction task.

Hypothesis 2:   In group 2 (high spatial ability) mean completion times of participants who follow diagram-based instructions will be significantly faster than participants who follow text-based instructions in the molecule construction task.

Hypothesis 3:   Mean completion times of group 2 (high spatial ability) will be significantly faster than group 1 (low spatial ability) in the text-based condition.

Hypothesis 4:   Mean completion times of group 2 (high spatial ability) will be significantly faster than group 1 (low spatial ability) in the diagram-based condition.

The following two illustrative examples (8.8) demonstrate how the research question or goal can be formulated in qualitative research using the grounded theory method. Once you have articulated the reasoning behind your research project, you will present your research question. The examples above demonstrate how this can be done effectively. It is important to note that these formulations are centralised around exploration as opposed to presenting predictions.

Example 8.8   From Timlin-Scalera et al., 2003

The following research questions were considered to gain a better understanding of the process of help-seeking of the present sample of white, middle- to upper-middle-class male adolescents:

(a) What are the mental health needs of this population?

(b) Under what circumstances, if any, would they seek help from a mental health professional for their personal needs?

(c) What factors might specifically motivate them to seek help from a mental health professional if they had a personal problem, or inhibit them from seeking that form of help?

(d) If they would not, or have not sought help from a mental health professional, what other coping skills or resources, if any, have they used in the past and for what issues?

(e) What are their perceptions of the roles of their school and community counsellors and mental health professionals?

(f) Do these adolescents perceive a need for changes that would better serve their mental health needs or make seeking professional help a more accessible and viable option?

8.4   Common Pitfalls

The following are some common traps that you should try to avoid when preparing and writing your introduction chapter.

1. Trying to read everything

As already noted, if you attempt to read all the literature you will never be able to finish the reading. You have a strict time scale to adhere to so your reading cannot continue to such lengths. Remember the purpose of the literature review is not to provide a summary of all the published work that relates to your research question, but a survey of the most relevant and significant work.

2. Reading but not writing

As you may have already noticed, it is much easier to read yet another article as opposed to writing about what you have already read. Writing takes much more effort, but it helps you to make sense of and find relationships between the work you have read. You will continue reading articles throughout the entire research process; the writing you start early will not be the final piece of work, but it acts as a very good foundation and facilitates the production of a seamless introduction.

3. Not keeping reference information as you go

Students sometimes come to writing their references section and realise that they have forgotten to keep the information they need. The only solution in this situation is to invest the time in the library tracking down all the sources that were read, and going through the introduction to find which information came from which source. This process is very time consuming, and inevitably eats into valuable time needed in other areas of the research process. In order to avoid this pitfall, always keep this information in your notes, and always put references into your writing.

8.5   Checklist

- Have you addressed a significant psychological phenomena, making clear the relevance to the advancement of psychological knowledge?
- Have you shown appropriate consideration of relevant theoretical and empirical literature?
- Have you stated your research questions clearly and explicitly?
- Does your introduction run from the general to the specific?
- Is your writing style clear and convincing?

Summary

The purpose of the literature review is to present the reasoning or justification behind your project, and present a critical examination of the existing research that is significant to the research you are carrying out. Preparing the literature review is far from being a mechanical process, rather it comprises science and art. The scientific aspect comes into play in that scientific articles must be reviewed and evaluated. Creative and subjective processes come into play in making sense of the body of literature which may require subjective judgements in determining which sources to emphasise, how to combine various sources and how to account for gaps in knowledge on a topic so that a cohesive syntheses of the literature occurs.

A major difficulty students often face is deciding on what research to include in the literature review. You should review several older classic works in the area as well as more current research but remember that you should only include relevant information. Length should not be used as a substitute for tight organisation and clear writing; it is important that you continue the same logic of concise and precise writing throughout the introduction. Sternberg (2003) notes that it is very important that your arguments are valid and internally consistent with the literature that your have reviewed.

There are a number of ways to highlight the importance of your study. One way that this can be achieved is to illustrate that the concept is a common part of everyday life, by giving examples or by providing statistical evidence, therefore demonstrating the pervasiveness of the concept. A second strategy is to illustrate its significance. You can also demonstrate that the concept has captured the interest of other researchers, i.e. precedence. Two final strategies involve showing how your study corrects a previous weakness or builds on and extends on past research.

Once you have articulated the reasoning behind your research project, you should present your research question and hypotheses. The statement of your research question tells the reader the intent of your study and sets the stage for what is to follow. There are a number of pitfalls that should be avoided, from trying to read everything, reading and not writing, to failing to keep reference information as you go.

Further Reading

Hart, C. (2002) *Doing a Literature Review: Releasing the Social Science Research Imagination*. London: Sage Publications.

Meltzoff, J. (1999) *Critical Thinking about Research: Psychology and Related Fields*. Washington, DC: APA.

Sternberg, R. J. (2003) *The Psychologist's Companion: A Guide to Scientific Writing for Students and Researchers* (4th edn). New York: Cambridge University Press.

Examples were taken from the following psychology projects that were presented in part fulfilment of the requirements of Bachelor of Arts, Department of Psychology, American College, Dublin:

Woods, J. (2004) *Mood dependent memory in eyewitness testimony: the effectes of negative mood regulation at recall on the accuracy of reports*.

O'Loughlin, S. (2005) The Influence of Unilateral Forced Nostril Breathing on Performance of Lateralised Cognitive Tests in Trained and Untrained Participants.

Barry, S. (2004) The Effects of Spatial Ability on the Learning of Complex Scientific Instructional Material.

9

SAMPLING CONSIDERATIONS

Objectives

On reading this chapter you should:

- understand the importance of sampling considerations;
- understand the difference between probability and non-probability sampling;
- be aware of the four popular types of probability sampling; and
- be aware of the five popular types of non-probability sampling.

Overview

This brief chapter deals with the important issue of sampling for your research project. Sampling issues are important for both quantitative and qualitative methods of inquiry, but they are considered at different times during the research process. For example, in qualitative research they are generally most important during the simultaneous data-analysis and data-collection phase, while in quantitative research they are most important during the planning and design stage of the research process. Section 9.1 deals with the importance of sampling considerations for your research project. Section 9.2 describes the four popular probability sampling techniques, while Section 9.3 describes five popular non-probability techniques.

9.1   Sampling Considerations

During your research methods courses, you would have learned about the importance of external validity, which is essentially the ability to generalise from your sample to the population of interest. It is important to be aware that this ability to generalise is greatly affected by the sample of participants in your study. A representative sample is one in which the characteristics of the participants reflect the characteristics of the population you are generalising to. Therefore it is very important that your sample is representative. Another important factor to bear in mind is that the population of interest depends on your research question, and that the validity of your outcomes and the conclusions of your study will greatly depend on your sample being representative. Sampling techniques are classified as either probability sampling or non-probability sampling.

9.2   Probability Sampling

Probability sampling procedures give us greater confidence that the sample efficiently represents the population of interest because they utilize some form of random selection of participants. In probability sampling each participant or element has some known specifiable probability of being included in your sample. There are a four popular probability techniques as seen in Figure 9.1, which are outlined below.

1. Simple random sampling (SRS)

Simple random sampling utilises an unsystematic, random selection process, where every member of the population has an equal chance of being selected. There is no bias in SRS that can lead to persons with certain characteristics having a higher probability of being selected than persons without those characteristics. SRS requires that you have a list of all members of the population, known as the sampling frame, which you can randomly select from. You can randomly select your participants using random number tables or by using a random-number generator, of which there are many available on the internet.

2. Stratified random sampling

Stratified random sampling is a useful procedure when you need to randomly select subgroups of participants for your sample. There are a number of types of stratified random sampling, for example proportional or quota random sampling and equal allocation stratified random sampling. Proportional random sampling allows for the sample to be taken using simple random sampling for each of the subgroups (for example, male and female), according to their representation proportionately to the entire group.

Equal allocation stratified sampling is used when the same percentage of the group members is selected from each group, using simple random sampling, regardless of the total size of the group. The result of both types of sampling should be a sample that represents each of your subgroups.

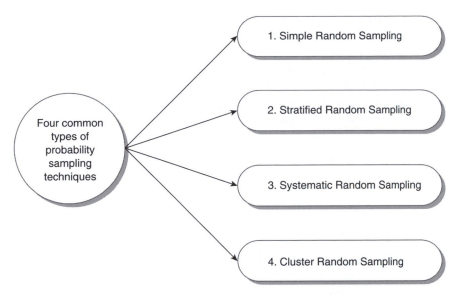

Figure 9.1   Four popular probability sampling techniques

3. Systematic random sampling

Systematic random sampling utilises a systematic random-selection process. Some ordered or systematic criteria is used from a randomly arranged sampling frame. For example, when a list of the members of the target population is compiled, a name on the list is chosen as the starting point, and then every 10th participant is selected. This is a very quick and easy sampling technique to use.

4. Cluster random sampling

The fourth type of probability sampling is generally used when it is beyond the researchers' ability to compile a complete list of the population of interest, but it is possible to get a complete list of the groups or clusters that make up the population. Simple random sampling is applied to the representative 'clusters' to select the clusters in which all members will participate. This type of sampling is very economic for large populations.

9.3   Non-Probability Sampling

Qualitative researchers generally work with small sample sizes and study them in a lot of depth, as opposed to quantitative researchers who usually work with large sample sizes and are more concerned with statistical significance. Qualitative samples are usually purposive (Morse, 1989), based on non-probability sampling as opposed to random samples based on probability sampling.

The main difference between non-probability and probability sampling is that non-probability sampling does not involve random selection and probability sampling does. From this, an important question arises: does this mean that non-probability samples aren't representative of the population? Fortunately the answer is not necessarily. With non-probability samples, you may or may not represent the population well. The following section will deal with five popular non-probability sampling techniques as illustrated in Figure 9.2.

1. Purposive sampling

In purposive sampling, you sample with a purpose in mind. For example, you would usually have one or more specific predefined groups that you are seeking. Purposive sampling can be very useful for situations where you need to reach a targeted sample quickly and where sampling for proportionality is not the primary concern.

2. Theoretical sampling

Here you recruit participants to your study as features of potential interest are identified through, for example, the interview process – each interview you conduct provides a slice of data on which you can build. Therefore through simultaneous involvement in data collection and analysis, you avoid becoming overwhelmed by volumes of general unfocused data that do not lead to anything new. This cumulative process is known as theoretical sampling, and is dealt with in more detail in Unit 3 of the book, which deals with qualitative methods of inquiry.

3. Convenience Sampling

Convenience sampling is probably the most commonly used sampling technique by undergraduate psychology students when recruiting the participants for their study. It is also very common for undergraduate psychology students to use other undergraduate students as their participants. If you use a convenience sample it is very important that you describe the composition of your participants in the participants section of your methodology, as the composition and type of sample that you have selected has implications for the external validity and the conclusions that you can draw from your analysis. This point is covered a number of times in Units 2 and 3 of the book.

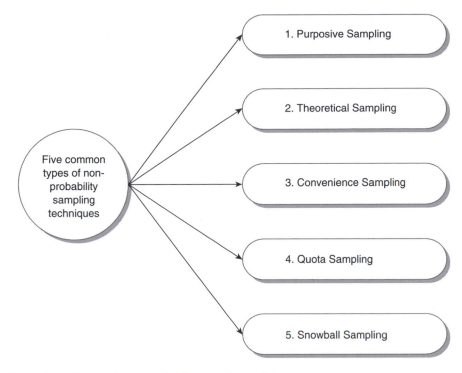

Figure 9.2   Five popular non-probability sampling techniques

4. Quota sampling

In quota sampling, you select people non-randomly according to some fixed quota. There are two types of quota sampling: proportional and non-proportional. In proportional quota sampling you want to represent the major characteristics of the population by sampling a proportional amount of each. For instance, if you know the population has 40% women and 60% men, and that you want a total sample size of 100, you will continue sampling until you get those percentages and then you will stop. So, if you've already got the 40 women for your sample, but not the 60 men, you will continue to sample men. Even if legitimate women respondents come along, you will not sample them because you have already 'met your quota'. The key issue is that you decide on the specific characteristics on which you will base the quota, on the basis of your research question.

Non-proportional quota sampling is a bit less restrictive. In this method, you specify the minimum number of sampled units you want in each category. Here, you're not concerned with having numbers that match the proportions in the population. Instead, you simply want to have enough to assure that you will be able to talk about even small groups in the population. This method is the non-probabilistic analogue of stratified random sampling in that it is typically used to assure that smaller groups are adequately represented in your sample.

5. Snowball sampling

In snowball sampling you begin by identifying someone who meets the criteria for inclusion in your study. You then ask them to recommend others who they may know who also meet the criteria. Although this method would hardly lead to representative samples, there are times when it may be the best method available. Snowball sampling is especially useful when you are trying to reach populations that are inaccessible or hard to find. For instance, if you are studying drug users you are not likely to be able to find good lists of drrug users. However, if you identify one or two, you may find that they know other drug use and how you can find them.

Summary

Sampling techniques are essential in the design of both quantitative and qualitative methods of inquiry. Four popular types of probability sampling include simple random, stratified random, systematic random and cluster sampling. Five popular non-probability sampling techniques include, purposive, theoretical, convenience, quota and snowball sampling.

Further Reading

Cochran, W. G. (1977) *Sampling Techniques (Probability & Mathematical Statistics)*. London: John Wiley & Sons.

10

SOURCING MATERIALS AND MEASURES FOR PSYCHOLOGICAL RESEARCH

Objectives

On reading this chapter you should:

- be aware of the major sources for both published and non-published psychological tests and measures, which are of potential use for your project;
- be aware of the sources for psychological equipment for your project;
- understand the ethical issues involved in using tests and measures for your psychology project;
- be able to evaluate potential tests and measures for your project, by assessing the reliability and validity claims made by them; and
- have a practical understanding of the different types of reliability and validity, and how they can affect your project.

Overview

Students often have difficulty with the practical task of actually sourcing materials, measures and equipment for their undergraduate project. Due to the magnitude of psychological measures and equipment available, it is not surprising that undergraduate psychology students find themselves in this situation. In fact, many post-graduate students and long-standing researchers have similar difficulties with this respect, and they too can invest significant time into researching and sourcing the materials and measures that are available in the field. Section 10.1 provides useful information on how to source both published and unpublished tests and measures, and therefore to save valuable time for the undergraduate researcher of psychology.

Section 10.2 briefly deals with ways to source psychological apparatus for your project. Most institutions have general equipment that is usually available for students to use; however, if a piece of apparatus is unusual you may need to source it for yourself. Following this, Section 10.3 deals with the very important issue of ethics for test users. Regardless of whether you use a published or non-published measure in your research project, it is vital that you have received permission from the author, and acknowledge this in your methodology.

Sourcing measures and materials is only one part of the process. It is crucial that you choose measures that have high reliability and validity. Therefore Section 10.4, details the necessary considerations that should be made when deciding on a measure. The different types of reliability and validity are outlined, and the relationship between the different perspectives is exemplified. Some words of caution are also given for interpreting both the reliability and validity of a measure, in an attempt to aid the undergraduate student in becoming an objective and knowledgeable consumer of the vast number of psychological materials and measures that are available.

10.1   Sourcing Materials and Measurements

For experimental projects, once you have operationalised your variables (which is dealt with in Unit 2 of the book), you can then decide on what psychological-testing instruments or materials you need. There are thousands of testing and assessment tools available today, so it is very important that you choose ones that are both reliable and valid. Once you begin this search, you will soon see that some are free to use, while others are quite expensive, and some are limited to qualified psychologists (or can be used under their supervision), while others are accessible to the general public. This section will deal with the various issues related to locating and finding psychological tests, with specific reference to the print and online resources that are useful to the undergraduate psychology student, as seen in Table 10.1.

Published tests and measures

An excellent starting place for sourcing tests and measurements are the testing references available at your university library. These references provide comprehensive and directive information on tests, and provide valuable information regarding who publishes the test and how to evaluate it.

The Sixteenth Mental Measurements Yearbook (MMY) (2005) has been the standard source for information about and reviews of educational and psychological tests for many years. For an index to all volumes (or editions), you can search the web-based index. The online database equivalent of *Mental Measurements Yearbook* contains descriptive information and critical reviews of new and revised tests published over the past 30 years. The database covers thousands of commercially available tests in categories such as personality, developmental, behavioural assessment, neuropsychological, achievement, intelligence and aptitude, educational, speech and hearing, and sensory

Table 10.1   Major sources of materials and measures for psychologists

Sources of published tests and measures

- *The Sixteenth Mental Measurements Yearbook (MMY)* (2005), published by the Buros Institute for Mental Measurements, Lincoln, NE
- *Tests in Print (TIP)* published by the Buros Institute for Mental Measurements, Lincoln, NE
- *Tests* published by Pro-Ed, Inc., Austin, TX
- *Test Critiques* published by Pro-Ed, Inc., Austin, TX
- *The Comprehensive Handbook of Psychological Assessment: Four Volume Set,* published by John Wiley & Sons Ltd, Chief Editor Michel Hersen (2003)

Sources of unpublished tests and measures

- *PsycINFO*™
- *Directory of unpublished experimental measures* published by C. Brown Publishers
- *Measures of Psychological Assessment: A Guide to 3,000 Original Sources and their Applications* published by the Institute for Social Research
- *Health and Psychosocial Instruments (HAPI)* published by Behavioral Measurement Database Services
- *The Educational Testing Service (ETS) Test Collection*

motor. It also contains additional information on the extent to which reliability, validity, norming data, scoring and reporting services, and foreign-language versions are available. A free version is also available on the internet as *Mental Measurements Yearbook Test Reviews Online*; however, it does not contain reviews.

Tests in Print (TIP). is a bibliographic encyclopaedia of information on every published and commercially available test in psychology and achievement. The most current volume is the 2002 sixth edition. There are no critical reviews or psychometric information on the tests – detailed information on individual tests is available in other reference books such as *MMY*. *TIP* was created to serve as a master index to the whole Buros Institute reference series on tests, including the 15 *MMY*s and the monograph series. The only criterion for inclusion is that the test be in print and available for purchase or use.

Tests is a comprehensive reference for assessments in psychology, education and business. The most current edition is the 2003 fifth edition. The text is also a bibliographic encyclopaedia, containing information on thousands of testing instruments in psychology, education and business. It provides concise descriptions of tests, with each entry including the test title and author, the intended population, the test's purpose, the major features, the administration time, the scoring method, the cost and availability, and the primary publisher. Also, a scanning line uses coded visual keys to indicate whether the test is self- or examiner-administered. *Tests* does not contain evaluative critiques or data on reliability, validity or norms – this information can be found for selected instruments in *Test Critiques*.

Test Critiques is updated annually, and is designed to be a companion to *Tests*. It contains supplemental information including psychometric information such as reliability, validity and norm development. Tests are chosen for inclusion based on research on the most frequently used psychological, educational and business-related tests.

The Comprehensive Handbook of Psychological Assessment: Four Volume Set is an innovative reference which presents essential information on the four major classes of psychological assessment instruments, including intelligence/ neuropsychological, personality (both objective and projective), behavioural and industrial/organisational. Each volume contains information on the history of the specific branch of testing, the range of tests, theoretical considerations, psychometric concerns, range of populations, cross-cultural factors, use with people with disabilities, legal/ethical considerations, computerisation and future development. Individual chapters consider these topics as they relate to specific instruments. As a result, these volumes are indispensable for clinicians and researchers in these areas. Volume 1, Intellectual and Neuropsychological Assessment, is edited by Gerald Goldstein and Sue R. Beers. Volume 2, Personality Assessment, is edited by Mark J. Hilsenroth, Daniel L. Segal and Michel Hersen (Editor-in-Chief). Volume 3, Behavioral Assessment, is edited by Stephen N. Haynes, Elaine M. Heiby and Michel Hersen (Editor-in-Chief). And finally Volume 4, Industrial and Organisational Assessment, is edited by Jay C. Thomas and Michel Hersen (Editor-in-Chief).

Unpublished tests and measures

It is useful to note that psychological measures are not limited to published tests – there are numerous unpublished or non-commercial inventories and measures that exist in the behavioural sciences literature. It is difficult for the undergraduate student to know where to find these measures; however, once you know where to look, the process becomes straightforward. The following paragraphs details such sources.

PsycINFO™ can be used to locate references to testing instruments. Use the Classification Code for Tests (222.cc) or consult the PsycINFO™ Thesaurus for appropriate descriptors. (Searching for either 'assessment instrument in the Special Features field or 'test/survey appended' in the Form Content field can also be productive when looking for complete instruments appended to journal articles.)

Directory of unpublished experimental measures contains eight volumes from 1974 to 2003. They contain lists of non-commercial, experimental measures, with very short descriptions, and were created to enable researchers to determine what types of non-commercial experimental test instruments are currently in use. The entries are not evaluative, but do include information about reliability, validity and related research, if available.

Measures for Psychological Assessment: A Guide to 3,000 Original Sources and their Applications is another useful resource. Although it contains a wealth of references to experimental measures and corresponding research, this text is outdated, as it was last published in 1975. It is a helpful resource when looking for a specific measure appearing in the literature during the 1960s or early 1970s, but you would want to consult a more recent measure that is appropriate for your need.

Health and Psychosocial Instruments (HAPI) is another useful computerised database. Many measures created or modified for specific studies appear in journals, but never become commercially available, this database publicises their existence and allows researchers and students to benefit from past work and avoid re-creating existing instruments. *HAPI* uses controlled vocabulary descriptors from APA's *Thesaurus of Psychological Index Terms and the National Library of Medicine's Medical Subject Headings (MeSH)*. The database, which is updated quarterly, contains over 15,000 instruments, most appearing in the literature between 1985 and the present. One particularly useful feature is that reliability and validity can be used as keywords to access instruments with tested psychometric properties. You could, for instance, search for all instruments in your area with demonstrated test–retest reliability, construct validity or both. *HAPI* is available at many college libraries through BRS Information Technologies. Now, it is also available on CD-ROM, which is updated twice a year.

The Educational Testing Service (ETS) Test Collection database contains records on over 10,000 tests and research instruments, and is also available on the internet as *ETS Test Collection*. These offer information on a multitude of educational and psychological tests cited in the literature but unavailable commercially. This includes both never-published and out-of-print tests. Users who purchase the microfiche may reproduce tests for their own use. Currently, there are over 800 tests included, with new sets of tests prepared annually and added to the cumulative set. These can be purchased as a set or by individual title, and an annotated index is available with each set. Also available is the *Cumulative Index to Tests in Microfiche* (1975–87), which indexes all tests available for the first 13 sets of *Tests in Microfiche*. This reference is available at many college and university libraries.

10.2   Sourcing Psychology Apparatus

Your university will stock a number of experimental apparatus, that are usually available for students to use for their undergraduate psychology projects. However, if your institution is quite small and does not have a particular apparatus that you need to carry out your project, you may have to source it for yourself. The company *Lafayette Instrument* has a wide range of apparatus, that can be ordered online. Their life-sciences section covers areas as diverse as biofeedback systems, psychomotor, learning and memory, sensory and perception, and reaction timing.

10.3 Ethics for Test Users

Whether you use published or non-published tests in your research project, it is vital that you have received permission from the author. This is fairly straightforward when the test has been published. For unpublished tests you must contact the test author and request permission to use their test, and secure their permission in writing if the material is copyrighted.

Locating the author may be a difficult process, particularly if the measure is several years old. The first step to take in such situations is to go back to the journal article: where the article lists the author's organisational affiliation or university, you should find contact information. If this fails, directories published by scientific and professional associations such as the APA, the PSI and the BPS could provide you with a more current address and phone number for the author. This is useful if the article is several years old and the author has moved since the article was published. If these attempts to locate the author fail, contact the publisher holding the copyright to the original material and request permission from the publisher. No matter how difficult this process may seem, you should make every effort to contact an author or copyright holder to secure permission before using any test or other instrument.

Sometimes, an author may have some conditions attached to the use of a measure. For example, the author may want a copy of your results afterwards, including the raw data, as they often want to add this to their ongoing analysis of their measure. Or if you have translated the measure into a different language, the author may want a copy of the translated measure to add to their collection. If you make any such agreements with authors of tests and measures, it is very important that you uphold your end of the bargain.

10.4 Evaluating Measures

The goal of measurement is to assign numbers to behaviours, objects or events so that they correspond in some meaningful way to the attribute that you are going to measure. You should aim at selecting measures, where the variability in the numbers assigned  reflects, as accurately as possible, the variability in the attribute being measured. For example, if you weigh yourself on a bathroom scale three times in a row, you expect to obtain the same weight each time. If, however, you weigh

140 pounds the first time, 108 the second time and 162 the third time, then the scales are unreliable – they can't be trusted to provide consistent weights. Therefore for a measure to be reliable, its results should be repeatable when the behaviours are re-measured. It is important to note that if you use a measure that is unreliable in your project, then you will not obtain meaningful data. As already outlined in Chapter 2, poor science is unethical, as poor conceptualisation and design will end in results that have no use or real meaning for furthering scientific knowledge.

Reliability

The basic idea of reliability is reflected by the word 'consistency'. The way in which reliability is conceptualised by researchers can take one of three basic forms:

1. To what degree has a person's measured performance remained consistent across repeated testing? – *Test–Retest Reliability.*
2. To what extent do the individual items that go together to make up a test or inventory consistently measure the same underlying character? – *Internal Consistency Reliability.*
3. How much consistency exists among the ratings provided by a group of raters? – *Inter-rater Reliability.*

Each reliability technique produces a single numerical value, known as the reliability coefficient. This value is simply an indicator of the data's consistency, and generally takes a value between 0.00 and +1.00. The purpose of the following sections is not to go through the calculations of each type of reliability, rather it is to explain the logic involved. Therefore, in assessing the suitability of a particular measure, you will understand how the author has conceptualised reliability, and whether it suits your purpose. Also in explaining the logic the hope is that you can become a better critical consumer of the measurements available.

1. Test–retest reliability

If you are measuring variables that should be stable over time, then a reliable measure should give the same or a very similar reading at different points in time. To calculate this index, researchers generally measure a group of participants twice on the same measure. The time period between two testing sessions can be very short, for example a day, or very long, for example a year or more. Taking this variability in the length of time between testing sessions, it is important to note that high coefficients of test–retest reliability are far more impressive when the time interval between sessions is long. It is advised

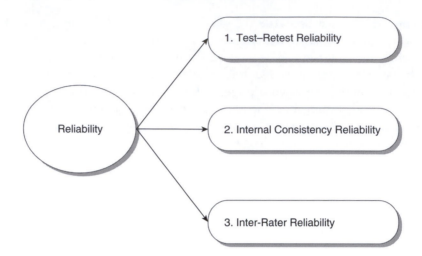

Figure 10.1   Three major sources of reliability

that you look to see what the time interval between test sessions of a potential instrument is. If you pay no heed to this issue, and use the measure anyway, the reader or examiner of your project will certainly take your claims about reliability with a grain of salt.

2. Internal consistency reliability

Some measures may report the internal consistency reliability, instead or as well as the inter-rater reliability (see below). This is the most common reliability quoted, but ideally at least one of the other measures of reliability should also be quoted. Internal consistency reliability is defined as consistency across the parts of a measuring instrument, with the parts being individual questions or subscales. There are three very popular procedures for calculating the internal consistency that you will probably encounter when evaluating potential measures for your project: the split-half reliability coefficient; Kuder-Richardson #20; and the cronbach alpha. The cronbach alpha is probably the most commonly used and most versatile approach. This technique simply gives a value for all the items on the measure correlated with each other.

3. Inter-rater reliability

The index of inter-rater reliability gives the degree of consistency among raters. There are a number of popular procedures for inter-rater reliability known as Kendall's Coefficient of Concordance, which is often used for ranked or ordinal data, Cohen's Kappa is similar but is used for nominal data, and Pearson's Product–Moment Correlation which is suitable for interval/ratio data.

Warnings regarding reliability

It is important to note that different methods or reliability reflect different perspectives. For example, a high coefficient of stability doesn't mean internal consistency is high also. It is also important to realise that reliability coefficients apply to data, not to measuring instruments. Reliability is theoretically and computationally related to the data produced by the use of a measuring instrument, not to the measuring instrument itself as a stand alone measure. It is of paramount importance that you understand that reliability is a property of the scores produced by the administration of a measure and, as you will see in later chapters, this is why it is very important to cite the reliability from your own investigation, as well as the measure's documented reliability. A final warning is concerned with the fact that reliability is not the only criterion that should be used to assess the quality of data. Another very important criterion is validity, which will be dealt with next.

Validity

Validity can be defined as 'accuracy'. Data are valid to the extent that the results of the measurement process are accurate. In assessing the quality of potential measures for your project, it is vital that you are aware of the relationship between reliability and validity. It is possible for research data to be highly reliable even though the measuring instrument does not measure what it claims to measure. However, an instrument's data must be reliable if they are valid. High reliability is a necessary but not sufficient condition for high validity.

Different types of validity

There are three popular ways of viewing validity: content validity criterion-related validity and construct validity.

1. Content validity

When deciding on the best inventory for your project, an important question concerns the degree to which the various items jointly cover the material that the measure is designed to measure. Content validity is often determined by experts carefully comparing the content of the measure against an outline that specifies the instrument's claimed area or field. This subjective opinion from subject matter experts (SMEs) establishes or doesn't establish the content validity of an instrument.

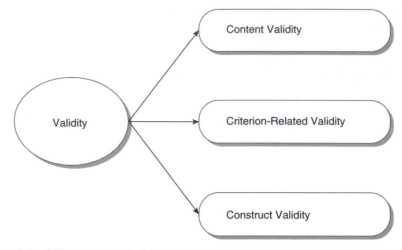

Figure 10.2   Different types of validity

2. *Criterion-related validity*

To establish criterion-related validity, researchers assess the degree to which new measurements provide accurate measurements by comparing scores from the new instrument with scores on a relevant criterion variable. For example, a new intelligence test might correlate itself with the Stanford Binet.

3. *Construct validity*

Construct validity is very important in psychological research. This type of validity addresses whether the construct being measured by a particular instrument is a valid construct, and also whether the instrument is the best one for measuring it. Many measuring instruments are developed to reveal how much of a personality or psychological construct is possessed by the respondents to whom the instrument is administered.

To determine the degree of construct validity, it is common to provide correlational evidence showing that the construct has a strong relationship with certain variables that it should be related to, and a weak relationship with other variables, that it shouldn't be related to. It is also customary to conduct a factor analysis on the scores from the new instrument.

Warnings about validity claims

To assist you in evaluating potential measures for you research project, you need to be aware of some concerns regarding validity claims. You must always be on guard for unjustified claims of validity and for cases where the issue of validity is not addressed at all. Remember that reliability is an essential but not sufficient condition for validity. Do not be coaxed into an unjustified sense of security concerning the accuracy of research data by a technical and persuasive discussion of consistency.

Summary

Sourcing materials and measures can be a very time-consuming task, especially if you are unaware of the major sources of both published and unpublished measures. Whether you use published or non-published measures in your psychology project, it is extremely important that you have received permission for the author beforehand. There are a number of issues to be considered when choosing a measure to use for your psychology project. The objective is always to use a measure that has high reliability and validity and that has been well established. It is also very important that you choose a measure that does in fact measure how you have operationalised your variables of interest. Reliability addresses the consistency of a measure, while validity refers to its accuracy. Just because the data resulting from a particular measure may be highly reliable, it doesn't mean that it measures what it purports to measure. However, a measure's data must be reliable if it is in fact valid. It is important to realise this distinction, and to thoroughly evaluate the appropriateness of a particular measure, for the aims of your study.

Further Reading

Anastasi, A. and Urbina, S. (1997) *Psychological Testing* (7th edn). Upper Saddle River, New Jersey: Prentice Hall.
Borsboom, D. (2005) *Measuring the Mind: Conceptual Issues in Contemporary Psychometrics*. Cambridge: Cambridge University Press.
Kline, P. (1999) *Handbook of Psychological Testing*. London: Routledge.

UNIT 2
QUANTITATIVE METHODS OF
INQUIRY

Introduction

The long-standing quantitative approach to inquiry emphasises precise measuring of variables and testing hypotheses that are usually linked to general casual explanations. Quantitative researchers are usually concerned about issues of design, measurement and sampling, because their deductive approach emphasises detailed planning prior to data collection and analysis.

Quantitative methods of inquiry have a long tradition. Chapter 11, *Quantitative Methods of Inquiry*, outlines some of the most significant characteristics of the method. Over the years, numerous models have been developed to portray the steps involved in quantitative research. Models are very useful for the undergraduate psychology student to help prevent feelings of being lost amidst the research process. Such models should be viewed as being flexible as opposed to cast in stone. The logic of experimental design, a simple concept that often surprises students, is described as referring to arranging the overall structure of your experiment in order to see the effects of the independent variable on the dependent variable as clearly as possible under controlled conditions. Quantitative methods of inquiry can vary from interventionist (experiments) to non-interventionist (correlational and differential research). Quantitative researchers will often focus extensively on operationalising variables into measurable entities during the planning and designing stage, occurring before conducting the actual research.

Chapter 12, *Analysing Quantitative Data*, deals with the rational tasks of processing and making sense of the data obtained for analysis. The appropriateness of a statistical procedure in answering your research question depends on a number of things: your research question, your research design and the type of data that you have collected. Due to space limitations, the computations and logic behind statistical techniques can be found elsewhere, as they are beyond the scope of a book of this nature. An example of a differential study is utilised to work through the steps involved in hypothesis testing. Results that are highly significant and near significant are considered, along with the meaning of significance, from both a statistical and practical perspective.

Chapter 13, *Designing and Conducting an Experimental Based Project*, deals with the second stage of the model of the quantitative research process: the designing, planning and the specific methodology employed to answer the research question. The important role of the research question is again demonstrated: as no single experimental design is necessarily better than another, the suitability rests with the nature of the research question(s) being asked. The chapter also details the important stages of planning and designing your study. The stages involve operationally defining your research variables, deciding on who your participants should be, and what sampling technique to use to select your participants. The important decision of how to assign participants to the various levels of your independent variable in order to answer your research question is also dealt with, and what type of data to collect.

The next design decisions involve sample size, representativeness, power and statistical analyses. The final decision involves ethical considerations which were dealt with in considerable detail in Chapter 2. The importance of keeping a detailed record during this phase, and the role of the pilot study, are also noted.

Chapter 14, *Writing Up your Quantitative Methodology*, considers how, in the form of its various subsections, the methodology should contain all the information needed by another researcher to replicate your study. The design subsection should be a very precise and concise overview of the formal design and of the principal features of your study. The research question is described as being the major factor in determining the appropriateness of your design. Students often under-estimate the importance of a comprehensive participants section, therefore the detail that is needed is described. The materials subsection describes the information that should be reported for measures and for any apparatus used in your study. The procedure subsection and the importance of sufficient detail for replication are explained. Finally, the data management subsection is useful for describing any checks that you ran on your data and any cleaning up of the data that was necessary.

Chapter 15, *Writing Up your Quantitative Results Section*, describes how you have some choice in how you organise the presentation of your results. The results section of your project provides a concise yet comprehensive description of your results, including descriptive and inferential statistics. The fundamental purpose of the results section is to provide the data that will enable you to answer your research question. Therefore, you should organise the section so that the relevance of the data to the research questions and hypotheses that you set forth in the introduction are as clear as possible.

Chapter 16, *Writing Up your Quantitative Discussion Section*, illustrates how, in the discussion, you continue to make sense of your data by interpreting the results specifically in terms of the research question, and also in broader terms, in how this answer contributes to knowledge in the field of psychology. This emphasises the dual nature of psychological science as discussed in Chapter 1. The chapter exemplifies how the discussion should be structured and written for a quantitative project. The chapter also demonstrates how the interpretation phase represents the flip side of the problem specification aspect, encountered in Chapter 11. When defining the research problem or idea, the research literature was drawn upon, and guided you to important questions, clearly demonstrating a deductive flow of thought and reason. During this stage of the research process, it is illustrated how the answers obtained determine how accurate the theories predict new observations, relying on inductive thought and therefore reasoning, from the specific results of the study back to the generality of theory.

11

QUANTITATIVE METHODS OF INQUIRY

Objectives

On reading this chapter you should:

- be aware of the characteristics of the popular quantitative methods of inquiry;
- be able to use the model of the quantitative research process as an organisational tool for carrying out your project;
- understand the logic of experimental design;
- be aware of the different types of experimental designs;
- understand when it is appropriate to utilise a quasi-experimental design;
- understand when it is appropriate to use non-experimental designs;
- understand the critical role played by precise operational definitions for your research variables; and
- understand the important issues regarding how you measure your data.

Overview

Chapter 11 deals with quantitative methods of inquiry, including both experimental and non-experimental designs. Section 11.1 details some of the most pertinent characteristics of quantitative methods of inquiry. Section 11.2 introduces a model of the quantitative research process, which can act as an organisational tool for the undergraduate researcher. Section 11.3 focuses on experimental methods of inquiry in the quantitative paradigm, with the first discussion dealing with the logic of experimental design, a simple concept that often surprises students. It is described as referring to arranging the overall structure of your experiment in order to see the effects of the independent variable on the dependent variable, as clearly as possible under controlled conditions. The related concept of internal validity and external validity are then discussed. Two very popular experimental designs, the independent and dependent groups design, are introduced and are shown to answer research questions addressing causes of behaviours. Quasi-experimental designs are also introduced as an alternative method of inquiry when you are unable to manipulate your independent variable. Section 11.4 focuses on non-experimental methods of inquiry, in particular the survey method which encompasses both correlational and differential research designs. The important issue in quantitative research of conceptualisation and operationalisation are detailed in Section 11.5, and finally Section 11.6 deals with the theory of measurement.

11.1   Characteristics of Quantitative Methods of Inquiry

Almost all quantitative research relies on a positivist approach to science, and generally uses a linear research path, as demonstrated in Section 11.2. Quantitative research typically follows a reconstructed logic, in that the logic of how to do research is highly organised, and reconstructed into logically consistent rules and terms. The language is of hypotheses and variables, and emphasis is on the precise measuring of variables and testing hypotheses that are usually linked to general casual explanations.

Therefore quantitative researchers are usually concerned about issues of design, measurement and sampling because their deductive approach emphasises detailed planning prior to data collection and analysis. Quantitative researchers will often focus extensively on operationalising variables into measurable entities during the planning and designing stage, occurring before conducting the actual research. Quantitative research involves quantifying data in the form of numbers, which acts as an empirical representation of the construct or theory. Quantitative methods of inquiry can vary from interventionist (experiments) to non-interventionist (correlational and differential research).

11.2   A Model of the Quantitative Research Process

Quantitative methods of inquiry have a long tradition within psychology and the behavioural sciences. Over the years, numerous models have been developed to portray the linear steps involved in quantitative research. Quantitative models of the research process are constructed as useful representations of reality that can guide further thinking and research, and are therefore beneficial for the undergraduate psychology student to help prevent feelings of being lost amidst the research process, by adding structure and to organise the activities involved in producing their psychology project.

The model represents the major activities for quantitative research in the order that they logically occur. Such models should be viewed as being flexible as opposed to cast in stone. It is important to remember that, like any model, this model of the research process is (see Figure 11.1) not a complete representation of reality. It acts to simplify the complexity of psychological

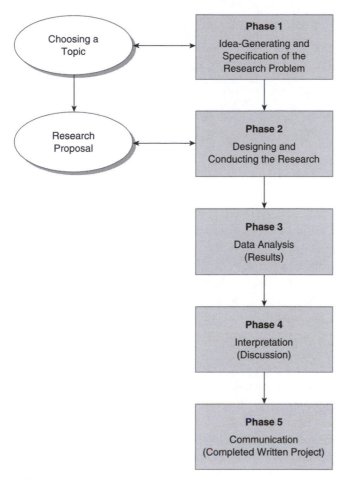

Figure 11.1   A model of the research process

research, and to identify the major aspects of the research process in order to make the process more manageable for the student.

Phase 1: Idea-generating and specification of the research problem (introduction)

The first stage of this model, the idea-generating and specification of the research problem, represents the introduction and literature review section of your research project. As demonstrated in Chapters 3 and 8, research begins with an idea. At this initial stage, a vague idea is sufficient to direct the researcher to an area where the idea can be developed and refined. The careful conceptualisation and phrasing of the research question is critical, because everything done in the remainder of the research process is aimed at answering that research question.

The question that you develop might involve a highly specific and precisely defined hypothesis. During Phase 1 of the research process, one works from the general to the specific using rational and abstract processes to systematically develop ideas towards a valid research question.

Phase 2: Designing and conducting your study (methodology)

Phase 2 of the model of the research process involves designing and conducting your study, and constitutes the methodology sections of your psychology project. Your methodology sections are specific and are structured around making observations and recording data in order to answer your research question. Before any data are collected, you must determine what types of observations are to be made and under what conditions. You will also decide on what methods will be utilised for recording the behaviours of interest in order to answer your research question. For example, will you be recording times of successful completion of a task, or participants responses on a specific topic?

Another very important design issue involves who your participants will be. The type of participants you recruit will have implications for generalising your results during the interpretation stage. However, you must also make sure that the type of measurements or materials you use are suitable for your participants. For example, if you were planning on using an aptitude test on children age 10 to 11 years of age, but the test was actually suited for 16-year-olds, you would run into serious problems regarding construct validity, and also all the data you record might be at a very low level therefore creating a floor effect in the data. Running a pilot study will help ensure such planning and design issues are ironed out before you commence your actual experimentation or research stage. During this stage you will also decide what type of statistical tests you will run in Phase 3. It is also essential that you make the necessary ethical judgements regarding your participants' welfare, etc. as dealt with in Chapter 2.

The undergraduate psychology student often views the conducting of the research or making the observations of the planned behaviours or responses as the actual research. Clearly the planning and designing phase set the foundation for this part of the process, and should never be neglected. Remember that the successful implementation of your research rests on rigorous design and planning.

Phase 3: Data-Analysis (results)

During Phase 3 of the model of the research process, the results or data-analysis phase, the focus remains on the specific. In quantitative approaches the focus is primarily on abstract rational processes of making sense of the data that you have collected. As already noted, the data-analysis procedures are selected in the design phase. In quantitative psychological research, the data will be in the form of numerical record. Statistical procedures are employed to describe and to evaluate numerical data and to determine the significance of the observations made. A key aspect to the successful completion of this phase of the research process is that you choose analytical procedures that are appropriate to the question being answered and the type of data that was collected.

Phase 4: Interpretation (discussion)

Phase 4, the interpretation or discussion phase of quantitative approaches, involves inductive reasoning, to interpret the specific results of your study and to make sense regarding the general theories presented in the introduction. Having analysed the data, you must continue to make sense of them by interpreting the results. For quantitative data this is usually in terms of how they help answer the research question, and how this answer contributes to the knowledge in the field. Therefore, the findings are put into a context that helps to relate them not only to your original questions, but also to other concepts and findings in the field. It is also hoped that the results of your study will suggest ways to expand or modify the theory in order to increase its usefulness and accuracy.

This stage represents the flip side of Phase 1, the problem-specification phase. When defining the research question, theories are used to guide you to important questions. Now the answer(s) that you have generated to those questions are used to determine how accurate the theories predict new observations and behaviour. In the problem-specification phase, you use deductive reasoning, going from general theory to the specific prediction. However, in the interpretation phase, you generally use inductive reasoning, going from the specific results of the study back to the generality of the theory. The train of thought involved is demonstrated in Figure 11.2.

Phase 5: Communication (write-up)

The final stage of the model is the important communication phase, which is so often neglected within models of the research process. As a social enterprise, a critical component is communication of the research findings. For undergraduate psychology students, the actual write-up of a research project along the accepted guidelines of the scientific community is an act of communication. This stage of the research process will be dealt with in significant detail in Chapter 25.

11.3   Experimental Methods of Inquiry

The logic of experimental design

Experiments, like all other methods of inquiry, are a means of answering questions, but more specifically of testing hypotheses and predictions. An

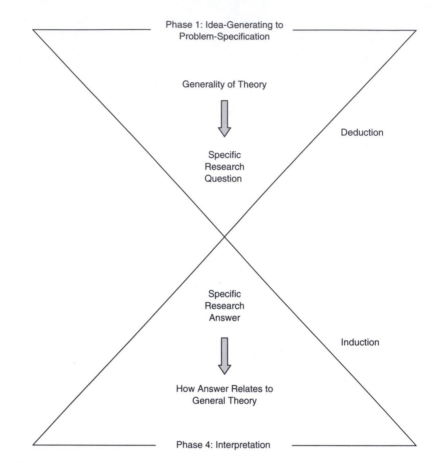

Figure 11.2   Train of thought involved in quantitative research

experiment is a tightly controlled investigation in which the researcher manipulates one or more factors under study – the independent variable(s) – to determine if such changes or manipulation have an effect on the dependent variable. Therefore, the logic of designing experiments refers to arranging the overall structure in order to see the effects of the independent variable as clearly as possible under controlled conditions.

Generally, true experimental studies have three important characteristics: random assignment of participants to the specified levels of the independent variable; manipulation of those levels; and the control of extraneous variables. The levels of the independent variable are manipulated by deciding what the levels are, how they are implemented, and how and when the participants are assigned and exposed.

As you will have learnt throughout your undergraduate psychology degree, no design affords the experimenter complete control. There will always by uncontrolled sources of variation because, as you can imagine, not every variation that affects a given outcome can be influenced in one design. Therefore, uncontrolled sources of variation are unavoidable in psychological research at all levels. However, all is not lost, a great deal of useful information can be gained from experimental designs that adequately control for the major sources of variation. The three general types of experimental control that can be applied to your psychology project are manipulation; holding conditions constant; and balancing.

It is very important that you match your design to the complexity of the issue and include only those variables that are required for generating meaningful results. For example, it makes no sense to employ a complicated multifactor design when the issue at hand is simply defined by a single variable. Introducing complex and unnecessary features into a design format is a waste of resources and may complicate interpretative issues by creating a fog which makes it difficult to see the essential result.

Internal and external validity

A carefully designed experiment will permit valid conclusions to be drawn about the effects of the independent variable on the dependent variable, so that you can conclude that manipulating the independent variable caused a change in the dependent variable. By means of experimental control you rule out inadvertent confounding, and the results reflect the effects of the intended variables. Underwood (1957) referred to this as the basic principle of experimental design, that is, you 'design the experiment so that the effects of the independent variables can be evaluated unambiguously'. This is, essentially, the internal validity of an experimental design. The external validity of an experimental design refers to how accurately you can generalise results to the population. This is dealt with again in Chapter 13.

Experimental designs

Your research question and hypothesis determine how you will assign your participants to the various levels of your independent variable. There are two common possibilities. First of all you can assign only some participants to each level. This type of design is known as a between-subjects design, an unrelated design, a non-repeated groups design or an independent groups design. The second approach is to assign each participant to every level of the independent variable, and is commonly known as a within-subjects design, a related or repeated measures design or a dependent groups design.

Consider the following hypothesis: participants who receive music for 20 minutes will have more creative scores than participants who receive no music. Here there is one independent variable, with two levels music and no music, and a single dependent variable creativity. The research question is concerned with investigating the differences in creativity between the levels of the

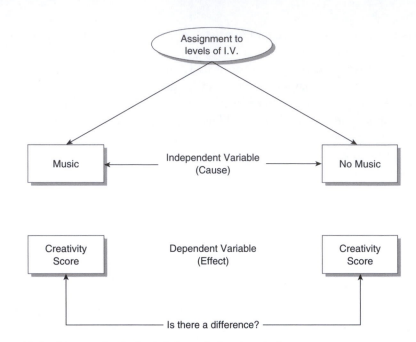

Figure 11.3   An example of a basic independent groups design

independent variable, music and no music, as illustrated in Figure 11.3. The appropriate design to answer this question would be an independent groups design, and if the data is interval ratio, an independent t-test would be the appropriate statistical analysis to run on the data in the analysis phase.

The advantage of the independent groups design is that it is safer than the within-subjects design because serial dependencies do not form and each participant's data expresses a fresh profile, free of the possible contaminating influence of experience, practice effects or transfer of training. Remember that this type of design is necessary for natural groups such as age and gender. On the negative side, you need more participants to fill the conditions and it is often more time-consuming. The results also run the potential risk of being confounded due to individual differences among the participants in the two groups. As you will recall from your methodology training, random assignment can prevent individual differences from acting as confounding variables.

The second approach is to assign each participant to every level of the independent variable as seen in Figure 11.4. Consider the following hypothesis, music increases creativity.

The within-subjects design is generally viewed as being more efficient than the between-subjects design, because the performance of each participant is compared across the different levels of the independent variable (i.e. experimental conditions). Each participant receives each level of the independent variable, hence less participants are needed to fill the conditions of the experiment. However, the efficient within-subjects design brings with it serious risks of

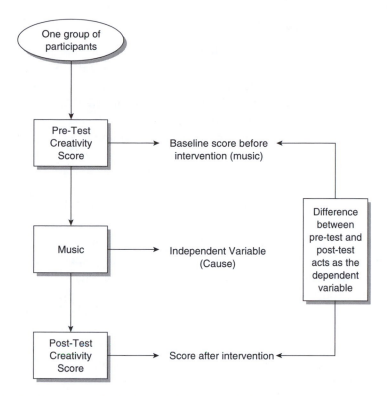

Figure 11.4   An example of a basic dependent groups design

carry-over effects from one level of the independent variable to the next, which could result in an invalid experiment. As you can imagine, carry-over effects are particularly serious if the conditions affect each other (or carry over) in different ways, for example if the experimental condition affects the control condition differently than the control condition affects the experimental condition.

One way to minimise carry-over effect among different levels of the independent variable is to counterbalance them. Using this technique, each level has the same chance of being influenced by confounding variables. In other words, you counter the effects of potential confounding variables by balancing them over the periods when the levels are administered.

Experiments need not be exclusively an independent groups design or a dependent groups design. It is often convenient to have some independent variable treated as between-subjects and others as within-subjects in the same experiment (assuming that the experiment has more than one independent variable). If one variable seems likely to cause transfer or carry-over effects (for example administering a drug), it can be made a between-subjects variable while the rest of your variables are within-subjects. This compromise is not as efficient as a pure within-subjects design, but is often safer. Remember to use the appropriate statistical analysis for a mixed design.

Quasi-experimental designs

Within quantitative psychology there has generally been a preference for experimental designs over other approaches; however, the experiment has limitations in its applicability to real-life situations. Consider the following research question: you are interested in determining whether child car seats prevent serious injury in a car crash compared to no car seat. In this situation you would not have control over participants to randomly assign them to the different levels of the independent variable (i.e. car seat and no car seat).

Quasi-experimental designs do not involve randomly assigning participants to conditions. Instead comparisons are made between people in groups that already exist. Therefore the quasi-experimental variable indicates that the variable is not a true independent variable manipulated by the researcher but rather is an event that occurred for other reasons. Quasi-experimental designs do not possess the same degree of internal validity as true experimental designs, because participants are not randomly assigned to conditions and the researcher may have no control over the independent variable. Fortunately, a well-designed quasi-experiment that eliminates as many threats to internal validity as possible can provide strong circumstantial evidence about cause-and-effect relationships. Consequently, the quality of a quasi-experimental design depends on how many threats to internal validity it successfully eliminates.

The non-equivalent groups' design pre-test-post-test design is a common design involving two groups: the quasi-experimental group and the non-equivalent control group. Each group is administered a pre-test, followed by the quasi-experimental group receiving the intervention, and then both groups receiving a post-test. There are a number of quasi-experimental designs that you can utilise depending on your research question – any general methodology textbook will outline the major designs.

11.4   Non-Experimental Methods of Inquiry

There are also some quantitative methods of inquiry that are not experimental in nature, for example survey research, and correlational and differential research. These methods do not involve manipulating variables; instead they utilise several basic research procedures to obtain information from people in their natural environments. The central instrument for obtaining information is the questionnaire. These types of designs utilise the same statistical methods of analysis as experimental research.

Survey research

Oppenheim (1992) draws a distinction between descriptive and analytical survey designs. Descriptive surveys answer questions such as how many, by providing a summary of opinions, attitudes or behaviour, which are also referred to as status surveys. Analytical surveys include correlational and differential studies, where the researcher looks at the relationships or differences between the sets of data. Survey research, therefore, is not a single research design (Schuman & Kalton, 1985), but an umbrella term for both correlational and differential research designs and descriptive surveys.

Correlational and differential research

Correlational research involves the measurement of relationships between variables. A critical feature is that the researcher does not manipulate the independent variable as in the case of the experiment. Instead, correlational research assesses the relationships among naturally occurring variables with the goal of identifying predictive relationships. A correlation exists when two different measures of the same people, for example, vary together, i.e. when scores of one variable covary with scores on another variable.

Correlational studies have less control than an experiment or quasi-experiment. Foster and Parker (1999) note that a correlational study is defined in terms of how the study is conducted as opposed to the statistics used to analyse it. Differential research involves investigating differences between groups that are defined by pre-existing variables, again the independent variable is not manipulated.

11.5 Conceptualisation to Operationalisation

The ability of psychology to carry out scientific research depends on psychologists' ability to measure psychological variables objectively and accurately. Every quantitative research project includes one or more sets of variables that the researcher manipulates and/or observes and measures. Any characteristic that can take on more than one value can act as a variable. Examples include speed, reaction time, psychological levels such as heart rate or blood pressure, etc. It is important to note that if the events of interest are static with no variation, they cannot serve as research variables for your study.

During the idea-generating and hypothesis-generation phase of your project, you consulted the research literature to develop conceptual definitions for your variables of interest. A good definition should have one clear, explicit and specific meaning, so that there is no ambiguity or vagueness attached to the concept or construct. As a cognitive process, conceptualisation involves thinking through the meanings of a construct. It is important to note that a single construct can have several definitions, for example leadership. Also, some constructs are highly complex and abstract, for example the self-concept. These complex constructs contain lower level concepts within them, for example self-esteem, which can be made even more specific, for example feelings of competence. Other constructs are simple and concrete, like hunger for example. When

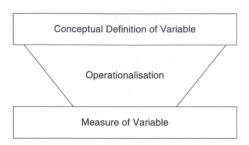

Figure 11.5   The process of operationalisation

developing definitions, you should be very aware of how complex and abstract a construct is, and the implications that arise from using complex constructs.

Through the process of operationalisation, conceptual definitions can be linked to a specific measurement of the variable as demonstrated in Figure 11.5. Therefore, by operationally defining variables, it is possible to test your hypotheses objectively. Strict operationalism did not last long in psychology, because equating a concept with a set of operations creates an arbitrary restriction on the concept. For psychologists, the problem with operationalism boiled down to how to accomplish it in practice when dealing with such complex psychological phenomenon as aggression, and creativity, etc. Despite the problem with the strict use of operational definitions, the concept has been of value to psychology by forcing researchers to clearly define the terms used in their studies (Hilgard, 1987). This is especially important when you consider that a lot of research in psychology concerns concepts that are open to numerous definitions.

To give an example within the area of leadership, there have been numerous definitions proposed by researchers, practising managers and leaders alike. There is little definition agreement within the field, which causes confusion and difficulty for the novice student. Yukl (2002) reasoned that this state of affairs was due to the word leadership being taken from the common vocabulary and incorporated into the technical vocabulary without being precisely defined.

Operational definitions are therefore concrete recipes for variables that allow you to talk about your variables in concrete specific, objective terms, rather than in abstract vague, subjective terms. One very important result of the precision resulting from operational definitions is that it allows an experiment to be repeated. Research variables are often operationalised by the measurement that is used to tap into the concept, as you will see next.

11.6   Theory of Measurement

When choosing your measure or apparatus it is very important to consider the type of data that is yielded from recording behaviours or responses in this way. This brings us on to the implications that different levels of measurement have for the data, for what types of analysis are appropriate to run, and what type of conclusions to be drawn. Levels of measurement are an abstract but important and widely used idea. The major task in measurement in research is to represent the research variables numerically. To measure a variable is to assign numbers that represent values of the variable. Measurement is essentially the assigning of numbers to observations in accordance with certain rules. The measurements you record for each participant constitute the data; these data are the bases for later analysis and interpretation. The way in which you assign numbers to the observations of your participants determines the scale of measurement to use. Furthermore the type of measuring scale that you employ in collecting your data helps determine which statistical inference test you should use to analyse your data.

A common method for classifying variables is to distinguish between continuous and discrete variables. The latter include nominal and ordinal data, while the former include interval ratio data.

Discrete variables

Nominal and categorical variables are discrete variables that have been classified into categories where no order is implied. They are created by assigning observations into various independent categories, and then counting the frequency of occurrence within those categories. Simply, this involves using numbers to label categories; therefore the only property that this type of variable possesses is identity hence the term categorical.

It is important to realise that nominal data possess no true mathematical properties and act only as labels. The only measure of average which can be used is the mode because this is simply a set of frequency counts. Hypothesis tests can be carried out on variables collected in the nominal form. The most likely would be the Chi-square test. However, it should be noted that the Chi-square is a test to determine whether two or more variables are associated and the strength of that relationship. It can tell nothing about the form of that relationship or where it exists, and therefore is not capable of establishing cause and effect.

The second type of discrete variables are ordinal and possess magnitude as well as identity. They provide information regarding greater than or less than, but do not tell how much greater or how much less. There are a number of statistical tests that are appropriate for ordinal variables. It is possible to test for order correlation with ranked data. The two main methods are Spearman's Ranked Correlation Coefficient and Kendall's Coefficient of Concordance. The other permissible hypothesis testing procedures are the Mann-Whitney U test, the Wilcoxon Rank Sum test, the Wald–Wolfowitz Sign or Run test, the Kolmogorov–Smirnov Z test, Kruskal Wallis, and the Friedman 2-Way Analysis. It is important to remember that the type of design employed in your study, along with the type of data and of course the research question being asked, should be considered in determining the appropriate statistical analysis to run on your data.

Continuous variables

Interval/ratio variables are the most sophisticated type of variable, and possess the properties of identity, magnitude, equal intervals between adjacent units and a zero point. There are a wide variety of statistical tests that can be run on interval/ratio data, so caution again must be given here. Always consider the research question and the design of your study in deciding on the appropriate statistical tests to run to test your hypotheses. T tests, ANOVA's, Pearson Correlations, Multiple Regressions and MANOVA's can all be carried out on parametric data, but their appropriateness rests with the research question and the design employed.

Summary

Quantitative research typically follows a reconstructed logic, as seen in the model of the research process. The logic of experimental design refers to the overall arrangement of your study, so that you can very clearly see the effects of the independent variable on the dependent variable, in a controlled fashion. The two very popular types of experimental design include the independent groups design and the dependent groups design. The quasi-experimental design is used when you cannot manipulate the independent variable. Survey research is non-experimental and covers designs such as correlational and differential, which utilise the same statistical analysis of experimental designs.

Conceptualisation to operationalisation involves developing clear and precise definitions of how your variables are conceptualised and measured. The type of data that you collect will have implications for the type of analyses that you can run later in the research process. It is also crucial that the type of data collected will enable you to answer your research question.

Further Reading

Clark-Carter, D. (2004) *Quantitative Psychological Research: A Student's Handbook.* Hove & New York: Psychology Press.

Field, A. and Hole, G. (2004) *How to Design and Report Experiments.* London: Sage Publications Ltd.

Harris, P. (2002) *Designing and Reporting Experiments in Psychology* (2nd edn). Buckingham and Philadelphia: Open University Press.

Mitchell, M. L. and Jolley, J. M. (2004) *Research Design Explained* (5th edn). Canada: Thomson/Wadsworth.

Shaughnessy, J. J., Zeichmeister, E. B. and Zechmeister, J. S. (2005) *Research Methods in Psychology.* International edition: McGraw Hill.

12

ANALYSING QUANTITATIVE DATA

Objectives

On reading this chapter you should:

- understand the two major trends involved in quantitative data analysis;.
- be aware of the steps involved in hypothesis testing using SPSS as a means of answering your research question;
- understand the important role played by exploratory data analysis;
- understand the importance of testing the assumptions of your planned inferential analysis;
- know what steps to take if your data is not normally distributed; for example, transforming your data;
- understand the importance of computing confidence intervals, effect sizes/measures of association, and tests of power to overcome the limitations of the null hypothesis test procedure;
- be able to deal with results that are highly significant, or nearly significant, and understand the meaning of significance; and
- be aware of the limitations of statistical computer software.

Overview

This chapter deals with the rational tasks of processing and making sense of the data you have obtained for analysis. While at the beginning stages of the research process you developed your research question, and then collected the data to enable you to answer your research question, at this stage in the process you go about answering your research question. Therefore, as noted throughout the text, the appropriateness of a statistical procedure in answering your research question depends on a number of things: your research question, your research design and the type of data you collected. Section 12.1 deals with two popular approaches to quantitative data analysis put forward by Cronbach (1957): experimentalists and correlationists.

Due to space limitations, the computations and logic behind statistical techniques can be found elsewhere, as they are beyond the scope of a book of this nature. Appendix A shows you how to run some of the popular statistical tests using SPSS. The following sections use an example to work through the steps involved in hypothesis testing. Section 12.2 focuses on hypothesis testing as a means of answering your research question using SPSS V14, and demonstrates how statistical procedures are used to describe and to evaluate numerical data and determine the significance of observations Section 12.3 highlights the importance of stating your hypothesis in a quantitative research project, as the hypothesis(es) that you have generated provide the general framework for your study and delineate the problem and the variables under investigation. Section 12.4 goes on to emphasise the important role of exploratory data analysis (EDA) as a means of getting to know the data, and to test for assumptions of normality, before reporting the descriptive statistics. Section 12.5 focuses on the third step, running the appropriate inferential test, including descriptives, confidence intervals, effect size and power. Section 12.6 deals with Step 4, interpreting your results, and focuses on SPSS outputs.

Section 12.7 considers results that are highly significant and near misses, while section 12.8 focuses on the meaning of significant results. Finally Section 12.9 gives a warning regarding the use of statistical packages and reading SPSS outputs.

12.1 Quantitative Data Analysis

The primary goal of data analysis is to determine whether our observations support a claim about behaviour (Abelson, 1995). There are two major trends within quantitative data analysis. The first is comparing groups using analysis of variance and based on data from experiments. The second approach is focused on exploring relationships based on data usually from non experiments. Cronbach (1957) referred to these two groups as experimentalists and correlationists. The experimentalists generally use t-tests and ANOVAs to test their claims, while the correlationists use correlations and regression analysis. Also note that in differential research it is also customary to run t-tests and ANOVAs to test for differences.

In carrying out your quantitative psychology project, your aim is to analyse and answer your research question, based on your sample data. This entails drawing conclusions that extend beyond the data that you have collected. As was previously mentioned, your data represent a sample of the target population. The importance of ensuring that your sample is representative of your population is highlighted for this reason. In order to make predictions about the larger population of which the sample is only a part, it should represent the population. Such predictions as these, based upon your sample data but designed to extend beyond your sample in terms of generalisations, are called inferences, hence the name inferential statistics. Inferential statistics, therefore, are a group of statistical techniques and procedures that allow you to generalise your findings beyond the actual data obtained in your study. Inferential statistics also include estimating parameters.

Quantitative researchers use two types of inferential tests based on the type of variables used; remember continuous and discrete variables in the previous chapter. Parametric tests refer to a general label covering those statistical procedures that require that the sample data under analysis be drawn from a population and be normaly distributed. Parametric tests also require that the samples are taken independently (when more than one population is being sampled they have the same variance or a known ratio of variances), the data collected is interval ratio and all arithmetic operations can be performed. Parametric tests are more powerful and efficient than non-parametric tests.

Non-parametric tests are a class of statistical procedures for determining relations between variables which can be used without making assumptions about particular parameters of distributions. Therefore these tests are distribution free but not assumption free, each particular procedure is dependent on certain criteria. For example, to use the χ^2 your data must be randomly selected, and each case must have at least five occurrences.

12.2 Hypothesis Testing as a Means of Answering your Research Question Using SPSS v14

Hypothesis testing is a very popular method in quantitative research for answering research questions. Due to the increasing number of undergraduate psychology students using SPSS to run their statistical analysis, the text incorporates SPSS into the steps involved in hypothesis testing. There are a number of stages involved in the chain of reasoning for hypothesis testing. When reviewing the literature, you may have come across studies that have not utilised all of the steps below. In order to overcome the limitations of the null hypothesis significance test procedure as a way of answering your research question, it is important that you go through each step as illustrated in Figure 12.1.

To demonstrate the four steps proposed for hypothesis testing an example of some differential research is presented. The research question was whether different exercise levels had an impact on women's general health. The hypothesis was that the higher the level of exercise the more positive a woman's general health would be. The independent variable was exercise level and had three levels: did not exercise, exercised for fun and exercised competitively. The dependent variable was their self-attribution of their general health which was operationalised using a questionnaire. The lower the value on the questionnaire meant the more positive general health was.

STEP 1: State your hypothesis(es)

STEP 2: Carry out exploratory data analysis (EDA) and test assumptions

STEP 3: Run appropriate inferential test, including descriptives
confidence intervals, effect size and power

STEP 4: Make sense of your results

Figure 12.1   Steps involved in hypothesis testing using SPSS

12.3   Step 1: State your Hypothesis

As previously discussed, when conducting your quantitative research project in psychology, the hypothesis(es) that you have generated provide the general framework for your study and delineate the problem and the variables under investigation. The hypothesis to be tested is called the null hypothesis and is given the symbol 'Ho'; the null hypothesis is the hypothesis of no relationship or no difference. The alternative hypothesis, known as 'Ha', is often considered as the research hypothesis and is also known as the experimental hypothesis, i.e. the researcher is looking for a relationship or a difference, and attempts to reject the Ho in favour of the Ha. It is very important to realise that you do not make any reference to the null hypothesis in your study – you simply apply this logic in deciding whether you obtained significance or not.

If your research question involves investigating whether there is a significant difference between two groups on a particular variable and your data is interval ratio, then the independent t-test is the appropriate test to run on your data. However, if your research question involves investigating whether there is a significant difference between more than two groups, for example between three groups, then it is not appropriate to use the independent t-test. It is possible to run multiple t-tests, however, multiple t-tests increase the probability of making a Type I error. This is illustrated in the following example: Suppose you are comparing five groups, which makes 10 pairs of t-tests, using the formula:

$$1 - (1 - \alpha)^C$$

$1-(1-0.05)^{10} = 40$, therefore you have a 40% chance of making a Type I error, compared to 5% using the ANOVA. Consequently, if you have three of more comparison groups, it is appropriate to run the one-way non-repeated ANOVA.

In the example, the hypothesis was that the higher the level of exercise the more positive a woman's general health would be. It is important to note that, in this case, our hypothesis is one tailed as we have stated a direction. It is expected that women who exercise competitively will have more positive general health compared to the other two levels, and that women who exercise for fun will have more positive general health that those who do no exercise at all.

12.4   Step 2: Exploratory Data Analysis and Testing for Normality

When analysing your data, you are confronted with a decision regarding what kind of statistical analysis to perform on your data in order to answer your research question(s). Although you probably decided during the planning and designing stage of your project what type of statistical tests to run, you have to test the assumptions for using the tests now that your data has been collected. This can be achieved through exploratory data analysis and running tests of normality.

Before you begin to run any inferential statistics on your data, it is very important to get a sense of the data. You should inspect your data very carefully, get a real feel for it, and in some ways make friends with it (Hoaglin, 1991). Exploratory data analysis helps ensure that you run the most appropriate statistical test. As an explorer, you first need to describe what you see. Exploratory Data Analysis, also known as EDA (Tukey, 1977), is an approach for data analysis that employs a variety of techniques, mostly graphical in nature, to maximise insight into a data set, to uncover the underlying structure, to detect important variables, to extract outliers and anomalies, and to test underlying assumptions.

The particular graphical techniques employed in EDA are often quite simple, consisting of various techniques of plotting the raw data, such as histograms, lag plots and probability plots. They also consist of plotting simple statistics such as mean plots, standard deviation plots, box plots and main effects plots of the raw data. A lag plot checks whether a data set is random or not. Random data should not exhibit any identifiable structure in the lag plot. Non-random structure in the lag plot indicates that the underlying data are not random. Box plots (Chambers, 1983) are an excellent tool for presenting variation information in data sets. Box 12.1 below goes through the steps for running some exploratory data analysis using SPSS V14. The dependent variable in the example, women's general health, is referred to as ghqtot.

Box 12.1   Running a exploratory data analysis using frequencies and a histogram using SPSS V14

Main Menu → **Analyse** → **Descriptive Statistics** → **Frequencies to open up dialog box**

→   Transfer your DV (ghqtot) into the **Variable** box.

→   Click into **Charts** to reveal the **Frequencies: Charts** dialog box.

→   In **Chart Type** click the **Histogram** button, and tick the **With Normal Curve** option

→   **Continue**

→   Back in the **Frequency** dialog box, click into the **Statistics** button to reveal the **Frequencies: Statistics** dialog box. Under **Percentile Values** tick **Quartiles**.

→   Tick **Percentiles** to specify your desired percentile, for example, 95th, by typing 95 and click **Add**.

→   Under **Dispersion**, tick the **Std. Deviation**, and **Minimum** and **Maximum** options.

→   Under **Central Tendency**, tick the **Mean** and **Median** options.

→   Click **Continue**.

→   **Ok** to run the analysis

The steps outlined in Box 12.1 generated the SPSS Output 12.1 above. The table includes information regarding the percentile range of the data, central tendency and dispersion. Figure 12.2 shows the histogram with normal curve imposed for the ghqtot data for the participants.

Tests of normality and transformations

Many statistical procedures assume that the variables are normally distributed. A significant violation of the assumption of normality can seriously increase the chances of the researcher committing either a Type I (over-estimation) or Type II (under-estimation) error, depending on the nature of the analysis and the non-normality. Micceri (1989) points out that true normality is very rare in psychology. Thus, one reason that researchers utilise data transformations is to improve the normality of variables.

ghqtot

N	Valid	113
	Missing	0
Mean		56.7699
Median		54.0000
Std Deviation		12.31942
Minimum		32.00
Maximum		89.00
Percentiles	25	48.0000
	50	54.0000
	75	63.0000
	95	81.6000

SPSS Output 12.1 Some EDA statistics

N = total number of participants.

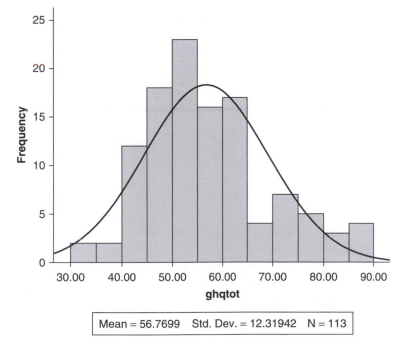

Mean = 56.7699   Std. Dev. = 12.31942   N = 113

Figure 12.2   Histogram with normal curve imposed for the ghqtot scores

There are several ways to tell whether a variable is normally distributed or not. Throughout the literature, researchers tend to report 'eyeballing the data' or visual inspection (Orr et al., 1991). This type of analysis by eye can be achieved through the exploratory data analysis just mentioned. Analysis of Figure 12.2 illustrates the difficulty in this situation of determining by eye whether the general health data (ghqtot) is in fact normally distributed or not. This is why some researchers are more concerned with objective assessments of normality. These can range from simple examination of skewness and kurtosis to inferential tests of normality, such as the Kolmorogov–Smirnov, or the Shapiro–Wilk tests. The steps involved in running the Kolmorogov–Smirnov using SPSS are outlined in Box 12.2 below.

Box 12.2   Running a one-sample Kolmorogov–Smirnov using SPSS V14

Main Menu → Analyse → Nonparametric Tests → one-Sample K-S (to reveal dialogue box)

→ Transfer DV to **Test Variable List**, and make sure the default **Normal** checkbox is ticked.

→ Click **Options** to reveal **One-Sample Kolmogorov–Smirnov Test: Options** dialog box, and choose **Descriptive and Quartiles**. Click **Continue** and then **OK**.

→ **Continue → OK**.

Both the Kolmorogov–Smirnov and the Shapiro–Wilk tests are similar in that they compare your sample data to normally distributed data, with the same mean and standard deviation. If the tests are insignificant then your data is not significantly different to a normal distribution and you can assume normality of your data. Following the steps outlined in Box 12.2, SPSS generated the outputs shown below. Output 12.2 shows the descriptive statistics of the 113 GHQ scores, while Output 12.3 shows the results of the Kolmogorov–Smirnov Test of goodness of fit. Analysis of Output 12.3 shows that the data are normally distributed, because the sample data was not significantly different from the normally distributed data that it was compared to.

If you find that your data is not normally distributed, there are a few simple manipulations you can try on the data, before resorting to running the non-parametric equivalent statistical test. For example, you could delete outliers from your data. It is important to consider your ethics here, and ensure that

	N	Mean	Std.Deviation	Minimum	Maximum	Percentiles		
						25th	50th(Median)	75th
ghqtot	113	56.7699	12.31942	32.00	89.00	48.0000	54.0000	63.0000

SPSS Output 12.2   Descriptive statistics of the Kolmogorov–Smirnov Test of goodness of fit

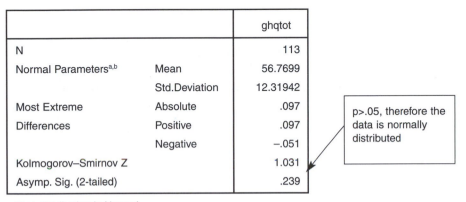

		ghqtot
N		113
Normal Parameters[a,b]	Mean	56.7699
	Std.Deviation	12.31942
Most Extreme	Absolute	.097
Differences	Positive	.097
	Negative	−.051
Kolmogorov–Smirnov Z		1.031
Asymp. Sig. (2-tailed)		.239

p>.05, therefore the data is normally distributed

a Test distribution is Normal.
b Calculated from data.

SPSS Output 12.3   One-Sample Kolmogorov–Smirnov Test

you use such a procedure with caution – it should never be used for the purpose of adjusting your p-value as this could be viewed as scientific fraud.

Handling outliers can be a difficult process. You need to consider whether the values represent natural variability or are fluke values or mistakes in data collection and recording. During EDA, use box plots to help identify outliers. It is possible for mid-outliers to naturally exist in your data, while severe outliers are often mistakes. Mid-outliers can be normalised through transformation, while severe outliers must be deleted from your data set to achieve normality. It is important that you do not delete more than 5% of your data, and if you have more than 5% severe outliers there is probably something else going on in the data. There is debate regarding whether outliers should be removed or not. For example, Judd and McClelland (1989) argue that outlier removal is desirable, honest and important, while Orr et al. (1991) hold the opposite view.

Data transformations are often necessary under the conditions of non-independence or non-normality. Data transformations are the application of a mathematical modification to the values of a variable, that is, simply transforming your data on another scale. Such a process, often referred to as change of scale or transformation of coordinates, has nothing to do with the way the distribution function is displayed in a graph. There are a number of possible data transformations, from adding constants, multiplying, squaring, raising to a power, or converting, to logarithmic scales, inverting and reflecting, and taking the square root of the values as demonstrated in Box 12.3 below.

These three transformations have been presented in the relative order of power, ranging from the weakest to the most powerful. It is good practice to use the minimum amount of transformation necessary to improve normality of your data.

There are two types of skew that can occur in your data: positive and negative. The three types of transformations mentioned above work by compressing the right side of the distribution more than the left side, and are therefore very effective on positively skewed distributions. If you find that you have a negatively skewed distribution, it is very important that you reflect the distribution first, add a constant to bring it to 1.0, apply the transformation and then reflect again to restore the original order of the variable.

Box 12.3   Three popular types of data transformation

1. Square-root transformation
   When a square-root transformation is applied, the square root of every value is taken.

2. Log transformations
   Logarithmic transformations are a class of transformations, rather than a single transformation. A logarithm is the power (exponent) to which a base number must be raised in order to get the original number. Any given number can be expressed as y to the x power in an infinite number of ways. Popular log transformations include the log base 10 (Log10) and the Natural Logarithm, where the constant e (2.7182818) is the base.

3. Inverse transformation
   To take the inverse of a number (x) involves computing $1/x$. This makes very small numbers very large, and very large numbers very small. This transformation has the effect of reversing the order of your scores. Therefore, you must be careful to reflect, or reverse the distribution prior to applying an inverse transformation. Therefore to carry out a reflection of your data, you multiply each value by (−1) and then add a constant to the distribution to bring the minimum value back above 1.00 distribution to bring the minimum value back above 1.0. Then, once the inverse transformation is complete, the ordering of the values will be identical to the original data.

Some warnings regarding the use of data transformations

It is clearly evident that data transformations are valuable tools for achieving normality in your data. However, like all statistical tests and manipulations, they must be used appropriately. It is common for statistical texts to gloss over this issue, leaving students unprepared to use these tools effectively and appropriately. As already noted, the transformations mentioned above reduce non-normality by reducing the relative spacing of scores on the right side of the distribution more than the scores on the left side. Altering the relative distances between data points raises issues in the interpretation of the data. If done correctly, all data points remain in the same relative order as prior to transformation. This allows you to continue to interpret results in terms of increasing scores. The important point then is that you must be careful when interpreting results based on transformed data.

Suggestions for good practice

- Always run EDA before you run any statistical analysis. To neglect this important step leads to an increased chance of drawing incorrect conclusions from your data.
- Familiarise yourself with the requirements of the statistical tests you plan to use on your data in order to answer your research question.
- Utilise the removal of outliers and data transformations with care.

12.5 Step 3: Run Appropriate Inferential Test, Including Descriptives, Confidence Intervals, Effect Size and Power

The next step involves carrying out the appropriate inferential to test your analysis hypothesis(es). In the example, the research design involved three levels of the independent variable, and the data was interval/ratio, and our hypothesis involved testing to see if there was a significant difference between the three levels of exercise with regard to general health. Therefore it was appropriate to run a one-way non-repeated ANOVA to test our hypothesis.

In the example there were unequal numbers.(n's) in the three groups, therefore it was appropriate to select the Scheffe post hoc analysis. However, if there had been equal numbers in each group, it may have been appropriate to run the Tukey post hoc analysis. This point will be returned to later in the chapter.

In carrying out your appropriate statistical test, it is important that you make sure to instruct SPSS to calculate the descriptive statistics, confidence intervals, estimates of effect size and power. In calculating these measures you will overcome some of the limitations of the null hypothesis significance test procedure, and in turn strengthen the conclusions that can be drawn from your analyses.

Box 12.4   Running a one-way non-repeated ANOVA using SPSS V14

Main Menu → Analyse → General Linear Model → Univariate

→ Transfer your DV into the **Dependent Variable** box.

→ Transfer you IV into the **Fixed Factor(s)** box.

→ Click into **Post Hoc** to reveal the **Univariate: Post Hoc Multiple Comparisons for Observed Means** dialog box.

→ Transfer IV grouping variable to the **Post Hoc Tests** box and click **Scheffe** (because of unequal numbers in the three groups)

→ **Continue**.

→ Back on the **Univariate** diolog box, click into the **Options** button. Tick **Descriptives, Estimates of Effect Size, Observed Power** and **Homogeneity tests**.

→ At the bottom of the dialog box, check that the **Significance Level** has a default setting of .**05**, and that the corresponding **Confidence Intervals** are set at 95%. Click **Continue**.

→ Back on the **Univariate diolog** box, click into the **Plots** button to reveal the **Univariate: Profile Plots** dialog box. Transfer your IV to the **Horizontal Axis,** and click on the activated **Add** button to transfer the name of IV to the Plots box below.

→ **Continue**.

→ **OK** to run the analysis.

12.6   Step 4: Make Sense of your Results

The final stage in hypothesis testing concerns making sense of your results. SPSS generates a number of tables and figures for the one-way non-repeated ANOVA. The first table in the SPSS output shows the three levels as defined by the independent variable, exercise level. This table is useful for checking that the independent variable has been defined accurately.

Between-Subject Factors

		Value Label	N
Levels	1	Don't	24
	2	Fun	49
	3	Competitive	40

SPSS Output 12.4   First table generated for one-way non-repeated ANOVA

It is important to summarise your data in a meaningful way. This is usually achieved by carrying out descriptive statistics on the data, and also through graphical displays. It is important that you choose ways of describing and summarising your data that are the most informative. For example, what happened in your study as a function of the factors of interest? What trends and patterns do you see in the data? And which graphical display best reveals these trends and patterns in your data? When using SPSS, your descriptive analysis can be run at the same time as your inferential analysis.

Descriptive Statistics

Dependent Variable: ghqtot

Levels	Mean	Std.Deviation	N
Don't	62.7500	13.75010	24
Fun	57.8980	11.40951	49
Competitive	51.8000	10.73265	40
Total	56.7699	12.31942	113

Participants that exercise competitively had the lowest most positive score for general health.

SPSS Output 12.5 Second table generated for one way non-repeated ANOVA

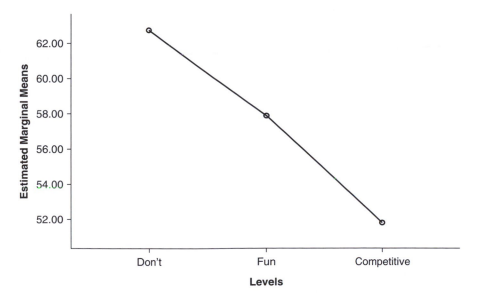

Figure 12.3   Profile plot of the three means of the three exercise levels

Levene's Test of Equality of Error Variances[a]
Dependent Varaible: ghqtot

F	df1	df2	Sig
1.189	2	110	.308

Tests the null hypothesis that the error
variance of the dependent variable is equal
across groups.
a Design: Intercept+levels

The p-value/significance value for Levene's F Statistic is 0.308, therefore the groups do not differ significantly regarding HOV, therefore the three groups are comparable

SPSS Output 12.6   Third table generated for one-way non-repeated ANOVA

The third table, SPSS Output 12.6, gives the results of Levene's Test for Equality of Error Variance. Analysis of the table indicates that the assumption of homogeneity of variance (HOV) is met.

Interpreting P value

SPSS generates the actual significance probability, which means that you can interpret the significance of your analysis quite simply, by determining whether this value if greater than or less that .05. A value greater than .05 is insignificant while a value less than .05 is significant. Analysis of SPSS Output 12.7 indicates that there was a significant difference between the three groups (don't exercise, exercise for fun, and exercise competitively) with regard to general health ($F = 6.957$; $df = 2, 110$; $P < .05$).

Effect size

It is important to indicate something about the magnitude of your significant result by calculating an effect size. There are various effect size indices, which are usually conveyed by means of a decimal number between 0 and 1.0. These analyses are used in an effort to probe the practical significance of your findings. The most common index used for the ANOVA in SPSS is partial η^2; however, it is important to note that ω^2 gives a more realistic value than partial η^2. ω^2 can be calculated using the following formula:

$$\omega^2 = \frac{(g-1)(F-1)}{(g-1)(F-1)} + N$$

You can obtain the F value from SPSS Output 12.7, therefore F = 6.957, g refers to the number of levels of the independent variable or the number

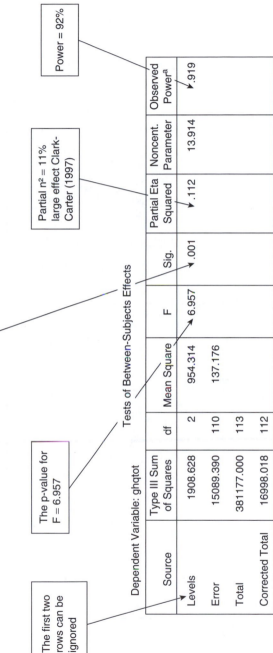

The first two rows can be ignored

The p-value for F = 6.957

SPSS generates the actual significance probability. You can interpret the significance of your analysis quite simply, by determining whether this value is greater than or less than .05. A value greater than .05 is insignificant while a value less than .05 is significant.

Partial n² = 11% large effect Clark-Carter (1997)

Power = 92%

Tests of Between-Subjects Effects

Dependent Variable: ghqtot

Source	Type III Sum of Squares	df	Mean Square	F	Sig.	Partial Eta Squared	Noncent. Parameter	Observed Power[a]
Levels	1908.628	2	954.314	6.957	.001	.112	13.914	.919
Error	15089.390	110	137.176					
Total	381177.000	113						
Corrected Total	16998.018	112						

a. Computed using alpha = .05

SPSS Output 12.7 Fourth table generated for one-way non-repeated ANOVA

Dependent Variable: ghqtot
Scheffe

Significant differences P < .05, and confidence intervals do not include 0.

Insignificant differences P > .05, and include 0 in the confidence intervals.

Multiple Comparisons

(I) Levels	(J) levels	Mean Difference (I–J)	Std. Error	Sig.	95% Confidence Interval	
					Lower Bound	Upper Bound
Don't	Fun	4.8520	2.91808	.255	−2.3891	12.0931
	Competitive	10.9500*	3.02408	.002	3.4459	18.4541
Fun	Don't	−4.8520	2.91808	.255	−12.0931	2.3891
	Competitive	6.0980	2.49578	.055	−.0952	12.2911
Competitive	Don't	−10.9500*	3.02408	.002	−18.4541	−3.4459
	Fun	−6.0980	2.49578	.055	−12.2911	.0952

Based on observed means.

* The mean difference is significant at the .05 level.

of comparison groups which = 3, and N refers to the total number of participants = 113.

$$\omega^2 = \frac{(3-1)(6.957-1)}{(3-1)(6.957-1)} + 113$$

$$\omega^2 = .095$$

$$\omega^2 = 9.5\%$$

Clark-Carter (1997) recommends that you consider an effect size < 1% (<0.01) as a small effect; that between 1–10% (0.01–0.10) as a medium effect; and a value > 10% (>0.1) as a large effect. What becomes apparent is that the ω^2 value of 9.5% is lower than the partial η^2 value of 11.2%; this is because the ω^2 value accounts for the positive bias of the partial η^2, and is hence a more realistic value of effect size.

For t-tests it is useful to calculate the effect size, which involves determining to what degree Ho is false from your sample data. The most common procedure yields estimates that are standardised in the sense that they take into account the amount of variability in your data. When interpreting effect size indices for t-tests, known as 'Cohens d' you should utilise the criteria established by Jacob Cohen (1988): .20 = small, .50 = medium, and .80 = large effect size.

Reporting the effect size improves the quality of your project, by attending to the issue of practical significance in addition to evaluating whether or not there was statistical significance.

Power

The concepts of statistical power are covered in detail in a number of texts, for example Cohen (1988) and Lipsey (1990), but for our purposes it is sufficient to say that the term statistical power denotes the likelihood of getting significance (Cohen, 1988). As you will see in Chapter 13, power depends on the types of statistical analysis that your run on your data – parametric tests are deemed more powerful than non-parametric tests. Power increases as your sample size increases, and it decreases with increasing sampling variance. Chapter 13 details the use of prospective power analysis when planning your study. During data analysis it is also appropriate to conduct a retrospective power analysis. Fortunately SPSS allows for retrospective power analysis as these calculations can be quite elaborate. Analysis of SPSS Output 12.7 indicates a power value of 92% which is a very impressive value.

You can also carry out power analysis when you obtain an insignificant result. When an insignificant result is supplemented by a power analysis that yields a high value close to 1.0, you are showing that you had a large enough sample size so as to make it unlikely that an important finding was missed due to a type II error. This illustrates that you had a good design, and can be used for your discussion.

Analysis of the summary ANOVA table does not indicate which of the comparison groups are contributing to the significant difference that was found between the three groups. It is necessary to analyse the post hoc multiple comparisons table to determine which group(s) contributed to the significant difference. In this situation it was appropriate to run the Scheffe as the three groups had unequal numbers of participants. The Scheffe is not as powerful as the Tukey. The Scheffe, like most post hoc comparison tests, provides confidence intervals, which are a very useful way of conveying the meaning of a significant result that goes beyond the hypothesis test. For example, analysis of SPSS Output 12.8 indicates that there was a significant difference between the group that did not exercise and the group that exercised competitively ($MD = 10.95$; $P < 0.05$; $CI\ 95 = 3.4459 -18.4541$), and that the true mean difference lies between 3.4459 and 18.4541.

12.7   Results that are Highly Significant and Near Misses

The level of significance plays a highly important role in hypothesis testing. In a practical sense it functions as a dividing line, where statistical significance is located on one side of the line and the lack of statistical significance on the other. Because the level of significance plays such an important role, both pragmatically and conceptually in hypothesis testing, it is included when the decision about significance is reported. With the level of significance set at .05, the most popular alpha level, a decision to reject Ho is summarised by the notation $P < .05$, while a decision not to reject Ho is summarised by $P > .05$. You can also provide evidence as to how strongly the data challenge Ho – you can inform the reader if you exceeded the level of significance by a wide margin, or if you just missed the level.

If P is much larger than alpha, then your situation is straightforward. However, if P was equal to .06 when alpha was set at .05, many researchers would consider this a near miss. This type of situation was observed in SPSS Output 12.8 above: the significance level for comparing the group that exercised competitively with the group that exercised for fun was ($P = .055$). Therefore, in these situations, researchers often use the phrases given in Box 12.5.

Other researchers insist that anything over .05 is insignificant and should not be viewed as anything else. It is therefore very important that you get advice from your supervisor if some of your data appears to be a near hit or a near miss.

Box 12.5 Common phrases for near hits

- That they achieved marginal significance
- Their findings approached significance
- There was a trend towards significance
- Results indicate borderline significance

12.8 The Meaning of Significant Results

If $P < .05$, you can assert that your results were significant. However, one should note that the word significant means something different when it is used in conjunction with the hypothesis test procedure than when used in everyday language. It is crucial that you understand the statistical meaning of the term. A statistically significant finding may not be very significant at all. In our everyday language, the word significant means important or noteworthy. Within the inferential context, a significant finding is simply one that is not likely to have occurred if Ho is true, that the Ho being tested has been rejected. It does not necessarily mean that the results are important.

Therefore, whether or not a statistically significant result constitutes an important result is influenced by:

- the quality of the research question, as mentioned in previous chapters. A worthwhile question will generally have practical significance
- the quality of the research design that guides the data collection.

While you researched the literature at earlier stages in the model of the research process, you may have come across journal articles that summarised carefully conducted empirical investigations that lead to significant results, yet the study itself seems to be quite insignificant. Therefore, in order for your project to yield important and practically significant findings, the research question should be answering some important and worthwhile issue.

12.9 A Warning about Statistical Packages and Reading SPSS Outputs

In order to use the computer statistical packages effectively you must have a good knowledge of research design and statistics. Remember that the computer is not able to determine what research design you used, or the rationale behind the use of that design.

Take the following example carrying out an advanced statistical procedure like the MANOVA. Following the advice given in some textbooks can be problematic here – you need to have an understanding of how the design relates to your research question. Some books advise students to focus on the MANOVA output, while other books advise to delete this table and focus on the between and within summary tables. The rationale for deciding on which tables to read is not being made explicit in these texts; therefore the role of the research question needs to be addressed here, for example if you are interested in looking at random effects then it is appropriate to analyse the MANOVA table. However, if you are interested in investigating differences between or within your groups, then there is no need to look at the MANOVA table. As you can imagine this is leading to confusion for students, and again highlights the importance of the research question in governing the choice of design and analysis.

Summary

The appropriateness of a statistical procedure in answering your research question depends on a number of things: your research question, your research design and the type of data you collected. Cronbach (1957) distinguished between two popular approaches to quantitative data analysis: experimental and correlational. The four steps involved in hypothesis testing using SPSS are: stating your hypothesis; exploratory data analysis and testing assumptions of normality; running the appropriate tests, including descriptives, confidence intervals, effect size and power; and finally, the fourth step involves interpreting your results. It is important to consider practical importance as well as statistical significance. It is also crucial that you understand the role of the research question for interpreting SPSS outputs, and that you realise that SPSS will do exactly what you tell it. Therefore, if you tell it to run an analysis that is not appropriate to answer your research question, the computer package will run the analysis – it does not know that you have made a mistake.

Further Reading

Clark-Carter, D. (2004) *Quantitative Psychological Research: A Student's Handbook*. Hove and New York: Psychology Press, Taylor & Francis group.

Field, A. and Hole, G. (2004) *How to Design and Report Experiments*. London: Sage Publications Ltd.

Harris, P. (2002) *Designing and Reporting Experiments in Psychology* (2nd edn). Buckingham and Philadelphia: Open University Press.

Kinnear, P. R. and Gray, C. D. (2004) *SPSS 12 Made Simple*. Hove and New York: Psychology Press, Taylor & Francis group.

Kirk, R. E. (1996) Practical Significance: A concept whose time has come. *Educational & Psychological Measurement*, 56, 746–59.

—————— 13 ——————

DESIGNING AND CONDUCTING AN EXPERIMENTAL RESEARCH PROJECT

Objectives

On reading this chapter you should:

- be fully cognisant of the central role played by designing and planning your study;
- be able to make important design decisions in order to ensure that your project is both internally and externally valid;
- be aware and understand the sequence of decisions involved in the design and planning of your study; and
- You should understand the important issues regarding how you measure your data.

Overview

Chapter 13 deals with the second stage of the model of the quantitative research process: the designing, planning and the specific methodology employed to answer your research question. In Section 13.1 the important role of the research question is again demonstrated – as no single experimental design is necessarily better than another, the suitability rests with the nature of the research question(s) asked.

Section 13.2 describes the important stages of planning and designing your study, with the caution that if you fail to plan, you plan to fail. Decision 1 involves operationally defining your research variables. This is related to Phase 1 of the model of the research process, the idea-generating to problem-specification. The second design decision focuses on who your participants should be. This has implications for the external validity of your study, and so it is of great consequence that you define your sample depending on the constructs and hypotheses that you are investigating and that your sample reflects your target population. Decision 3 involves using the most appropriate sampling technique to select your participants. Decision 4 deals with the importance of how to assign participants to the various levels of your independent variable in order to answer your research question. Decision 5 deals with what type of data you will collect. The type of data collected must enable you to answer you research question, and the type of data, meaning how it was actually observed and measured, has implications for the type of analyses that can be run later on.

The sixth design decision – representativeness, sample size, power and statistical analyses – are then dealt with. These issues are often neglected by students, which has detrimental effects on the quality of their research project. It is essential that you consider how many participants you require to adequately represent your target population, and to ensure that you have sufficient power to achieve significance. The final decision involves ethical considerations which were dealt with in considerable detail in Chapter 2.

Section 13.3 deals with conducting your study, that is, making the observations and collecting the data. The importance of keeping a detailed record during this phase is also noted. Section 13.4 deals with the role of the pilot study. Carrying out a pilot study allows you to spot flaws in your design and methodology and to rectify them. Finally, section 13.5 presents a checklist for designing an experimental project.

13.1   The Importance of the Research Question

One of the major tasks for psychologists is to provide a description of human behaviour and to investigate its underlying processes. The uniqueness and power of the experimental method is that it allows you to go beyond description towards providing answers as to how and why a particular behaviour comes about. Therefore, if you have developed a research question that addresses causes of behaviour, it will be appropriate to carry out an experimental research project in order to answer your research question. As you will have learnt through your methodology courses, the experiment deals with the four goals of the scientific method, description, prediction, understanding and control.

You will also have learnt that no single experimental design is essentially better than another and that the suitability of a given design rests with the nature of the research question(s) asked. It makes no sense to utilise a very complicated multifactor design, when the issue at hand is quite simple, for example to investigate if there is a significant difference between how males and females perceive their intelligence. Remember that introducing complex and unnecessary features into an experimental design format is a waste of time and resources. More importantly for the undergraduate student, this may complicate interpretative issues. It is more appropriate to carry out a simple and clear project well, as opposed to carrying out a complex project badly. The scientific principle of parsimony comes into play again here. When your project is being graded, an important consideration will be whether you matched the design to the complexity of the issue, and whether you included only those variables that were required for generating meaningful results.

This being said, students often worry that their design is too simple, especially when they have just learnt that another student has a more complicated design. Again, complexity does not translate into a better project; scientific rigour, clarity and insightfulness *do*, however.

13.2   The Importance of Planning and Designing your Study

⚠ IF YOU FAIL TO PLAN, YOU PLAN TO FAIL.
Clearly this very important planning stage is imperative to the success of the research project; basically, if you fail to plan, you plan to fail. Therefore, the success of your psychology project can rest on this stage. As already noted, the research question will dictate the design of your study and the type of analysis that you will run on your data. At the planning and designing stage there are a number of decisions to be made before any data are collected. You must determine which observations will be made, under what conditions, and what methods will be employed for recording the observation of your participants.

As already noted, how you record your observations will have implications later on for the type of analyses that can be run on the data. For example, if you record reaction times, your data would be interval/ratio, it would therefore be appropriate to run parametric analyses. However, if you record discrete or categorical data which is nominal, it would be appropriate to run non-parametric analyses. Furthermore, the inferences made later on cannot outrun the data that was collected. Figure 13.1 illustrates the seven important design decisions involved in carrying out a well-planned and designed experimental study.

Decision 1: Operationalising your variables

As already noted in Chapter 11, the process of operationalisation involves linking conceptual definitions of a variable to a specific measurement of it. Therefore your first step in planning and designing an experimental-based project is to operationalise your variables in order to test your hypothesis objectively and ultimately answer your research question. Consult Chapter 11, which dealt with this issue in detail.

Decision 2: Who will your participants be?

No matter how carefully you describe the measuring instruments and procedures of your study, and regardless of the levels of appropriateness and sophistication of the statistical techniques you will use to analyse the data, your results will be meaningless unless there is a clear indication of your sample. Population variables can influence the external validity of your study. The

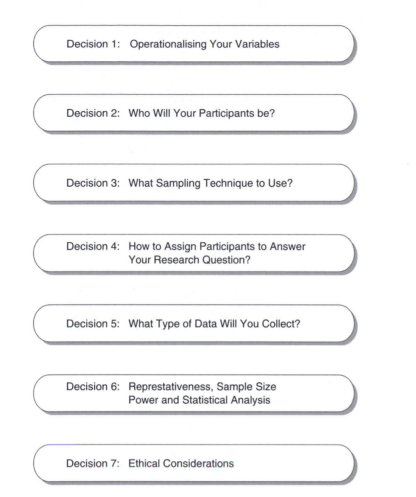

Figure 13.1   The decisions involved in designing your study

external validity of your study allows you to accurately generalise the results of your study to your target population. Therefore defining your population is a very important design consideration, because it defines the population that you can generalise your results to.

In order to define your population you should create selection criteria based on your research question in order to recruit your sample, that is, the characteristics you require for allowing people to participate in your study. The criteria that you use to define your sample will also define the population that it represents; therefore you need to create selection criteria so that the sample is representative of your target population.

Defining your sample first depends on the constructs and hypothesis being investigated. For example, when studying the behaviour of children, the sample and population should be composed of children of a specified age. It is very important to note that a population is by no means a fixed entity, defined by one variable. Members of a population can differ along many variables; for example the population of children consists of males and females, from different cultures and with different abilities. How well your results generalise to the population will depend on how much your sample has in common with the population in terms of all the participant variables that can influence or confound your results. In this regard, your sample should reflect the important characteristics of the population that you are studying.

Decision 3: What sampling technique to use?

As already noted in Chapter 9, the external validity of your study is greatly affected by the sample of participants in your study. A representative sample is one in which the characteristics of the participants reflect the characteristics of the population; therefore it is very important that your sample is representative. Another important factor to bear in mind is that the population of interest depends on your research question, and that the validity of your outcomes and the conclusions of your study will greatly depend on your sample being representative. Consult Chapter 9 for the popular probability and non-probability sampling techniques.

Decision 4: How to assign participants to answer your research question

The next decision involves how you will assign your participants to the various levels of your independent variable(s). This decision will be determined by your research question and hypothesis. As already noted in Chapter 11, there are two common possibilities. First, you can assign only some participants to each level – this type of design is known as a between-subjects or an independent groups design. The second approach is to assign each participant to every level of the independent variable, and is commonly known as a within-subjects design or a dependent groups design.

Decision 5: What type of data will you collect?

The next stage involves deciding on what type of observations to make, and what methods you will employ for recording your data. You will also decide on what type of measure to use to operationalise your research variables. Often the dependent variable is closely connected to the measuring instrument used to collect the data, and as you will see in the examples given in the following chapter, the dependent variable is often operationally defined as being equivalent to the scores on the measurement. Chapter 10 detailed

The choice which statistical test can legitimately be used for data analysis depends largely on which scale of measurement has been employed. Furthermore, the inferences that can reasonably be drawn from a study should not outrun the data observed.

Figure 13.2   Implications of scaling

useful sources of both published and non-published tests and measures, and equipment that are useful at this stage.

As already noted in Chapter 11, it is vital that you collect data that will answer your research question. The type of data that you collect will have implications for the type of analysis that you can run on the data later. It is important that you understand the different types of data to ensure that you record the most appropriate type to answer your research question.

Decision 6: Representativeness, sample size, power and statistical analysis

Once you have made decisions regarding your population and sample, and the type of design required to investigate your research question, you now need to decide on how many participants you require to adequately represent your target population, and to ensure that you have sufficient power. To maximise external validity, the general rule is the more the merrier. The larger the sample the more of the population is being observed, and therefore your sample is more likely to include all relevant types of participants.

Many students neglect to consider power during the design stage. It is important to realise that well-designed experiments must ensure that power will be reasonably high to detect a significant result. Otherwise an experiment is hardly worth doing. Most textbooks contain detailed discussions of the factors influencing power in a statistical test, for example what kind of statistical test is being performed, as some statistical tests are inherently more powerful than others. In general, the larger the sample size, the higher the power. However, increasing sample size involves more time and effort. Consequently, it is important to make the sample size 'large enough' but not wastefully large. A word of caution is needed here because greatly increasing the sample size, for example to 1,000 participants, would probably give you significance for every test you ran on your data – trivial differences are detected regardless of whether the tests make any sense to run on the data, so you should never under-estimate the importance of practical significance and logic.

On the one hand you want to use a sample size that is sufficiently large enough to give the statistical tests that you will run on your data adequate power, while on the other hand you don't want to use a sample size too small as to make the probability of obtaining significance too low. Therefore, you must get the balance right.

The level of error in your experimental measurements can also affect power. Measurement error acts like noise that can lose the signal of real experimental effects. Consequently, anything that enhances the accuracy and consistency of measurement can increase statistical power.

It is very useful, therefore, to calculate the required sample size for your groups to ensure that the statistical test you plan to run on your data will have adequate power. One can usually perform special analyses prior to running the experiment, to calculate how large a sample is required – this is known as prospective power analysis. Due to the difficulty involved in calculating prospective power analysis, a number of computer packages have been developed to run the computations for you, for example PASS, Power & Precision, nQuery Advisor, Stat Power and GPOWER, most of which have free trials.

Decision 7: Ethical considerations

As already noted in Chapter 2, there are a number of ethical issues to consider at the planning stage of your study, for example upholding scientific rigour, the dignity and welfare of your participants, and making risk–benefit judgements. Refer to Chapter 2 to refresh yourself with the important ethical considerations.

13.3   Conducting your Study

Conducting your study, making the observations and getting the data are the most familiar aspects to undergraduate students who often see this as actually doing the research. Throughout this phase of the research process you will carry out the procedures that you decided on during your planning phases. Basically, you will be making observations of the participants' behaviour under the conditions that you have specified, therefore the earlier phases serve as preparation for making empirical observations, and the remaining phases focus on using those observations (i.e. processing, interpreting and communicating them). It is clearly evident that scientific research can be seen as a process of inquiry that revolves around its most central aspect – making empirical observations.

It is advisable that you keep a diary of your experimental procedure as you go, as this will facilitate the writing of a concise and precise methodology section, which is very important for replication purposes as already mentioned. If possible, you should try and write your methodology as your carry it out. Students are warned not to try and write this section from memory, at a later date. A scantily written method section will lose you marks, regardless of how sophisticated your data analyses and other sections are.

13.4   Pilot Study

Running a pilot study is a very important aspect of conducting your project. It allows you to spot flaws in your methodology before you actually conduct the study. The pilot study allows you to see whether the instructions and the task are understood by participants. It is very common that the pilot study will reveal the need to make adjustments to either the instructions, procedure or recording devices. When changes have been made, do another pilot test to make sure that all is now running smoothly. Although conducting a pilot study may appear time-consuming, this form of quality control saves you time in the long run, and improves the scientific rigour of your project.

13.5   Checklist

- Is your design adequate to answer your research question?
- Is your independent variable appropriate given the nature of the research question?
- Are the levels of the independent variable appropriate?
- How will you assign your participants to the levels of your independent variable?
- Have you operationally defined your variables sufficiently?
- How will you measure your data?
- Will your measurements be accurate?
- Have you selected the appropriate sampling technique to recruit your participants?
- Will the sampling technique yield a representative sample?
- Do you plan to carry out a pilot study?

Summary

Rigorous planning and designing of your study is of great significance. No matter how sophisticated your analysis, or the connections and implications you draw from your data, they are meaningless unless the design and methodology you have employed answer your research question. There are a number of design decisions that you should attend to. These include operationalising your variables, deciding who your participants will be, how to select your participants, how to assign your participants to answer your research question and what type of data to collect. You should also consider your sample size, representativeness and power considerations, and of course your ethics. You should carry out a pilot study before you launch into your experimentation. This will enhance the quality of your design, and will also save you time in the long run.

Further Reading

Clark-Carter, D. (2004) *Quantitative Psychological Research: A Student's Handbook*. Hove and New York: Psychology Press: Taylor & Francis.

Field, A. and Hole, G. (2004) *How to Design and Report Experiments*. London: Sage Publications.

Harris, P. (2002) *Designing and Reporting Experiments in Psychology* (2nd edn). Buckingham and Philadelphia: Open University Press.

Mitchell, M. L. and Jolley, J. M. (2004) *Research Design Explained* (5th edn). Canada: Thomson/Wadsworth.

14

WRITING UP YOUR QUANTITATIVE METHODOLOGY

Objectives

On reading this chapter you should:

- understand the importance of concise and precise detail for writing up your methodology;
- be aware of the various subsections that make up the method section; and
- be able to write up your methodology subsections with enough detail for replication.

Overview

Section 14.1 deals with writing up your methodology section of your project. In the form of its various subsections it contains all the information needed by another researcher to replicate your study. The division of the method into the subsections of design, participants, materials and apparatus are dealt with in the following sections using examples from students that I have supervised. Section 14.2 describes the design subsection as a very precise and concise overview of the formal design of the principal features of your study. The research question is described as being the major factor in determining the appropriateness of your design. Section 14.3 deals with the second subsection of your methodology, the participants. Students often under-estimate the importance of a comprehensive participants' section, so the detail that is needed is described. Section 14.4 details the materials subsection and describes the information that should be reported for measures and for any apparatus used in your study. Section 14.5 deals with the procedure subsection and the importance of sufficient detail for replication is explained. The data-management subsection is described in Section 14.6. Finally, Section 14.7 presents a checklist to assist you in writing up the methodology section of your project.

14.1   Writing up the Methodology

It is advisable that you write up the methodology section of your project while you are carrying it out. However, due to time constraints, it is not always possible for students to do this. If you have kept a diary or made notes during the planning, designing and carrying out of your project, you will be able to refer to those when writing up this section. It is not a good idea to try and write this section from your memory.

The method in the form of its various subsections contains all the information required by another researcher to replicate the experiment. It therefore gives a detailed account of the practical aspects of conducting your project.

According to the APA Manual (2001):

> the method section describes in detail how the study was conducted. Such a description enables the reader to evaluate the appropriateness of your methods and the reliability and the validity of your results. It also permits experienced investigators to replicate the study if they desire to do so. (p. 17)

It is customary and beneficial to divide your methodology into sections labelled design, participants, materials, procedure and data management (see Figure 14.1).

It is also imperative for you to realise that a detailed and precise methodology allows your reader and marker to make an informed decision as to whether you used an appropriate design to answer your research question, and whether the methodology you employed was appropriate, etc.

14.2   Design Subsection

The design subsection is a very precise and concise overview of the formal design of the principal features of your study. The design you utilise is contingent on the nature of the research question(s) you have asked. You must describe the independent variables and how they were operationalised, and also the conditions selected to represent the different levels of them. It is also important to describe the dependent variables and how they were operationalised, and the units used to measure them. You should state the various experimental and control groups, and briefly state how participants were assigned to these groups. It is also useful to state the experimental hypotheses, to illustrate the appropriateness of the design for answering your research question(s). It may also be useful to present a contingency table illustrating the formal design of your study. The following example illustrates what information should go into the design section.

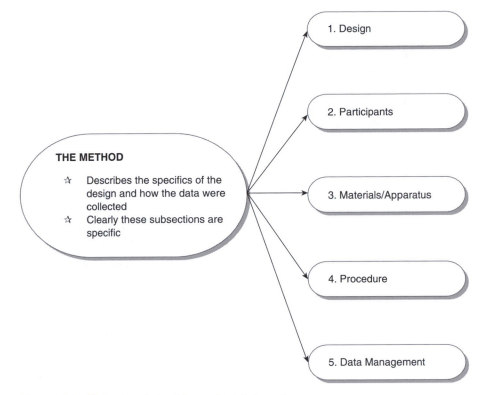

Figure 14.1   Five subsections of the methodolody section

Example 14.1   From Barry, 2004

An independent groups' design and a within-groups design were used to investigate spatial ability and the learning of complex scientific instructional material. The independent variables were the participants' level of spatial ability and the instructional format. Participants' spatial ability was determined using the Purdue Visualisation of Rotations Test (Bodner & Guay, 1997), while the instructional design followed either a text- or diagram-based format. The dependent variable was the participants' ability to construct complex molecular models, measured by recording the time for successful completion of the task in seconds. The formal design of the present study is presented in Table 14.1 below. It was expected that mean completion times would be significantly faster for both high and low spatial ability participants when diagrammatic-based rather than text-based instructions were being followed. It was further expected that the high spatial ability participants would have significantly faster completion times than the low spatial ability participants using both text-based and diagram-based instructions.

(Continued)

(Continued)

Table 14.1   Contingency table of formal design of the present study

	Text-based	Diagram-based
Group 1 (High spatial ability	n = 16	n = 17
Group 2 (Low spatial ability)	n = 15	n = 16

14.3   Participants Subsection

This is the second subsection of the methodology. Students often skim over this section, failing to realise the importance of a comprehensive participants section. The APA Publication Manual (2001) clearly describes the purpose and content of the participants subsection as follows:

> Appropriate identification of research participants and clientele is critical to the science and practice of psychology, particularly for assessing the results (making comparisons across groups), generalising the findings, and making comparisons in replications, literature reviews, or secondary data analyses ... (p. 18)

Begin by reporting whether your sample was randomly or conveniently selected. This is an important distinction to make, and has many implications for your study including external validity. Report the total number of participants, major demographic characteristics, mean age, age range and gender. Give the total number of participants, and the number assigned to each experimental condition. If some participants fail to complete the experiment, state how many.

Describe your participants in terms of those variables that are more likely to have an influence on your dependent variable(s). For example, when a particular demographic is a dependent variable or an independent variable, or is important for interpreting the results, describe the group specifically.

The APA Manual also warns that 'conclusions and interpretations should not go beyond what the sample would warrant' (2001, p. 18). The issue of external validity and generalisability comes into play here. The type of participants that took part in your study will dictate the generalisations which can be made based on your findings later on, as already noted in the previous chapter.

Students often under-estimate the importance of a comprehensive participants section, and simply report the age range and mean age for the group A comprehensive participants section is of paramount importance, as it provides a more complete picture of the sample, which has implications for the replication of your study. An example of the participants section is presented next.

Example 14.2   From O'Loughlin, 2005

Participants were selected by means of convenience sampling. The non-yoga sample were obtained from the undergraduate psychology classes in the American College Dublin. The yoga sample was obtained through the Irish Yoga Association. Altogether there were 69 participants; 38 non-yoga and 31 yoga experienced in pranayama. Yoga participants' level of experience with pranayama ranged from 4 months to 20 years, with a mean of 5.2 years. The age range of all participants was 19–63, (M = 32.75). The age range of non-yoga participants was 19–33, (M = 24.5), and the age range of yoga participants was 27–63, (M = 43.2). In total there were 12 males and 57 females. In the yoga condition there were 30 females and 1 male, and in the non-yoga there were 27 females and 11 males. All participants were right handed (as determined by self report and a handedness inventory) and were free of nasal obstruction at this time of the experiment

---

Summary of what should be included:

1. Describe the number of participants per condition, including a breakdown by gender.
2. The age range and mean of the overall sample. If there is a lot of variation between groups then include an age breakdown of the groups.
3. Major demographics.
4. Selection process and how participants were assigned to conditions.

14.4   Materials Subsection

In this subsection, you should describe any instruments, questionnaires or measures used, and state their reliabilities and validities. The different types of reliabilities and validities were dealt with in chapter 10. Example 14.3 presents the materials subsection detailing the relevant information required for a pen and paper measure of motivation.

Example 14.3   Sources of Motivation Inventory (Barbuto & Scholl, 1998)

Motivation sources were measured using the Motivation Source Inventory (Barbuto & Scholl, 1998). The SMI is a 34 item self-report inventory. A seven point response format is used ranging from (1) strongly disagree to (7) strongly agree.

The inventory measures five sources of motivation, Intrinsic Process, Instrumental, Self-Concept External, Self-Concept Internal, and Goal Internalisation. Examples of each subscale are given below.

(Continued)

(Continued)

Intrinsic Process – 'I only like to do things that are fun'
Instrumental – 'A day's work for a day's pay'
Self-Concept External – 'It is important to me that others approve of my behaviour'
Self-Concept Internal – 'Decisions I make will reflect high standards that I've set for myself'
Goal Internalisation – 'I would not work for a company if I didn't agree with its mission'

The SMI has reported coefficients alpha ranging from 0.70 to 0.91 and produced a goodness-of-fit index of 0.92 (Barbuto and Scholl, 1998)

Standard laboratory equipment such as tables, chairs, stopwatches, etc. can usually be mentioned, without detail. However, it is very important that you detail specialised equipment obtained from commercial suppliers, by providing the model number of the equipment and the supplier's name and location. Remember the importance of replication. If someone was to replicate your study, they need to know where you got any specialised equipment from. Equipment that has been custom made or that is very complex may be illustrated by a drawing or a photograph, as seen in Example 14.4 below. You should also include a detailed description of complex equipment in an appendix.

Example 14.4   From O'Loughlin, 2005

Nostril dominance was determined using 10 × 12cm aluminium metal plates with arches marked 1cm apart (see Figure 1). In this method, the 'Zwaardemarker method' proposed by Gertner, Podoshin and Fradis (1984), the participant holds a metal plate in a horizontal position under his/her nose and slowly exhales through the nostrils. Nostril dominance is determined by measuring the area of condensation on the plate. The dominant nostril produces a larger area of condensation which lasts for longer.

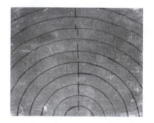

Figure 14.1   Metal plate used for measuring nostril dominance

Aearo E.A.R. brand compressible foam earplugs were used as nose plugs to block one nostril, in the right and left nostril breathing conditions.

14.5   Procedure Subsection

The procedure section is just as important as any other subsection in the method-ology. Yet students often fail to outline in enough detail how they conducted their study. Do not take anything for granted, no matter how obvious the details of how you carried out your study are from the other subsections, you must still explicitly state what you did in sufficient detail. Therefore, you must explain what the par-ticipants did, or what was done to them during your investigation. It is also useful to include a verbal account of instructions given to the participants.

APA Manual (2001) states that the procedure:

> should tell the reader what you did and how you did it in sufficient detail so that a reader could reasonably replicate your study. (pp. 14–15) At the beginning of this section you should detail how you selected your participants. If you used a random sample, you should explain how you did this.

14.6   Data-Management Subsection

Not all universities will espouse the inclusion of this subsection. It is therefore very important that you check with your supervisor before including this section in your methodology. Some researchers advocate placing this section in the results section as opposed to the methodology. I think that it is useful to position your data management at the end of your methodology as it can improve the flow of your project by integrating the results section to follow.

If you are including this subsection, you should include any reliability checks you ran on your data once it was inputted into SPSS. For example, if you check some of your raw data against your inputted data to ensure that it was inputted correctly, you should mention this. If you cleaned up your data following your exploratory data analysis, you should also mention this, as well as the percentage of data that you omitted and why. Refer back to Chapter 12 if needed.

If you have used any standard measurements or you have developed your own measurement, it is beneficial to carry out reliability checks like those mentioned in Chapter 10 in order to ascertain the internal reliability of your own study. You can then discuss the internal reliability in your discussion. For example, if your study demonstrates high reliability, it gives more weight to your findings and conclusions.

14.7   Checklist

- Is your design adequate to answer your research question?
- Is your independent variable appropriate given the nature of the research question being asked?

- Are the levels of the independent variable appropriate?
- Were the variables of interest operationally defined appropriately?
- How accurate and valid are your measurements?
- Are the controls appropriate?
- Could you replicate the study based on the procedure given?

Summary

Your methodology section contains all the information required by another researcher to replicate your study. The design subsection provides an overview of the formal design of the principal features of your study, and should reflect the research question. The role of a comprehensive participants subsection is often under-estimated. This section should contain information regarding central demographics of interest, and how participants were assigned to conditions, including a breakdown by gender. The materials subsection describes the measures and apparatus used, including information regarding their reliability and validity. The procedure subsection, gives a step by step account of how you carried out your study, with enough detail for replication. And finally the data-management subsection can be included to describe how you managed your data, for example reliability checks and any changes made to your data following exploratory data analysis.

Further Reading

Clark-Carter, D. (2004) *Quantitative Psychological Research: A Student's Handbook.* Hove and New York: Psychology Press, Taylor & Francis.

Field, A. and Hole, G. (2004) *How to Design and Report Experiments.* London: Sage Publications.

Harris, P. (2002) *Designing and Reporting Experiments in Psychology* (2nd edn). Buckingham and Philadelphia: Open University Press.

Mitchell, M. L. and Jolley, J. M. (2004) *Research Design Explained* (5th edn). Canada: Thomson/Wadsworth.

Illustrative examples were taken from the following psychology projects that were presented in part fulfilment of the requirements of Bachelor of Arts, Department of Psychology, American College Dublin.

O'Loughlin, S. (2005) The Influence of Unilateral Forced Nostril Breathing on Performance of Lateralised Cognitive Tests in Trained and Untrained Participants.

Barry, S. (2004) The Effects of Spatial Ability on the Learning of Complex Scientific Instructional Material.

15

WRITING UP YOUR QUANTITATIVE RESULTS SECTION

Objectives

On reading this chapter you should:

- understand the structure of the results section;
- understand how to present your results in the body of your text; and
- be able to streamline your results.

Overview

Chapter 15 deals with writing up your results section. Section 15.1 deals with the structure that your results section should take. There is far more agreement on what should be included in quantitative results sections as opposed to qualitative, so this makes the task somewhat easier. Section 15.2 deals with the first section of your results, which involves reviewing your aims and hypotheses. Next, Section 15.3 deals with your descriptive statistics, which act to summarise your data in an easy format. Your inferential statistics are then presented in the following Section 15.4, and then section 15.5 deals with the conclusion section. Section 15.6 focuses on presenting tables and graphs in your results section, and Section 15.7 presents some guidelines for writing your results. Finally, Section 15.8 presents a checklist.

15.1   Structure of the Results Section

The results section of your project provides a concise yet comprehensive description of your results, including descriptive and inferential statistics as seen in figure 15.1. You have some choice in the way that you organise the presentation of your results. The fundamental purpose of the results section is to provide the data that will enable you to answer your research question.

Therefore, you should organise the section so that the relevance of the data to the research questions and hypotheses that you set forth in the introduction, are as clear as possible. Students often fall into the trap of organising their results based on the use of certain statistical tests rather than the relevance of findings to the initial set of hypotheses.

Don't interpret the results here, only report them. A guiding principle is to stick to the facts. The APA Manual (2001) states:

> The results section summarises the data collected and the statistical treatment of them. First, briefly state the main results of findings. Discussing the implications of the results is not appropriate here. Mention all relevant results, including those that run counter to the hypothesis. Do not include individual raw scores or raw data, with the exception, for example, of single-case designs or illustrative samples. (p. 20)

15.2   Review of Aims and Hypotheses

A results-section paragraph begins by stating the purpose of your study; this aims to keep your project flowing and to keep the structure of your project consistent with other sections. Remember that the reader, at any point of reading your project, should know where they have been, where they are and where they are going.

In example 15.1, the aims of the research are revisited and the independent and dependent variables are restated.

Example 15.1   From O'Loughlin, 2005

The effect of unilateral forced nostril breathing on performance of tests of verbal and spatial ability were investigated. The independent variables were breathing condition and group (yoga/non-yoga). The dependent variables were performance on Miller verbal analogy, alphanumeric mental rotations and Vandenberg and Kuse mental rotations tests.

It was hypothesised that, following a 30 minute breathing period, participants in the unilateral right nostril breathing condition would perform significantly better on the verbal analogies test than participants in the unilateral left nostril breathing condition. It was further predicted that yoga participants in the unilateral right nostril breathing condition would perform significantly better on the verbal test than non-yoga in the unilateral right nostril breathing condition.

It was also hypothesised that, following a 30 minute breathing period, participants in the unilateral left nostril breathing condition would perform significantly better on mental rotations tests than participants in the unilateral right nostril breathing condition or the control condition. It was also further predicted that yoga participants in the unilateral left nostril breathing condition would perform significantly better on spatial tests than non-yoga in the unilateral left nostril breathing condition.

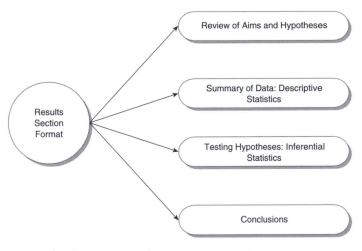

Figure 15.1   Format of the results section

15.3   Summary of Data: Descriptive Statistics

The next thing to do is to identify the descriptive statistics used to summarise the results for your dependent variable (D.V.), for example the mean and standard deviation. The purpose of your descriptive statistics is to summarise your data in a readily comprehensible form. There are a number of ways that you can do this; for example, you can present a summary of your descriptive statistics across conditions in the form of a table or a figure. However, it is important that you do more than merely present a table or figure. You must direct the readers' attention to the highlights of the data in the table or figure, focusing especially on the aspects of the results that are consistent with (or discrepant from) the hypothesis you proposed in the introduction. The same data should not be reported in both a table or a figure – tables can provide a more concise description of the results, while figures make it easier to see trends or patterns in the data. The example below demonstrates these points well.

Example 15.2   From Barry (2004)

Descriptive statistics

When all participants in the present study had completed the Purdue Visualisation of Rotations Test, they were split into two groups: Group 1 (low spatial ability) and Group 2 (high spatial ability). Descriptive statistics for both groups are presented in Table 1 below. Table 1 illustrates that for Group 1, the age range was between 17 and 32, with a mean

(Continued)

(Continued)

age of 22.8. The range of scores on the 20-item Purdue Visualisation of Rotations Test was between 2 and 9, with a mean age of 6.06 and a standard deviation of 2.21. The completion times for the molecule construction task ranged between 189 seconds and 558 seconds, with a mean completion time of 352.58 seconds.

For Group 2, Table 1 shows an age range between 18 and 31, with a mean age of 22.3. The range of scores on the 20-item Purdue Visualisation of Rotations Test was between 10 and 18, with a mean of 12.65 and a standard deviation of 2.44. The completion times for the molecule construction task ranged between 203 seconds and 465 seconds, with a mean completion time of 308.32 seconds.

Table 15.1 Descriptive statistics for Group 1 (low spatial ability) and Group 2 (high spatial ability)

	N	Minimum	Maximum	Mean	Standard Deviation
Group 1					
Age	33	17	32	22.82	3.93
Spatial Test Score (/20)	33	3	9	6.06	2.21
Task Completion Time (secs)	33	189	558	352.58	87.96
Group 2					
Age	31	18	31	22.32	3.5
Spatial Test Score (/20)	31	10	18	12.65	2.44
Task Completion Time (secs)	31	203	465	308.32	82.45

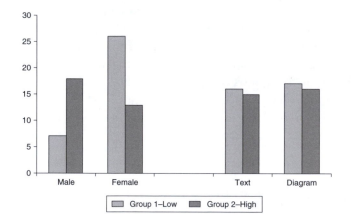

Group 1–Low   Group 2–High

Figure 1 Frequency distribution for gender, spatial ability and instructional design

The frequencies for gender and instructional design in Group 1 and Group 2 are illustrated in Figure 1 above. Group 1 consisted of 33 participants (7 males and 26 females), 16 of whom followed text-based instructions, while 17 followed diagrammatic-based instructions. Group 2 was made up of 31 participants (18 male and 13 female), 15 of whom followed text-based instructions, while 16 followed diagrammatic-based instructions.

What becomes very apparent from the above example is that there is a supporting thread of English throughout. It is crucial that you don't just present a table, followed by a figure, and expect the reader to know what they mean. You should always refer to tables and figures in the body of your text. A good rule of thumb is that if your take away all your tables and figures, your text should still make sense.

15.4   Testing Hypotheses: Inferential Statistics

In this section, it is important that you report your data analysis with sufficient clarity for someone else to be able to replicate them based on your description. For each statistical test, you must report the name of the test, the value of the test statistic, the degrees of freedom (df) and the significance level. When your results are significant you should also report the confidence level and the effect size; this makes results more meaningful, provides context and gives an indication of practical significance of results. When results are insignificant, do not report confidence intervals.

Statistical presentation of results

There are a number of ways that you can present your statistical results in the body of your text. The APA (2001) suggest the following, ($\underline{F}$ (2, 110) = 6.957; $\underline{P}$ < .05). Another popular approach is to underline the statistical notation and to include the degrees of freedom separately for example, (F = 6.957; df = 2, 110; P < .05). You should always consult with your supervisor to check which of these approaches your university supports.

15.5   Conclusions

You should always finish your results section with a conclusion. Like the introduction and discussion, the results section also benefits from a clear beginning, middle and end. This structure also facilitates the flow of your project as already discussed; it helps the reader to navigate throughout your project.

15.6   Presenting Tables and Graphs

If you have multiple t-tests or ANOVAs to present in your results section, you should put all your t-test results in one table and all your ANOVA results in another table. To make a separate table for each statistical test run on your data would make this section very bulky and hard to follow. Therefore the goal with presenting your tables is to streamline them – imagine that you are stripping away all the unnecessary fat so that your results section represents the heart, brain and muscle of your analysis; in other words, include all the vital information.

When labelling your tables and figures remember that they should be able to stand alone without the text; therefore it is crucial that the titles you give them describe what is in the tables and figures. Vague titles are inadequate for presenting your results.

15.7   Guidelines for Writing Up your Results Section

There are a number of common mistakes made by undergraduate psychology students when writing up their results section, so you should take note of the following:

- Do not teach the reader statistics.
- Do not interpret your results, you should only report them.
- Avoid vaguely labelled titles and figures.
- Make sure that your text makes sense independently of your tables and figures.
- Make sure that you have a thread of prose throughout your results section.
- Make sure that you make reference to any tables and figures that you present in your results section.
- Make sure you present your descriptive data before you present inferential data.
- Make sure that you include all the data that you intend to discuss in your discussion section.

15.8   Checklist

- Were the analyses run appropriately to answer the research question?
- Are the assumptions for the use of the statistical tests met?
- Was adequate descriptive data provided including means and standard deviations, in order to gain an understanding of the data?
- Were the inferential or analyses clear and logical?
- Are there any errors in the calculation or presentation of results?
- Are the tables and figures clearly labelled and presented?
- Were the conclusions validly based upon the data and analysis?

Summary

The results section of your report provides a concise yet comprehensive description of your results, including descriptive and inferential statistics. You have some choice in the way that you organise the presentation of your results. The fundamental purpose of the results section is to provide the data that will enable you to answer your research question. Therefore, you should organise the section so that the relevance of the data to the research questions and hypotheses that you set forth in the introduction, are as clear as possible.

Further Reading

American Psychological Association (2001) *Publication Manual of the American Psychological Association* (5th edn). Washington, DC: American Psychological Association.

Clark-Carter, D. (2004) *Quantitative Psychological Research: A Student's Handbook.* Hove and New York: Psychology Press, Taylor & Francis.

Field, A. and Hole, G. (2004) *How to Design and Report Experiments.* London: Sage Publications Ltd.

Harris, P. (2002) *Designing and Reporting Experiments in Psychology* (2nd edn). Buckingham and Philadelphia: Open University Press.

Rudestam, K. E. and Newton, R. R. (2001) *Surviving Your Dissertation: A Comprehensive Guide to Content and Process* (2nd edn). London: Sage Publications Ltd.

16

WRITING UP YOUR QUANTITATIVE DISCUSSION SECTION

Objectives

On reading this chapter you should:

- understand what the discussion contains; and
- understand the importance of making good on the claims that you made in the introduction section.

Overview

Having analysed your data, this chapter illustrates how in the discussion, you continue to make sense of your data by interpreting the results specifically in terms of the research question, and also in broader terms, in how this answer contributes to knowledge in the field of psychology. Therefore emphasising the dual nature of psychological science discussed in Chapter 1. Section 16.7 deals with what the discussion section exemplifies how the discussion should be structured and written for a quantitative project.

Examples will illustrate how findings are put into a context that helps to relate them not only to the original research questions, but also to other concepts and findings in the field. The chapter also demonstrates how the interpretation phase represents the flip side of the problem specification aspect, encountered in Chapter 11. When defining the research problem or idea, the research literature was drawn upon, and guided you to important questions, clearly demonstrating a deductive flow of thought and reason. During this stage of the research process, it is illustrated how the answers obtained to the questions determine how accurate the theories predict new observations, relying on inductive thought, therefore reasoning from the specific results of the study back to the generality of theory. Finally Section 16.4 presents a checklist.

16.1   What the Discussion Contains

By the time you have collected your data, and analysed it, and you have written up your results section, you may feel as if you have completed the research process. This is quite a common experience, which inevitably means that some students do not do justice to the interpretation of their results, and the write-up of the discussion section. It is very important that you do not fall into this trap.

The discussion holds much weight regarding the quality of your project, and therefore warrants as much consideration as the introduction and other sections. In the discussion, you have the opportunity to move beyond your data, and make creative insights regarding your findings and existing theory and research, clearly giving students an opportunity to develop their own independent critical thinking. This point is made very well by Abelson (1995, p. 13):

> High quality evidence, embodying sizable, well articulated and general effects, is necessary for a statistical argument to have maximal persuasive impact, but it is not sufficient.

When your data analysis is completed, you must construct a coherent narrative that explains your findings, counters opposing interpretations and justifies your conclusions. The discussion should be written in a style and tone consistent with the introduction, so that your project flows. The discussion is also the culmination of your research project, where you tie all the other sections together and make a statement about your original research question. In the discussion section you state what you have discovered, and what you think these findings mean. Unlike the results section, the discussion contains more than just facts, here you draw conclusions and interpretations from your data.

APA Manual (2001) states:

> After presenting the results, you are in a position to evaluate and interpret their implications, especially with respect to your original hypotheses. You are free to examine, interpret, and qualify the results as well as to draw inferences from them. (p. 26)

Although it is important to convince the reader of the aptness of your interpretation of your data and of your speculations, it is very important that you do not go too far beyond the evidence of your data, and draw unjustified conclusions. It is also important that you are up front about unanswered questions.

It is also important that you do not restate the data. As the APA manual (2001) states:

> Similarities and differences between your results and the work of others should clarify and confirm your conclusions. Do not, however, simply reformulate and repeat points already

made; each new statement should contribute to your position and to the reader's understanding of the problem. You may remark on certain shortcomings of the study, but do not dwell on every flaw. Negative results should be accepted as such without an undue attempt to explain them away. (p. 26)

Restatement of essential findings

The discussion begins with a statement of the essential findings, in which you should give particular attention to how your findings support or refute your original hypothesis. You do not repeat the descriptive statistics in this summary, nor do you include actual inferential results. In the introduction and literature-review section of your project, you made claims in the form of hypotheses and research questions. Therefore the purpose here is to answer your research question and also to validate your claims.

Assess the quality of your study and consider methodological flaws

In order to thoroughly assess what your results really mean, you must assess the quality of your piece of research. The first thing that you should think about is the internal validity of your study, that is, how sure are you that the change in your independent variable caused the change in your dependent variable. In other words, how sure are you that your experimental manipulations were responsible for your significant findings. You should go back to your methodology and the design of your study, and critically evaluate them. You should ask yourself questions like:

- Were there any confounding variables that I did not control for?
- Were there any flaws in how I conducted the study?
- Were my variables operationalised and measured appropriately?
- Did my measures have good construct validity? Did they measure what they were supposed to measure?
- Were my measures reliable?
- Was there a high level of measurement error?
- Were there any floor and ceiling effects?
- Did all my participants understand what they were required to do?

In assessing the quality of your study, it is important that you strike a balance between the strengths and weaknesses of your study. Remember that if you really rip your study to shreds, and list methodological flaws upon methodological flaws, the question arises as to whether you put sufficient thought and energy into the design of your study. Not only that, but it raises the ethical issue and questions whether you conducted good, valid research.

Also, if you have too many methodological flaws this will undermine the conclusions that you can draw from your findings.

When assessing the strengths of your study, you should think about what improvements you made after your initial pilot study. It is also advisable to think critically about your sample. Were they representative of the general population or were they selected from a specific group? Did you randomly select your participants or did you recruit a convenient sample? If your participants were not randomly assigned you need to determine whether your sample was biased in any way. This can be done by going back to your participants section and reminding yourself of your group composition. Did you determine an adequate sample size to ensure that your planned statistical tests had adequate power to detect significance before you recruited participants? As already mentioned, measurement error can affect your study; it can act like noise that loses the signal of real experimental effects. It is also useful to discuss the documented reliability of any measures that you utilised. As noted in Chapter 14, if you have calculated the reliability for the data of your own study, i.e. the internal reliability of your study, it can be discussed here. High internal reliability gives more weight to your findings and conclusions, and also demonstrates scientific rigour.

It is also useful to carry out your debriefing session shortly before you write up your discussion. Carrying out a debriefing session is a practice of good research ethics, but it also has a potential scientific or research benefit. The debriefing session gives you a very valuable opportunity to tap into the thoughts of your participants regarding the research situation, therefore assisting in the development of a phenomenological context (Jones & Gerard, 1967) in which to interpret your results. This sort of information can really improve your understanding and interpretation of your results, and may even provide some promising leads for future research.

The two examples below illustrate that it is not sufficient to merely list methodological flaws, but it is also important that you consider how they may have influenced your results.

Example 16.1 From O'Loughlin, 2005

The final factor which may have influenced the findings of the present study, is that some of the yoga participants had practiced breathing techniques, including alternative nostril breathing, just prior to the commencement of the experiment. While this factor was not controlled for, it would certainly need to be avoided in future research. As stated previously, alternative nostril breathing is a technique, which is purported to have a balancing effect on the hemispheres of brain. This effect is believed to occur through the equal and alternate stimulation of the right and left hemispheres. Thus, it is possible that the breathing techniques used prior to the experiment had already influenced hemispheric activity and thus reduced the effect of unilateral forced nostril breathing in these participants.

Example 16.2   From Barry, 2004

The experimental phase of the present study revealed some methodological flaws. ... there were some participants in the study for whom English was not their first language. As a result, the text condition of the molecule construction task may have been more difficult for the non-fluent English speakers, as some of the words used in the instructions (e.g. iodine, bromine, etc.) were not commonly used English words. ... Thus, future studies with fewer time and resource constraints should tailor the instructions to match the language of the participant, and emphasise the importance of reading the instructions carefully all the way through.

Theoretical implications

You should include a description of how your findings relate to the relevant literature, most of which should be cited in the introduction. As seen in Example 16.3, you should discuss how they are similar or, if your results are different, how they differ. You should also attempt to resolve and deal with these differences by suggesting reasons for why they might have occurred.

Example 16.3   From O'Loughlin, 2005

The findings were only significant for unilateral right nostril breathing increasing verbal performance in yoga participants. However, the general trends suggest a contralateral relationship between unilateral forced nostril breathing and lateralised hemispheric activity, as measure by lateralised cognitive tests. This provides some support for the yogic belief that unilateral forced nostril breathing stimulates the opposite hemisphere. It also provides support for Werntz et al.'s (1983, 1987) interpretation of increased amplitude in the contralateral hemisphere reflecting increased cortical activity during unilateral forced nostril breathing.

Careful consideration of findings that fail to support your research question

This point is related to your methodological flaws. If some of your findings are statistically insignificant, you should assess whether there were any features of your study that may have attributed to you failing to find significance, as demonstrated in Example 16.4.

Example 16.4   From O'Loughlin, 2005

Aside from the specific details regarding contradictory results, a possible reason why the present study failed to find a significant effect of unilateral left nostril breathing on spatial ability was because the right hemisphere is not as specialised for performance of spatial tasks as the left hemisphere is for performance of verbal tasks (Corballis, 1997). While mental rotation is acknowledged as depending highly on right-hemisphere processes, and has been found to activate the right hemisphere more reliably than other mental visuopatial (Deutsch et al., 1988), there is some evidence for a left-hemisphere involvement in mental rotations (Langton & Warrington, 2000). Corballis (1997) suggests that although there is evidence for a right-hemisphere bias in mental rotations, it is unlikely that this bias approaches the degree of left-hemisphere dominance for language-related tasks. Thus, it is possible that the present study failed to find a significant effect of unilateral left nostril breathing on spatial performance because the spatial tests were not purely a measure of right hemisphere activity.

However, do not be too hasty to attribute your insignificant results to flawed experimental design. If you find that your study is sound, then you should suggest an explanation for the discrepant results.

Careful consideration of rival explanations of your findings

It is also beneficial to consider any rival explanations of your findings, as demonstrated in Example 16.5

Example 16.5   From O'Loughlin, 2005

The contradictory findings between the present study and Jella et al. (1993) are also of interest as Vandenberg and Kuse mental rotations were used in both experiments. There are a number of factors that could have contributed to these differences. In the study by Jella et al. (1993) the number of participants per condition was larger and they used a within-subjects design. They had 51 participants per condition in the unilateral left nostril breathing condition while the current study only had 25 in this condition.

Practical applications of your study

As you already know from your methodology and theory courses in psychology, there is nothing as practical as a good theory (Lewin, 1936). It is therefore important to consider the practical applications of your findings, as demonstrated in Examples 16.6 and 16.7.

Example 16.6   From O'Loughlin, 2005

...it is possible that unilateral forced nostril breathing could be used as a means of helping people to fully utilise their cognitive abilities, by selecting the hemisphere best suited to specific task performance. It is also possible that unilateral forced nostril breathing could contribute to the treatment of psychopathologies in which lateralised dysfunction is implicated.

Example 16.7   From Barry, 2004

... the use of 3D molecular models, such as the ones used in the present study, could help to make abstract chemical concepts more understandable for both high and low spatial ability learners. Pillary (1997) found that the use of models decreased the extraneous cognitive load on the working memory of the learner, resulting in an increase in performance on chemistry tasks.

Directions for future research

The next step in the discussion is to propose additional research that could be done on the problem under investigation. Students can often find this aspect of the discussion difficult; however, there are some very useful strategies that can be used here. For example, any unanswered questions, or areas that remain unresolved, can become directions for future research. However, it is important; again, that you do not merely list directions for future research. It is important, that they are logical and have a rationale. For any suggestions that your make, it is advisable that you elaborate on why the research would be worth doing, and what results might ensue, as demonstrated in the following example:

Example 16.8   From O'Loughlin, 2005

Although unilateral forced nostril breathing is purported to influence hemispheric activity by influencing the hypothalamus and thus influencing automatic activity (Shannahoff–Khalsa, 2001), it would be interesting to explore if unilateral forced nostril breathing or alternate nostril breathing has any effect on executive function. As the olfactory bulb located in the frontal cortex (Kolb & Wischaw, 2001), close to the areas responsible for executive functions, it is possible that any stimulating effects of unilateral forced nostril breathing would be stronger in this area.

Conclusions of your study

Remember that the discussion section can really make or break your project. It is vital that you put a lot of thought into it, and try to draw sophisticated and accurate conclusions from your data. You should also present the strongest and most important statement that arises from your results as your conclusion. You should aim to end your project as strongly as you begin it, with your opening paragraph. This also lessens the chance of the reader finishing your project and thinking, 'Well, so what?' You need to ensure that there is no ambiguity as to the importance of your study, as demonstrated in Example 16.9.

Example 16.9   From O'Loughlin, 2005

The present study demonstrated that unilateral right nostril breathing significantly increased verbal performance in yoga participants.

16.2   Checklist

- Have you provided a clear, overall statement regarding support or non-support of your research question?
- Have you discussed possible problems such as confounding variables and alternative explanations for your results?
- Have you discussed the theoretical applications of your study's findings?
- Have you discussed the strengths and limitations of your study?
- Have you discussed the practical applications of your study's findings?
- Have you suggested directions for future research?
- Is there an objective basis to the reasoning, or is the author proving what he or she already believes?
- Can you deconstruct the flow of the argument to establish whether it breaks down logically?
- Are the generalisations valid?

Summary

In the discussion, you continue to make sense of your data by interpreting the results specifically in terms of the research question, but also in broader terms; how does this answer contribute to knowledge in the field of psychology? The interpretation phase represents the flip side of the problem-specification aspect.

Further Reading

American Psychological Association (2001) *Publication Manual of the American Psychological Association* (5th edn). Washington, DC: American Psychological Association.

Clark-Carter, D. (2004) *Quantitative Psychological Research: A Student's Handbook*. Hove and New York: Psychology Press, Taylor & Francis.

Field, A. and Hole, G. (2004) *How to Design and Report Experiments*. London: Sage Publications.

Harris, P. (2002) *Designing & Reporting Experiments in Psychology*. Buckingham: Open University Press.

Sternberg, R. J. (2003) *The Psychologist's Companion: A Guide to Scientific Writing for Students and Researchers* (4th edn). New York: Cambridge University Press.

Examples were taken from the following psychology projects that were presented in part fulfilment of the requirements of Bachelor of Arts, Department of Psychology, American College Dublin.

O'Loughlin, S. (2005) The Influence of Unilateral Forced Nostril Breathing on Performance of Lateralised Cognitive Tests in Trained and Untrained Participants.

Barry, S. (2004) The Effects of Spatial Ability on the Learning of Complex Scientific Instructional Material.

UNIT 3

QUALITATIVE METHODS OF INQUIRY

Introduction

It is often argued that the qualitative method of inquiry is unscientific, Harré (1997) notes that it is not always clear just what is meant by such a criticism. Qualitative methods of data collection and analysis may not lead to numerical results; however, as the following chapters will demonstrate, they are nevertheless of great precision. Compared to quantitative methods of inquiry, qualitative research has less agreement on what constitutes the essentials due to the diversity of the field, and the differing guiding qualitative paradigms. In writing this section I chose to include methods and techniques that the undergraduate psychology student can use for their project.

Chapter 17, *Qualitative Methods of Inquiry*, is a brief chapter dealing with qualitative approaches to data collection. The importance of language and understanding the participants' frame of reference are highlighted. The chapter briefly describes some of the popular qualitative methods of data collection that are suitable for undergraduate research projects in psychology, for example the interview, observation, participatory action research and the case study.

Chapter 18, *Qualitative Data Analysis*, emphasises the characteristics of qualitative data analysis, and describes the process of coding as central. The important role played by conceptualisation for qualitative research is highlighted. It is explained that qualitative research involves forming new concepts and refining concepts that are grounded in the data, and that this concept formation is an integral part of the analysis phase which begins during data collection as opposed to prior to it. Memoing is also described, which usually occurs at the same time as coding. Meaning making, and the cognitive processes involved are described. The important issue of reflexivity is flagged, as are the issues of reliability and validity for qualitative research. The popular qualitative methods of data analysis that are suitable for undergraduate psychology projects are briefly described, including grounded theory, conversational analysis, discourse analysis, interpretative phenomenological analysis and protocol analysis.

Although qualitative data collection and analysis occur simultaneously and are very much contingent on each other, the semi-structured interview and grounded theory are dealt with in two chapters. The purpose of this partitioning is not to promote them as distinct processes, but purely to prevent information overload for the undergraduate psychology student. Chapter 19, *The Semi-Structured Interview as Part of Grounded Theory*, focuses on the semi-structured interview, which is a very popular data collection technique that can be combined with numerous qualitative data analyses, including interpretative phenomenological analysis and grounded theory.

Chapter 20, *Designing, Conducting and Analysing a Grounded Theory-based Project*, focuses on grounded theory, which is one of the most popular and well-developed qualitative methods. Grounded theory was the example of choice for this chapter, because the rigour of the approach offers the qualitative undergraduate student 'a set of clear guidelines from which to build explanatory frameworks that specify relationships among concepts' (Charmaz, 2000, p. 510). Qualitative research involves forming new concepts and refining concepts that are grounded in the data. Concept formation is an integral part of the data analysis phase and begins *during* data collection as opposed to before it. This iterative relationship between the interview as a data-collection technique and grounded theory as a data-analysis technique, are highlighted.

Chapter 21, *Writing Up your Qualitative Methodology*, demonstrates that, like quantitative research, it is customary to divide your methodology into sections. However, universal agreement as to what these subsections are does not exist as it does for quantitative methodology. A guiding structure involving six different subsections is proposed, where the student can use whichever subsections are suitable for their qualitative method of inquiry.

Chapter 22, *Writing Up your Qualitative Findings and Discussion*, deals with writing up the analysis and interpretation of a qualitative project, with a focus on grounded theory. The chapter also presents a format for this section of your report, again highlighting the importance of matching your format to the nature of the research question that you have asked and are now answering.

17

QUALITATIVE METHODS OF INQUIRY

Objectives

On reading this chapter you should:

- understand the interpretative nature of qualitative research, and the importance of the participants' frame of reference;
- be aware of the major characteristics of qualitative methods of inquiry; and
- be aware of the popular qualitative methods suitable for undergraduate research.

Overview

This brief chapter deals with qualitative approaches to data collection. Section 17.1 focuses on the characteristics of qualitative methods of inquiry. The importance of language and understanding the participants' frame of reference are highlighted. Section 17.2 briefly describes some of the popular qualitative methods of data collection that are suitable for undergraduate research projects in psychology, for example the interview, observation, participatory action research and the case study.

17.1   Characteristics of Qualitative Methods of Inquiry

Recently, within the field of psychology, there has been an explosion of interest in qualitative methods of inquiry. The *Journal of Applied Psychology*, known for its quantitative papers adhering to scientific rigour, now accepts articles utilising qualitative methodologies. It is difficult to define qualitative research because it does not involve the same terminology as ordinary science. Lofland and Lofland (1984) describe the approach as involving methods of data collection and analysis that are non-quantitative, while Berg (1989) defines it as focusing on 'quality', a term referring to the essence or ambience of something. Other researchers call it a subjective methodology, with your self as the research tool (Adler & Adler, 1987). In general, qualitative methods are concerned with describing the constituent properties of an entity, using rich illustrative accounts.

Within the qualitative approaches, language is the fundamental property of human communication, where interpretation and understanding are key. Therefore, analytical strategies are used that remain as close as possible to this symbolic system. The goal is to understand the participants' own frame of reference as opposed to testing a preconceived hypothesis on a large sample. There are a number of theoretical underpinnings within qualitative approaches. For example, phenomenology and interpretative phenomenological analysis focus on exploring the life world of the participant, in order to make sense of their personal and social world, while discourse and conversational analysis are concerned with describing the linguistic resources participants use during conversations.

In qualitative research, your assumptions, interests and purpose dictate what type of methodology you will use. Qualitative researchers are committed to understanding social phenomenon from the participants' own frame of reference, and examining how they experience the world. The importance of reality is what people perceive it to be; this point is captured very clearly by Douglas (1970, p. ix): 'the forces that move human beings rather than simply as human bodies … are meaningful stuff'. The aim is to understand, at a personal level, the motives and beliefs behind people's actions.

What makes a study qualitative is that it usually relies on inductive reasoning processes to interpret and structure the meanings that can be derived from the data. Distinguishing inductive from deductive inquiry processes is an important step in identifying what counts as qualitative research. Generally, inductive reasoning uses the data to generate ideas (hypothesis generating), whereas deductive reasoning begins with the idea and uses the data to confirm or negate the idea (hypothesis testing) (Holloway, 1997). The purpose of many qualitative methods of inquiry is to generate theory from the data, known as theory generation. However, the process does not end there, generally qualitative researchers also want to verify the theories that are generated from the data, which involves deductive reasoning.

17.2   Qualitative Methods of Data Collection

In qualitative research, data collection generally takes place alongside data analysis or making sense of the data. The most common and versatile method of conducting qualitative research – the semi-structured interview – will be dealt with in detail in Chapter 19. Other common methods of qualitative inquiry include both passive and participant observation and action research.

The interview

The interview is a popular tool for the systematic collection of verbal information. The interview as a method of inquiry is a useful way of accessing people's perceptions, meanings and definitions of situations and constructions of reality (Punch, 2005). The interview is a skilled activity, which is interpersonal in nature, and generally requires some training. There are three major types of interviews used in research: the structured, the semi-structured and the unstructured interview. With the structured interview, the interviewer asks a series of short specific pre-established questions, that usually have preset response categories. The interviewer asks each question in a specified order. Semi-structured interviews are dealt with in detail in Chapter 19. In this case, the ordering of the questions is less important, and the researcher is free to probe interesting areas that emerge and to follow the respondent's interests or concerns. Finally, the unstructured interview is an open-structured, in-depth interview, often referred to as an ethnographic interview. The type of interview that you employ will depend on the nature of your research question.

Observation

Psychologists have a long tradition of employing the observation method of inquiry (Irwin, 1980). There are a number of observation techniques; in quantitative research a structured approach is taken, where categories to observe are pre-defined, whereas qualitative research utilises a more unstructured approach, and observations are made in a natural open-ended fashion without the use of pre-determined categories. Participant observation is a very popular intense research method used by qualitative researchers; however, it is usually beyond the scope of undergraduate research. Participant observation involves social interaction between the researcher and the participants, often referred to as informants. Again the type of observation that you employ is related to your research question.

Participatory action research

Participatory action research is a relatively new approach to qualitative research, which is simply learning by doing. Participatory action research assumes that knowledge is rooted in social relations and is most powerful when produced collaboratively through action. If the aim of your research question is to develop a rich understanding through being part of the method of inquiry, then participative action research may be appropriate.

Qualitative case study

Case studies are often used in applied areas of psychology such as industrial and organisational psychology. The case study consists of a detailed investigation of people, usually over a period of time within their context. The aim of carrying out a case study is to provide an analysis of the context and processes which illuminate the theoretical issues under investigation (Hartley, 2004). Therefore, if the aim of your research is a detailed and rich understanding of contextual dynamic social processes, then the case study may be an appropriate method of inquiry.

Summary

In general, qualitative methods are concerned with describing the constituent properties of an event or experience using rich descriptive accounts. Qualitative researchers are committed to understanding social phenomenon from the participants' own frame of reference, and examining how they experience the world. Qualitative methods remain as close to the fundamental property of human communication (language) as possible, and view interpretation and understanding a key. Common qualitative methods include the interview, observation, participatory action research and the qualitative case study.

Further Reading

Brydon-Miller, M. (1997) Participatory action research: Psychology and social change. *Journal of Social Issues*, 53(4), 657–66.

Camic, P., Rhodes, J. and Yardley, L. (eds) (2004) *Qualitative Research in Psychology: Expanding Perspectives in Methodology and Design*. Washington, DC: APA.

Cassell, C. and Symon, G. (eds) (2005) *Essential Guide to Qualitative Methods in Organizational Research*. London: Sage Publications Ltd.

Hartley, J. (2004) Case Study Research. In C. Cassell and G. Symon (eds) *Essential Guide to Qualitative Methods in Organizational Research*. London: Sage Publications Ltd, pp. 323–33.

Holloway, I. (1997) *Basic Concepts for Qualitative Research*. Oxford: Blackwell Science.

McTaggart, R. (ed.) (1997) *Participatory Action Research: International Contexts and Consequences*. Albany: State University of New York Press.

Punch, K. F. (2005) *Introduction to Social Research: Quantitative & Qualitative Approaches*. London: Sage Publications Ltd.

Smith, J. A. (ed.) (2003) *Qualitative Psychology: A Practical Guide to Research Methods*. London: Sage Publications Ltd.

18

QUALITATIVE DATA ANALYSIS

Objectives

On reading this chapter you should:

- understand the importance of coding
- understand that conceptualisation in qualitative research is how the researcher organises and makes sense of data;
- be aware of the different types of validity and reliability for qualitative research; and
- be able to establish validity and reliability for your qualitative project.

Overview

Data analysis is the most complex and mysterious of all of the phases of a qualitative project. In order to generate findings that transform raw data into new knowledge, a qualitative researcher must engage in active and demanding analytic processes throughout all phases of the research. Understanding these processes is therefore an important aspect not only of doing qualitative research, but also of reading, understanding and interpreting it. Due to the simultaneous process of data collection and data analysis some researchers avoid using the term data analysis, Silverman (2003) uses the term interpreting, and Hammersley and Atkinson (1995) refer to making sense of the data. Although many qualitative methods of inquiry involve simultaneous data collection and analysis, these two processes have been partitioned into two chapters for organisation purposes. Section 18.1 looks at the characteristics of examining qualitative data. Section 18.1 describes the process of coding which is central to many qualitative data analysis approaches. Section 18.2 goes on to describe the role played by conceptualisation for qualitative research. It is explained that qualitative research involves forming new concepts and refining concepts that are grounded in the data, and that this concept formation is an integral part of the data analysis phase and begins during data collection as opposed to before it. Section 18.3 describes the importance of memoing, which usually occurs at the same time as coding.

Section 18.4 presents Miles and Huberman's (1994) 13 tactics for generating meaning in qualitative data analysis. Section 18.5 lists the cognitive processes involved in coding and qualitative data analysis. Section 18.7 deals with the important issue of reflexivity. Following this Section 18.8 describes some of the popular approaches to qualitative data analysis suitable for undergraduate psychology projects, including grounded theory, conversational analysis, discourse analysis, interpretative phenomenological analysis and protocol analysis. Finally Section 18.8 presents the different meanings that reliability and validity have for qualitative research, and describes the different types of validity.

18.1   Coding

Coding serves an important role in both quantitative and qualitative methods. In quantitative research, coding serves to condense or reduce the data so that it can be counted, in order to generate means and standard deviations for further statistical analysis. What becomes apparent is that there is a shift away from the original raw data towards summary data. The role of coding in qualitative research is significantly different; coding initially serves as a way of organising the data as opposed to a structure for counting it. The original data is preserved through the linking of codes; therefore, when codes are retrieved, the original data can be displayed.

Much of qualitative analysis is centred around the process of coding, whereby regularities in the data are discovered. In simple terms, codes are names, labels or tags that are assigned to represent the meaning of sections of data. These sections can be anything from large chunks of data to individual words. Codes not only attach meaning to data, but they also index the data, and provide a basis for storage and retrieval of data.

When you begin assigning codes or labels to pieces of data, these early codes make more advanced coding possible. This, in effect, allows for the summarising of data by pulling themes together and by identifying patterns (Punch, 2005). Therefore the advanced coding in the meaning-making process is contingent on these early codes. It is therefore of paramount importance that you spend sufficient time at the early stages developing your first basic codes. Don't be too quick to jump to advanced analysis; spend the time putting the appropriate foundations in place.

Punch (2005) distinguishes between two different types of codes: descriptive and inferential codes. Descriptive codes are your basic codes that describe the meaning of the data, but do not go beyond it. More advanced coding involves making inferences that can outreach the raw data. These types of inferences are usually made about patterns that are emerging from the basic or descriptive codes. These inferences can often depend on creativity and insight for seeing patterns and connections in the data.

At the initial coding stages, you can either have pre-defined codes that you are looking for in the raw data, or you can have a general coding framework already developed. On the other hand, you can start coding with no a priori planning, and literally let the initial codes emerge from the data. Which approach you take will ultimately rely on the purposes of your research. The skills involved in coding involve being able to identify different concepts under category headings, linking concepts that fit together, and organising the sets so that the categories show a good fit with the data (Foster & Parker, 1999). The coding process for grounded theory is dealt with in detail in Chapter 20.

18.2   Conceptualisation in Qualitative Data Analysis

As was demonstrated in Chapter 11, quantitative research involves conceptualising variables and refining the concepts as part of the measuring process and occurs before the data collection and analysis. However, qualitative research involves forming new concepts and refining concepts that are grounded in the data. This concept formation is an integral part of the data analysis phase and begins during data collection as opposed to before it. Therefore, conceptualisation in qualitative research is how the researcher organises and makes sense of data. The data is usually analysed by organising it into categories on the basis of themes and concepts. In qualitative research, more conceptualisation occurs after as opposed to before data collection, and is largely determined by the data.

Operationalisation in qualitative research is therefore significantly different to that in quantitative research. In quantitative research, variables were operationalised by linking a conceptual definition to a set of operations used in data collection. However, in qualitative research, conceptual definitions are developed during and after data collection. Operationalisation in a qualitative research project is a detailed description of how you collected and thought about the specific data that becomes the basis for your concepts. Therefore, it involves a post hoc description as opposed to an a priori planned procedure. Qualitative operationalisation describes how data is collected and interpreted, and includes the use of pre-existing techniques and concepts that were integrated with those that emerged during data collection.

18.3   Memoing

Memoing usually commences at the beginning of analysis together with coding. During the coding process, you will have numerous ideas which you will want to record. Memos are used to record these ideas, therefore creativity is involved. It is important to record all ideas as they happen.

Punch (2005) notes that memos can be substantive, theoretical, methodological and personal. When memos are substantive or theoretical they may suggest that deeper concepts still exist in the data, but have not yet emerged during coding, and can therefore direct data collection and point towards new patterns in the data. Substantive and theoretical memos are also important because they have conceptual content, and are therefore more than simply describing the data. Consequently they help you move from the empirical raw data of participants to a conceptual level. This is also important for induction because they move analysis towards developing propositions. Therefore memoing links coding to the development of propositions.

18.4   Generating Meaning

Miles and Huberman (1994) propose 13 tactics for generating meaning from qualitative data, as seen in Table 18.1.

Table 18.1   Miles and Humberman's (1994) 13 tactics for generating meaning

Seeing what codes/labels go with what	1.	Noting patterns and themes
	2.	Seeing plausibility
	3.	Clustering
Achieve more integration among diverse pieces of data	4.	Making metaphors
Seeing what is there	5.	Counting
Sharpening understanding	6.	Making contrasts and comparisons
Differentiation	7.	Partitioning variables
Seeing things and their relationships more abstractly	8.	Subsuming particulars into the general
	9.	Factoring
	10.	Noting relations between variables
	11.	Finding intervening variables
Systematically assembling a coherent understanding of the data	12.	Building a logical chain of evidence
	13.	Making conceptual/theoretical coherence

18.5   Cognitive Processes Involved

Morse (1994b) believes that all qualitative analysis, regardless of the specific approach, involves:

• comprehending the phenomenon under study;
• synthesising a portrait of the phenomenon that accounts for relations and linkages within its aspects;

- theorising about how and why these relations appear as they do; and
- recontextualising, or putting the new knowledge about phenomena and relations back into the context of how others have articulated the evolving knowledge.

These steps will inevitably vary depending on the research question and the context of your study; the steps help to illustrate a sequence of cognitive processes by which the raw data are transformed.

18.6   Reflexivity

During the interpretation process, the qualitative researcher has a much broader scope for making sense of the data collected, based on their intuitions, creativity and personal experience. Kvale (1996) refers to this interpretative process as 'personal subjectivity'. Fine (1992) postulates that it is therefore important that, as a qualitative researcher, you take a reflective stance in order to notice how you shape the very data that you study. Reflexivity refers to the recognition that the involvement of the researcher as an active participant in the research process shapes the nature of the process and the knowledge produced through it. There are two types of reflexivity involved in qualitative research: personal reflexivity and epistemological reflexivity. Epistemological reflexivity requires that you ask questions like: How has the research question defined and restricted what can be found? How has the design of the study and the method of analysis created the data and the findings? Reflecting on your own involvement is just as important as reflecting on the involvement of your participants. Personal reflexivity involves reflecting upon the ways in which your own values, experiences, interests and beliefs have shaped your research. Chapter 20 looks at some useful strategies that can be used by undergraduate psychology researchers to become accustomed to the process of reflection.

18.7   Approaches to Qualitative Data Analysis

There are many diverse approaches to the analysis of qualitative data. The term data analysis has different meanings among qualitative researchers and these interpretations have lead to different methods of analysis (Punch, 2005). The following section deals with some of the popular methods of data analysis. It is important to note that this is by no means an exhaustive list.

Grounded theory

Grounded theory is dealt with in detail in Chapter 19 and has been described as the most influential paradigm for qualitative research (Denzin, 1997). It even has a journal called *Grounded Theory Review* and a website devoted specifically to it. The main aim of this approach is to discover what kinds of concepts and hypotheses or propositions are relevant to the area you wish to understand. Therefore, grounded theory begins with a research situation and, within that situation, your task as researcher is to understand what is happening there from your participants' point of view. Grounded theory provides new insights into the understanding of social processes emerging from the situation in which they occur, without forcing and adjusting the data to previous theoretical frameworks (Glaser, 1995, 1998). Grounded theory is the appropriate qualitative analysis to apply to your data if you are interested in developing a theory that accounts for your data.

Ethnomethodology/conversational analysis

The aim of this approach is to identify the social organisation underlying the way that everyday social actions and activities are produced; in other words, exploring some of the observable processes occurring during conversations, and viewing them as examples of social behaviour with their own patterns and rules for conveying meaning. By focusing on the observable processes, conversations are described in terms of structure, strategies and what can be revealed about the mechanisms involved in this type of human communication.

The key difference between conversation and discourse analysis is that the initial analysis of the transcribed conversation is theory free in conversational analysis. This avoids imposing prior understandings and knowledge to the data. Ten Have (1999) details four rounds that a transcription should go through in getting it ready for analysis. Pomerantz and Fehr (1997) have developed five steps to aid in conversational analysis;

Step 1: Select a sequence of interest.
Step 2: Characterise the actions in the sequence, and identify distinctive features.
Step 3: Analyse how the speaker packaged their actions (e.g. by choice of words or images) and how these affect the recipient's options.
Step 4: Analyse how timings, turn-takings, pauses and interruptions affect how matter is understood.
Step 5: Try to discover identities, roles and relationships.

Discourse analysis

Discourse analysis focuses on talk and texts as social practices and on resources that are drawn on to enable practices. Discourse analysis rejects the traditional cognitive explanations of social interaction; therefore, rather than explaining actions as a consequence of mental processes, the focus is on how mentalist notions are constructed and used in interaction. What becomes apparent is that the discourse itself is viewed as a social practice. Discourse can be used to achieve different things, for example to make a point in an argument or to blame somebody.

There are a number of stages involved in carrying out a discourse analysis. Like conversational analysis, the first stage involves transcribing the data. The next stage is very intensive, and requires immersion in the data, in order for deeper levels of meaning to emerge. Coding follows from immersion, and finally the data is explored in terms of the way that things were expressed, and the interpretations and shared meanings, known as interpretative repertoires.

Interpretative phenomenological analysis

Interpretative phenomenological analysis, known commonly as IPA, focuses on exploring how participants make sense of their personal and social world (Smith & Osborn, 2003). The phenomenological approach is aimed at exploring the personal experience of participants, and emphasises the dynamic process involved. Like grounded theory, IPA is often combined with the semi-structured interview as a method of data collection, and also follows a systematic data-analysis procedure. This is a popular qualitative approach for undergraduate psychology students.

Protocol analysis

Protocol analysis is a rigorous methodology for eliciting verbal reports of thought sequences as a valid source of data on thinking (Ericsson, 2002). The assumption is that it is possible to instruct participants to verbalise their thoughts in a manner that doesn't alter the sequence of thoughts mediating the completion of a task, and can therefore be accepted as valid data on thinking. Once transcriptions have been developed, they are prepared and then segmented and coded.

18.8   Evaluating Qualitative Data Analysis

Similar to quantitative, Morrow (2005) proposes trustworthiness as a core criterion for quality and rigour in qualitative research. Another caution is made regarding the interpretation of qualitative data. Qualitative methods acknowledge the researcher as a pivotal part of the relational, collaborative process of inquiry (Stacey, 1991). Remember that the integrity of data is very important to the advancement of the knowledge base for psychology as a science.

Reliability

In quantitative research, reliability refers to consistency or dependability. Qualitative researchers resist the quantitative approach, and believe that such standardised measures ignore the benefits of having a variety of researchers with many approaches. Qualitative researchers consider a range of data sources and employ numerous measurement methods. Each researcher will produce different results, as data collection is an interactive process in which the researcher operates in an evolving setting, which dictates the mix of measures that are appropriate. Miles and Huberman (1994) noted that qualitative methods of data analysis need to be systematic, disciplined and transparent. Therefore, to ensure the reliability of your qualitative data analysis or meaning making, you should present your analysis and how you came to generate your interpretation in a very systematic and transparent fashion. This transparent and systematic approach enables the reader to determine whether your interpretation is reliable.

Validity

Qualitative research is based on subjective, interpretative and contextual data, whereas quantitative research attempts to control or exclude such elements as they are viewed as confounding and extraneous factors. Due to this conflict between the two approaches it is not really appropriate to use the same concept of validity for both. Therefore, to solve the dilemma of the measurement of validity, qualitative researchers have developed measurement concepts in line with the qualitative paradigm (Maxwell, 1992; Smith, 1996).

Maxwell (1992) developed four categories to judge the validity of qualitative research: descriptive validity, interpretative validity, theoretical validity and generalisability. Auerbach and Silverstein (2003) also developed an important category known as transparency.

1. Descriptive validity

Descriptive validity refers to the accuracy of the data (Maxwell, 1992). Here validity refers to how truthful the link between a construct and the data is. Qualitative researchers are more concerned with authenticity than validity. Authenticity refers to giving an honest, unbiased account of social life from the frame of reference of someone who experiences it every day. It is less concerned with linking abstract concepts to empirical data, and more concerned with giving a true portrayal of social life. The focus is therefore on capturing an inside view and providing a detailed account of how those being studied feel about and understand events.

The descriptive validity of your project may come into question if you have omitted data. A verbatim interview transcript would be descriptively invalid if

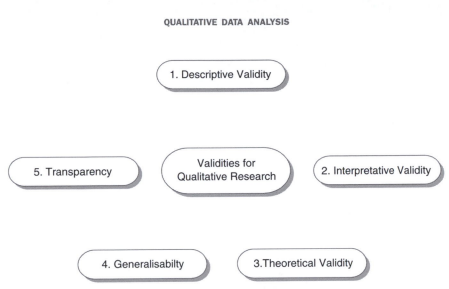

Figure 18.1   Different types of validity for qualitative research

you omitted features of the participants' speech, such as stress and pitch, that are essential to the understanding of the interview (Maxwell, 1992, p. 47). This is the most important type of validity for your qualitative project; without an accurate account of the formative data, all else is irrelevant (Glaser & Strauss, 1967).

2. Interpretative validity

A key question in assessing a piece of qualitative research is how did the researcher get to these conclusions from these data (Punch, 2005). Interpretative validity refers to how well you report your participants' meaning of events, objects and behaviours (Maxwell, 1992). What is paramount here is that you in fact report interpretations based on the participants' frame of reference as opposed to your own. You must emphasise the participants' view to others. It is very important to be truthful, and to try to establish a close link between your understanding and their actual frame of reference.

Smith's (1996) 'internal coherence' refers to whether the argument presented within your study is internally consistent and supported by your data. It is important that your interpretations are grounded in the data, but that they are also logical and make sense.

3. Theoretical validity

Theoretical validity 'goes beyond concrete description and interpretation and explicitly addresses the theoretical constructions that the researcher brings to, or develops during the study' (Maxwell, 1992, p. 50). In order to establish theoretical validity, you must ensure that there is coherence among your constructs, and that they fit together to form an accurate explanation of the phenomena under investigation. In a nutshell, your theory must fit your data.

4. Generalisability

Generalisability refers to the ability to apply the data, in this case the theory resulting from the study universally (Maxwell, 1992). In qualitative research, generalisability is not straightforward. As already mentioned, qualitative research is concerned with the concepts and perspectives of a select group; therefore the findings may only be applicable to this and similar groups.

Theory derived from grounded theory provides two levels of theory: abstract and situation specific (Auerbach & Silverman, 2003). Maxwell (1992) defined the abstract level as external generalisability, and the situation specific as internal generalisability. Situation-specific theory emerges from the repetitive themes and trends, and may be transferable to similar situations. At the abstract level, the theory is more holistic and general in nature. At this abstract level, it is possible to assess the generalisability of your theory.

5. Transparency

The issue of transparency is related to the reliability of your interpretations. Transparency measures how well you inform the reader of how you arrived at your interpretations (Auerbach & Silverstein, 2003). It is important that you provide enough information for the reader to understand the process that was involved in your interpretation, the method of sample selection, your research design, your interview protocol and your coding procedures. It is also useful to include your own epistemological viewpoints; for example, if you follow a feminist paradigm, you should include such information. Smith (1996) advises that you present sufficient evidence to enable the reader to assess your interpretation.

Many of these researchers have concluded that systematic, rigorous and auditable analytical processes are among the most significant factors distinguishing good from poor quality research (Thorne, 1997). Researchers are therefore encouraged to articulate their findings in such a manner that the logical processes by which they were developed are accessible to a critical reader, the relation between the actual data and the conclusions about data is explicit, and the claims made in relation to the data set are rendered credible and believable.

Summary

Conceptualisation in qualitative research is how the researcher organises and makes sense of data. Operationalisation in a qualitative research project is a detailed description of how you collected and thought about the specific data that becomes the basis for your concepts. Therefore, it involves a post hoc description as opposed to an a priori planned procedure. Qualitative researchers resist the quantitative approach to reliability, and instead consider a range of data sources and employ numerous measurement methods to ensure that the data is consistent.

Further Reading

Charmaz, K. (2000) Grounded theory; Objectivist and constructivist methods. In N. K. Denzin and Y. S. Lincoln (eds) *Handbook of Qualitative Research* (2nd edn). Thousand Oaks, CA: Sage Publications Ltd. pp. 509–35.

Coffey, A. and Atkinson, P. (1996) *Making Sense of Qualitative Data: Complementary Research Strategies*. Thousand Oaks, CA: Sage Publications Ltd.

Ericsson, K. A. (2002) Toward a procedure for eliciting verbal expression of nonverbal experience without reactivity: Interpreting the verbal overshadowing effect within the theoretical framework for protocol analysis. *Applied Cognitive Psychology*, 16, 981–7.

Have, P. Ten. (1999) *Doing Conversation Analysis: A Practical Guide*. London: Sage Publications Ltd.

Holloway, I. (1997) *Basic Concepts for Qualitative Research*. Oxford: Blackwell Science.

Miles, M. B. and Huberman, A.M. (1994) *Qualitative Data Analysis*. (2nd edn). Thousand Oaks, CA: Sage Publications Ltd.

Punch, K. P. (2005) *Introduction to Social Research: Quantitative and Qualitative Approaches*. (2nd edn). London: Sage Publications Ltd.

Smith, J. A. (2003) *Qualitative Psychology: A Practical Guide to Research Methods*. London: Sage Publications Ltd.

Strauss, A. and Corbin, J. (1998) *Basics of Qualitative Research*. Thousand Oaks, CA: Sage Publications Ltd.

19

THE SEMI-STRUCTURED INTERVIEW AS PART OF GROUNDED THEORY

Objectives

On reading this chapter you should:

- understand how to design and conduct a qualitative interview as a means of data collection;
- be able to transcribe your data for qualitative analysis; and
- understand the importance of reflexivity.

Overview

Section 19.1 introduces and details the qualitative interview as a method of data collection. The iterative relationship between the interview as a data-collection technique and grounded theory as a data-analysis technique is highlighted. Section 19.2 focuses on designing a qualitative interview-based study, and looks at important design issues, such as recruiting participants, appropriate sample size and theoretical sampling. The issues involved in constructing your interview guide are also dealt with, for example the importance of how questions are asked and how long each interview should be. Section 19.3 progresses to conducting the interview study. The need for a pilot study is exemplified, and practical and technical issues are dealt with. Section 19.4 outlines the process of transcribing your data, in order to prepare the data for the coding procedures involved in grounded theory. Finally Section 19.5 deals with reflexivity.

19.1 The Interview as a Method of Data Collection

The interview is one of the most popular methods of gathering data in qualitative research. There are numerous types of interview which can be considered qualitative. As is the case in psychology and the social sciences, terminology or too much of it becomes a problem for the undergraduate novice researcher. For example, qualitative interview techniques are often referred to as: semi-structured, unstructured, exploratory and in-depth interviews. In support of King's (2004) suggestion, the text will use the term qualitative research interview. Thus, qualitative research interviews are defined as an interview process, whose purpose is to gather descriptions of the life-world of the interviewee with respect to interpretation of the meaning of the described phenomena (Kvale, 1983, p. 174),

The goal of qualitative research interviewing is to see the research topic from the interviewees' perspective, and also to understand how and why they have come to have this perspective. In order to meet this goal, it is important that you do not impose too much structure, and that you include plenty of open-ended, clear questions. The key feature of the qualitative research interview is the nature of the relationship between you (the interviewer) and your participants. Unlike quantitative research, the relationship is seen as part of the research process itself.

19.2   Designing an Interview-Based Study

Recruiting participants

In qualitative research, you usually interview as many participants as necessary to find out what you want to know. This is not as simple as in quantitative methods, where we can run a power analysis to determine the appropriate number. Often you will be unable to determine your exact sample size until you are conducting your grounded theory analysis.

The range of participants in your sample will depend on your project's aims. Qualitative research always places a premium on diversity, in an attempt to illustrate the range of ways that a phenomenon is experienced. Sometimes you can determine the range of participants in advance. However, on other occasions, you may be unable to place such structure on participant characteristics. You may recruit participants to your study as features of potential interest are identified through the interview process; this is known as theoretical sampling and will be dealt with in detail in Chapter 20. At this point it is useful to be aware that your appropriate sample size will be determined by theoretical saturation. This means that you continue expanding the sample size until the interviews reveal no new data.

There is an inverse relationship between the amount of usable data gathered from each interview and the number of participants. Therefore, as the number of participants is increased, the amount of usable data that is generated decreases for each participant. What this also means is that the greater the amount of usable data you are able to gather from a single participant, the fewer participants you will require (Morse, 2000). This is an important point for the undergraduate psychology researcher and highlights the importance of thoroughly dissecting your data, and of course the importance of a thorough, well-designed interview guide.

Constructing your interview guide

The qualitative research interview is not based on a formal schedule of questions to be asked. It is therefore useful to develop an interview guide, which lists topics which you should attempt to cover in the course of your interviews. The guide could also involve some probes that could be asked to follow up responses and to elicit greater detail from participants. Glaser (1998) cautions against preconceived interview guides, and more fundamentally against forcing preconceived ideas and theories directly onto your data. However, the undergraduate psychology student does not have the scope for this approach, these it is beneficial to use an interview guide.

During your initial review of the literature, and the development of your research questions, you will have developed topics for your interview guide. This, however, is not the only source of topics; you could also ask subject matter experts for advice, and you could also rely on your own personal experience. Due to the flexible approach that qualitative methods take, it is important to remember that the development of your interview guide does not end at the start of your first interview. The guide can be modified throughout your interviews, adding topics that have emerged, and dropping and reformulating topics which are causing ambiguity or that consistently fail to elicit responses in any way relevant to your research topic.

Kici and Westhoff (2004) note that the interview guide should always consist of three sections: the opening, the main body of the interview and the closing. It has been recognised that the opening section of your interview is of paramount importance (Campion, 1998). There are a number of ways that you can build a comfortable climate for your interview, as seen in Table 19.1.

It is also advisable to start each interview with some easy questions, in order to ease the participants into the process. Remember that at undergraduate level, you should not ask any questions that will cause your participants any distress or embarrassment. It is possible to ask some sensitive questions, which should be left until the end of the interview; however, it is crucial that any sensitive questions have been passed by your supervisor, and the ethical review board at your college or university.

How questions are asked

The way in which questions are phrased during the interview influences the responses of your participants. Donaghy (1990) emphasises that the way in

Table 19.1   Ways to build a comfortable climate (Donaghy, 1990; Downs, 1980)

1.   Welcome the participant
2.   Introduce yourself
3.   Spend a few minutes on small talk about some current issue or about the weather
4.   Offer refreshments
5.   Use a warm and friendly tone of voice
6.   Sit beside the participant in comfortable chairs
7.   Give the participant a full orientation to the aims of your study
8.   Give an outline of the interview

which a question is asked is just as important as what is asked. Campion et al. (1998) found a correlation between formulation of interview questions and the reliability and validity of the interview data. It becomes abundantly clear that clarity of communication and of the formulation of your questions is of pivotal importance to the success of the interview process for gathering good, reliable and valid information. Cannell and Kahn (1968) flagged that formulating questions is one of the researcher's biggest problems. It is advisable that, as an undergraduate student who is relatively new to the interview process, you ask your supervisor to take a look at your questions, and to advise you during the construction of your interview guide.

Clarity can be achieved by formulating questions that are simple, clear and precise. Again we see the importance of parsimony within the research process, and the important roles played by precise and concise communication. King (1994) advises that you should avoid multiple questions. When a participant thinks about several aspects simultaneously, there is always a risk that they will give a partial answer or possibly become confused about the relevant question. It is more advisable to ask simple questions, which do not cause the participant any confusion regarding what you mean.

It is also of paramount importance that you do not ask any leading questions, as this will also affect the construct validity of your data by giving your participants a cue to the expected answer. Another important consideration is how you begin your questions. Seidman (1998) advises that you should start your questions with 'how' or 'please describe', because questions starting with 'why' warrant causal attributions. At the conclusion of each interview it is a good idea to end the interview on a good note. Remember your ethics.

How long should each interview be?

For an undergraduate project, interviews lasting between 40 and 60 minutes are usually deemed long enough. It is appropriate to consider the number of factors that you are interested in and to make sure that your interviews deal with them adequately. Therefore our universal rule applies, in that the aim of the research question will generally dictate the length of your interviews. As will become apparent in Chapter 20, there is no set number of interviews for when theoretical saturation will occur; the undergraduate psychology student is not expected to continue collecting and analysing data for a long period of time. It is acceptable to interview a minimum of five participants using the principal of theoretical sampling, for between 40 and 60 minutes each, resulting in approximately five hours of transcription.

19.3   Conducting the Interview

Pilot work and practical issues

As with quantitative research, it is vital that you carry out a pilot study when carrying out an interview-based study. Running a pilot study is a very important aspect of conducting your project. It allows you to spot flaws in your methodology before you actually conduct the study. The pilot study allows you to see whether the instructions and questions are understood by participants, and then adapt the study. It is very common that the pilot study will reveal the need to make adjustments to either the instructions, questions or recording devices. When changes have been made, do another pilot test to make sure that all is now running smoothly. Although conducting a pilot study may appear time-consuming, this form of quality control saves you time in the long run – it improves the rigour of your project and ultimately the validity of the conclusions that you derive from your findings and interpretation.

How you will record your interviews is another important consideration. There are a number of ways that you can do this. For example, you can record by audio-tape, video-tape, and by taking notes yourself. Using an audio-tape recorder is the most common method of recording, and is best suited to the undergraduate psychology student. Using a tape recorder allows you to concentrate on the purpose and the dynamics of the interview. The words, the tone and pauses are recorded in a permanent form that can be returned to again and again. Although a video recorder catches the visual aspects of the interview, the analysis of such data is too time-consuming for undergraduate psychology students. This is a medium of recording that you could possibly use as a post-graduate student. Many of the current computer packages for qualitative data support both audio and visual data.

Technical issues

It is very important that your tape recorder is in good working order. It is advised that you run maintenance checks before each interview to ensure that all is working. There is nothing worse than carrying out a great interview only to realise afterwards that nothing was recorded due to technical faults or human error.

It is also imperative that you record the interview conversations at an audible level, that is, clear and easy to hear. Again this issue can be ironed out during the pilot study. It is also important to conduct the interviews in a setting that is free from background noise. You should also make sure that the microphone is close enough to both the participant and yourself.

19.4   Transcribing

Transcribing one's own data is recommended as it can aid familiarity with material and hence benefit your findings and interpretation. However, this process can be time-consuming. Depending on the purpose of the research, not all interview data need be fully transcribed. You may be recommended to omit repetitive sections of dialogue or concentrate on transcribing attributional statements. Some supervisors may prefer the transcription and analysis of all interview material while limiting the number of interviews conducted. It is required that you state how transcription was managed within the methods section of your report. Regardless of the aims of your research, transcription involves listening to your tape-recorded interviews and translating spoken language into written language or text.

It is also important to ensure reliability and validity during the transcription process. Remember that your interviews will not be analysed directly from the tape recordings, the taped interviews are transcribed and then analysed. Every transcription from one context to another, in this case from oral to written, involves a series of judgements and decisions. It is therefore advisable that you run reliability checks on your transcripts. For example, you could ask a fellow student to transcribe a section of two or three of your transcripts, or to transcribe an entire transcript, and check whether there is a close match between your transcriptions and theirs.

Ascertaining validity of interview transcripts is more complicated than reliability. Kvale (1996) notes that the most straightforward approach is to determine what is the most useful transcription for your specific research purposes, as opposed to the question of what is the correct transcription. Therefore, the aims of the research question should dictate the appropriate type of transcription. For example, if you are interested in language and plan to carry out a discourse or conversation analysis, the inclusion of pauses, repetitions and the tone of voice are important aspects to be recorded.

19.5   A Note on Reflexivity

In order to take a reflexive stance, you should attend to your own experience during interviews, referred to as the pre-linguistic impact (Reissman, 1993). As noted in Chapter 18, there are a number of useful strategies that can be used by the undergraduate psychology researcher to become accustomed to the process of reflection: write your own presuppositions down at the beginning of your study and consult this list at each stage of the research process; keep a research diary in which you record your own feelings about the process; and finally listen to some of your taped interviews with a focus on your performance as an interviewer.

Tip for quality control

In order to check your interpretations of your data, why not get a fellow student to read a section of one of your transcriptions, and ask him or her to interpret the piece. Then cross-check this with your own interpretation to see if you interpreted it along the same lines.

Summary

The interview is one of the most popular methods of gathering data in qualitative research. The goal of the qualitative research interview is to see the research topic from the participants' perspective, and to understand how and why they came to have this perspective. Recognising the iterative relationship between data collection and data analysis is very important at the design stage. Theoretical sampling can help determine the appropriate sample size, along with the objectives of your project. Because the qualitative research interview is not based on a formal schedule of questions to be asked, it is crucial that you develop a comprehensive interview guide that lists topics which you should cover in the course of your interviews. Clarity of communication and the formulation of your questions is of pivotal importance to the success of the interview process for gathering good, reliable and valid information. It is vital that you carry out a pilot study. It is also important that you keep your recording equipment in good working order.

Transcribing one's own data is recommended as it can aid familiarity with your data – you are immersed in it – which clearly benefits your analysis and interpretation. Reliability and validity are also important considerations during the transcription process. Reflexivity refers to the recognition that the involvement of the researcher, as an active participant in the research process, shapes the nature of the process and the knowledge produced through it. Reflecting on your own involvement is just as important as reflecting on the involvement of your participants.

Further Reading

Kvale, S. (1996) *Interviews: An Introduction to Qualitative Research Interviewing.* London; Thousand Oaks, California: Sage Publications Ltd.

20

DESIGNING, CONDUCTING AND ANALYSING A GROUNDED THEORY PROJECT

Objectives

On reading this chapter you should:

- understand what is involved in carrying out a grounded theory analysis, from what makes up the basic elements, to the coding processes involved;
- understand the importance of the integrity of your data;
- understand how to carry out open, axial and selective coding on your data;
- be able to create memos to facilitate coding and reflexivity; and
- understand the importance of the issue of reflexivity.

Overview

Grounded theory is a process by which a researcher generates theory that is grounded in the data (Glaser & Strauss, 1967; Strauss & Corbin, 1998). The data for this approach can be collected through interviews, observations, personal journals, narratives or videos, etc. Chapter 19, therefore, dealt with the qualitative interview as a method of collecting data and designing a study for analysis using grounded theory. The data collected is then analysed by a coding procedure to illuminate patterns, themes or 'concepts that are the building blocks of the theory' (Strauss & Corbin, 1998, p.13). This procedure allows for the systematic analysis of the data and follows a given repeatable procedure. Consequently, grounded theory was the example of choice, because the rigour of the approach offers the qualitative student 'a set of clear guidelines from which to build explanatory frameworks that specify relationships among concepts' (Charmaz, 2000, p. 510).

Section 20.1 deals with the qualitative method and data analysis technique of grounded theory. Grounded theory is described as the appropriate qualitative analysis to apply to your data if you are interested in developing a theory that accounts for your data. Grounded theory is made up of three basic elements:

concepts, categories and propositions. Section 20.2 deals with the demanding simultaneous process of sampling, data collection and data analysis. The simultaneous coding process involved in grounded theory is outlined in Section 20.3, consisting of open, axial and selective coding, the aim of which is to develop meaning from the narratives of your participants. This meaning usually consists of a new theory that is generated from the data.

The data collection method that is most commonly used is interviewing, where the data has been transcribed into a narrative format as discussed in the previous chapter. Grounded theory investigates the emergence of categories during the careful and repeated reading of the transcripts. The goal is therefore to make explicit what is implicit in the text (Foster & Parker, 1999).

Section 20.4 deals with memo writing which usually begins at the same time as coding. Finally Section 20.5 focuses on reflexivity and presents some useful strategies for reflection. The design of the qualitative analysis computer program NVivo was strongly influenced by grounded theory. It is beyond the scope of this text to go through the workings of NVivo, so if you do not have a working knowledge of this program, Gibbs (2002) and Bazeley and Richards (2003) give useful descriptions of how to use NVivo for grounded theory.

20.1 Grounded Theory

Grounded theory is made up of three basic elements: concepts, categories and propositions. Concepts are the basic units of analysis, because it is from the conceptualisation of the data, not the data per se, that theory develops from. Corbin and Strauss (1990) explain that:

> theories cannot be built with actual incidents or activities as observed or reported; that is, from 'raw data'. The incidents, events, happenings are taken as, or analysed as, potential indicators of phenomenon which are thereby given conceptual labels. (p. 7)

The second element categories:

> are higher in level and more abstract than the concepts they represent...Categories are the 'cornerstones' of developing theory. They provide the means by which the theory can be integrated. (Corbin & Strauss, 1990, p. 7)

The third element of grounded theory are propositions. Propositions indicate the generalised relationships between categories and concepts. This third element was originally termed 'hypotheses' by Glaser and Strauss (1967); however, as the approach developed, researchers such as Whetten (1989) pointed out that 'propositions' was a more appropriate description. The reasoning behind this was that propositions involve conceptual relationships whereas hypotheses require measured relationships.

20.2 Sampling, Data Collection and Data Analysis: a Simultaneous Process

Guided by your research question, you will collect your first set of data, for example a transcript from your first interview. You analyse your first transcription before you carry out your second interview. Therefore your second interview will be guided by your first analysis. You recruit participants to your study as features of potential interest are identified through the interview process – each interview you conduct provides a slice of data on which you can build, as seen in Figure 20.1. This cumulative process is known as theoretical sampling.

It is important to note that the process of theoretical sampling depicted in Figure 20.1 gives a simplified account of events. The process does not have to follow the strictly linear path demonstrated; it is sometimes useful to go backwards to reassess your interpretation of something in your first analysis following from new insights gained from later analysis and data collection. Therefore through simultaneous involvement in data collection and analysis, you avoid becoming overwhelmed by volumes of general unfocused data that do not lead to anything new. The example below demonstrates the sampling technique known as snowballing dealt with in Chapter 9, which can be used in conjunction with theoretical sampling.

Example 20.1   From Timlin-Scalera et al. (2003)

The technique of 'snowballing' (Taylo & Bogdan, 1984) was used to obtain additional participants based on referrals or introductions from current participants. Snowballing was incorporated when it became clear that certain types of males, namely athletic and popular, had different perceptions of problems than less popular, less affluent, non-athletic males. Interviewees specifically from these two types of groups were sought to find out whether this theme would continue to emerge. Other themes that began to emerge from the interviews involved issues among gay males and males with learning disabilities. Again, an attempt was made to obtain additional interviewees with these characteristics.

During the coding procedure which is discussed in detail later in the chapter, your appropriate sample size will be determined by theoretical saturation (Glaser & Strauss, 1967; Strauss and Corbin, 1998). Theoretical saturation occurs: when no new or relevant data seem to emerge regarding a

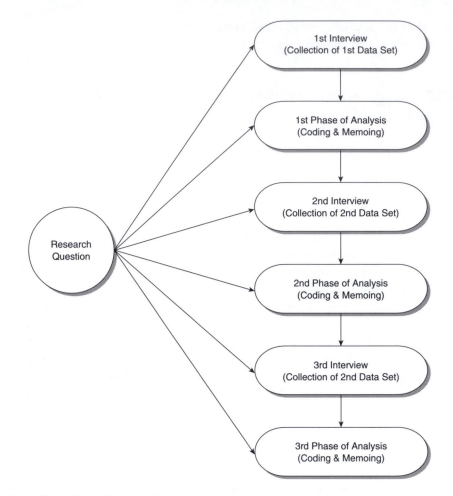

Figure 20.1   Theoretical sampling

category; when the category is well developed in terms of its properties and dimensions, demonstrating variation; and when the relationships among categories are well established and validated (Strauss and Corbin, 1998, p. 212), as illustrated in Example 20.2 below.

Example 20.2   From Timlin-Scalera et al. (2003)

The number of participants was based on when enough data had been gathered to reach a sufficient saturation point. That is, interviewing ceased when no new or relevant data were emerging, the category development was dense, and the relationships between the categories had been well established and validated (Creswell, 1998; Strauss & Corbin, 1990).

Although there is no set number of interviews for when theoretical saturation will occur, the undergraduate psychology student is not expected to continue collecting and analysing data for a long period of time, as this is clearly beyond the scope of the research project. Therefore, it is acceptable for the undergraduate student to interview a minimum of five participants, resulting in approximately five hours of data.

The quality of data can affect the sample size, which is why theoretical sampling is recommended when carrying out grounded theory. Theoretical sampling dictates that the researcher chooses participants who have experience of the specific phenomena under study. Therefore, you are in effect recruiting experts in the phenomena, which results in the best quality data (Glaser & Strauss, 1967). Theoretical sampling therefore acts as a quality-control mechanism.

20.3   Coding

Punch (2005) notes that what is essential in discovering a grounded theory is to find a core category, at a high level of abstraction, that is grounded in the data. Figure 20.2 illustrates the processes involved in grounded theory analysis. The first step involves developing concepts in the data, known as substantive codes. This is followed by finding relationships between the concepts, known as categories or theoretical codes, and finally conceptualising and accounting for these categories or relationships at a higher level of abstraction, known as core codes or propositions.

Although the three types of coding – open, axial and selective – are presented sequentially, it is important to note that they actually occur recursively according to the method of constant comparison. Constant comparison involves comparing each new piece of data to existing data, in order to develop conceptualisations of the possible relations between the various pieces of data, to generate coherent categories of meaning. The goal of this process is to create a theory grounded in the lived experiences of the participants, where the purpose of coding is to interpret and construct meaning out of the narrative data yielded from your participants.

Line-by-line open coding

Open coding is the first level of analysis, often referred to as initial coding, and involves selecting and naming categories from the analysis of your data. You begin by breaking open or fracturing your data, hence the term open coding. The idea here is that you open up the theoretical possibilities in the data (Punch, 2005). How you break your data down is a matter of dispute within the grounded theory research. Charmaz (2000) proposes line-by-line coding, as outlined by Glaser and Strauss (1967). However pieces of data can be as small as words or as large as a paragraph (Morrow & Smith, 2000), while

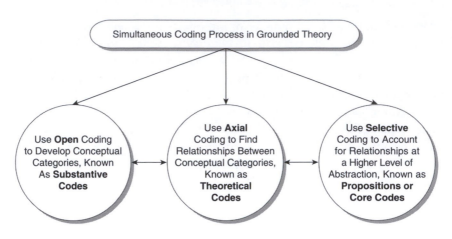

Figure 20.2   Simultaneous coding process in grounded theory

Rennie (1995) reports working with data pieces as large as a page or two of data. It is important to keep the aim of your research question in mind, when making decisions regarding the size of your pieces of data. For the undergraduate psychology student, line-by-line coding is advisable, as it is believed to focus the researcher to remain close to the text (Langdridge, 2004). As you analyse line-by-line, you look for conceptual categories implicit and explicit in that data, and the theoretical possibilities the data carry (Punch, 2005).

As already mentioned, open coding requires application of the comparative method as demonstrated in Example 20.3 below. This method gives you a feel for your data, directs you to the theoretical and conceptual issues lying behind the text, and gives you an insight into the deeper theoretical and conceptual levels that exist within them. In order to saturate the categories, data are initially broken down by asking simple questions such as what, where, how, when, how much, etc.

Example 20.3   From Timlin-Scalera et al. (2003)

The open-coding method began with close examination of the data by individual responses. During this phase of coding, each separate idea or incident in the data was considered and given a conceptual name. Each interviewee response was considered on its own at first to clarify the multitude of issues and topics that were discussed. Next, the data were broken down by identifying phenomena among all interviewee responses and grouped into categories. According to Strauss and Corbin (1990), line-by-line analysis is the most generative, and therefore a close approximation of this method was used in the present study. The categories were formed based on similarities of concepts found in the data. These categories were given conceptual labels or tentative names, and properties and dimensions of the categories were noted.

At first you compare data with data to find similarities and differences. Subsequently, you compare these coded units of meaning to other coded units of meaning, gradually you group your concepts into categories that encompass the units of meaning, as demonstrated in Example 20.3. To assist with this there are a number of techniques developed by Strauss and Corbin (1990) and Charmaz (2000) that are useful in helping you decide on what to code, as summarised in Figure 20.3.

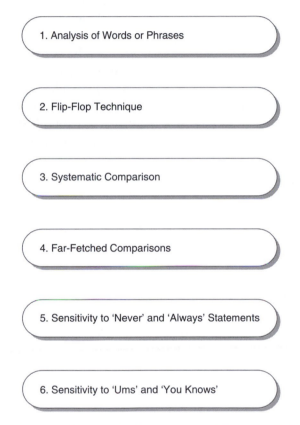

1. Analysis of Words or Phrases

2. Flip-Flop Technique

3. Systematic Comparison

4. Far-Fetched Comparisons

5. Sensitivity to 'Never' and 'Always' Statements

6. Sensitivity to 'Ums' and 'You Knows'

Figure 20.3   Techniques to initiate and facilitate open coding (Strauss & Corbin, 1967; Charmaz, 2000)

Analysis of words or phrases involves picking out a word or phrase that appears significant, and listing all possible meanings. You then consider which meanings apply by further examining your data/text. This strategy is very useful for facilitating generation of new meanings and ideas that you may have overlooked or that you may not have seen in the data. The **flip-flop technique**, involves comparing extremes on a given dimension. For example, if a participant mentions that age is related to ability to cope, see if you have an old and young participant in your study and investigate their responses. The third technique, **systematic comparison**, simply involves asking a series of questions to explore all the dimensions of two phenomena, relating to how do they differ, and how they are similar, as mentioned in the previous paragraph. Using **far-fetched comparisons**, consists of taking one element of the concept that you are examining and thinking of the most far-fetched or different example of some other phenomena that shares some characteristics with that concept. You then work through all the other elements of both phenomena to see if they shed any light on the original concept. Being **sensitive to statements of 'never' and 'always'** is also important. These types of statements are usually viewed as indicators to investigate the statements more closely – they often reveal hidden meanings in the data that may not be apparent on your initial reading of the transcript. Finally, being **sensitive to 'ums' and 'you knows'** can also be very useful for your meaning making. By exploring what they really indicate can shed light on meaning that you may have initially missed. As Charmaz (2000) describes, the participant may be struggling to articulate an experience, or the meaning may be simply related to culturally shared meanings that are taken for granted.

Axial coding

Axial coding is the next stage in the process after open coding. Whereas open coding fractures the data into concepts and categories, axial coding puts those data back together in new ways by making connections between a category and its sub-categories as demonstrated in example 20.4.

This is achieved by utilising a coding paradigm, i.e. a system of coding that seeks to identify causal relationships between categories. The aim of the coding paradigm is to make explicit connections between categories and sub-categories. This process is often referred to as the paradigm model and involves explaining and understanding relationships between categories in order to understand the event or experience to which they relate. Strauss and Corbin (1990) suggest a model in which you can identify six types of category or node (in NVivo). The goal behind this model is that each element has a causal influence on the next element, and that these causal conditions produced the event, and that the event caused the strategies in their contexts. These are also mediated by intervening conditions and produce actions and interactions that result in consequences, as shown in Table 20.1.

If you are using NVivo to organise your axial coding ideas, you can either use the node tree to set up a root node for each of your model elements and group all the instances as child nodes, or you can set up a subtree for each phenomenon and then just include the relevant model elements as its children. Gibbs (2002) and Bazeley and Richards (2003) give useful descriptions of how to use NVivo for grounded theory.

Table 20.1   Strauss and Corbin (1990) model

Model Element	Question
Causal conditions	What influences the central event?
Phenomenon/event	What is the central idea which a set of actions or interactions is directed at managing, or to which a set of actions is related?
Strategies	Is the event addressed purposeful or goal-oriented?
Context	Where or when do these events occur?
Intervening conditions	What conditions are shaping, constraining or facilitating the strategies that take place within their specified conditions?
Action/interaction	What strategies manage, handle and carry out an event under a set of perceived conditions?
Consequences	What outcomes, results of action or interaction results from the strategies?

Example 20.4   From Timlin-Scalera et al. (2003, p. 342)

After 'fracturing' the data during the open-coding phase, the researcher attempts to put it back together through axial coding (Strauss & Corbin, 1990). While continually consulting the notes and records of phenomena, as well as tentative categories and themes that were kept thus far, the transcripts were then reviewed multiple times during the axial-coding phase. At this point in the analysis, the data were arranged in yet new ways based on similarities or connections between the categories and their subcategories that were developed during open coding. Strauss and Corbin (1990), as well as Creswell (1998), presented a paradigm model in which the subcategories and categories are linked as a central phenomenon during axial coding by relationships, indicating causal relationships, context, intervening conditions and consequences for the phenomenon.

Selective coding

As you carried out your axial coding, a small number of phenomenon or themes will have begun to emerge as being of pivotal importance to your study, in that they are linked to many other elements of your model. Selective coding involves the process of selecting and identifying the core category and systematically relating it to other categories. It involves validating those relationships, filling in, and refining and developing those categories, which are then integrated together and a grounded theory is arrived at as seen in example 20.5.

Identifying your core category can be seen as a series of stages, the first involving the explication of the story line. At this point, you develop a story that brings together the majority of your elements. It is advisable that at undergraduate level you only choose one core category for your storyline. Remember that the storyline is your main argument, and ideally you should just have one. The next stage involves validation, using the paradigm model mentioned above, to generate hypothetical relationships between categories and using data from the field to test these hypotheses. Based on the outcomes of the previous stages, you refine your story line further. This completes the grounding of the theory, through theory construction and verification.

Example 20.5   From Timlin-Scalera et al. (2003, p. 342)

In the next phase of analysis, the researchers identified and presented a story line, which became the core category that integrated the categories previously identified (Creswell, 1998). This phase required that the researchers use all the materials they had been working on, including personal memos, notes, formal analysis, debriefing notes, and the interviewer's own thoughts that had been forming while conducting the study. Strauss and Corbin (1990) suggested that the following steps be used to aid in this process: formulating and identifying a story line, relating subsidiary categories around the core category, relating categories at the dimensional level by asking questions and making comparisons, validating those relationships against the data to complete its grounding, and filling in categories that may need further development.

In the final process of grounding the theory, a story line began to emerge from the data during the selective coding, and the researchers' task was to explicate the story line by connecting the categories in terms of their relationships to one another. While explaining the story line, the researchers linked actions and phenomena into interactional sequences to bring 'process' into the analysis (Strauss & Corbin, 1990). The authors described process as a way of giving 'life to the data' and connecting the data further with consequences and interactions among the phenomena.

20.4   Memo Writing

In grounded theory, memoing usually commences at the beginning of analysis together with coding. During the coding process, you will have numerous ideas which you will want to record. Memos are used to record these ideas, but also constitute the very process of analytical thinking itself (Gibbs, 2002). Therefore memos reflect your thinking and theorising as you proceed through the grounded theory coding process, and also reflect the general development of your analytical framework, as seen in Example 20.6.

> ## Example 20.6   From Timlin-Scalera et al. (2003)
>
> Throughout the data collection process, two different types of memos were kept. One set of memos took the form of a personal journal that included such information as reactions to interviews, specific notes on events that might have influenced the interviewer's mood or affect during certain interviews, and feelings about the process in general. The other set of memos were more objective comments and summaries that were written immediately after each interview. The personal journal served as a helpful way to process and reflect on reactions and outside factors that might have influenced the interview proceedings in any way. The practice of keeping reflective memos during the interview process has been highly recommended (Glaser & Strauss, 1967; Strauss & Corbin, 1990).

20.5   Reflexivity

As already noted in Chapter 18, there are a number of useful strategies that can be used by the undergraduate psychology researcher to become accustomed to the process of reflection:

1. It is useful to write your own presuppositions down at the beginning of your study, and consult this list at each stage of the research process.
2. Keep a research diary in which you record your own feelings about the process as seen in Example 20.6 above.
3. Listen to some of your taped interviews with a focus on your performance as an interviewer.

It is crucial that you realise that these techniques are only a means to an end of developing a habit of awareness and critical thinking regarding your involvement with your research and your participants. You should keep in mind that these techniques to improve your reflexive ability should never become mechanistic justification for the quality of your work, and at the other end of the spectrum, they should never become a licence for self-indulgence – remember your ethics.

Summary

Grounded theory is the appropriate qualitative analysis to apply to your data if you are interested in developing a theory that accounts for your data. The three types of coding – open, axial and selective – occur recursively according to the method of constant comparison. The first step involves developing concepts in the data, known as substantive codes. This is followed by finding relationships between the concepts, known as theoretical codes, and finally conceptualising and accounting for these categories or relationships at a higher level of abstraction, known as core codes or propositions. Memoing usually beings at the beginning of analysis, together with coding. It is important to keep track of your reflections and personal reactions during grounded theory.

Further Reading

Bazeley, P. and Richards, L. (2003) *The NVivo® Qualitative Project Book*. London: Sage Publications.

Charmaz, K. (2000) Grounded theory: Objectivist and constructivist methods. In N. K. Denzin and Y. S. Lincoln (eds) *Handbook of Qualitative Research* (2nd edn). Thousand Oaks, CA: Sage Publications Ltd. pp. 509–35.

Gibbs, G. R. (2002) *Qualitative Data Analysis: Explorations with NVivo*. Buckingham: Open University Press.

Holloway, I. (1997) *Basic Concepts for Qualitative Research*. Oxford: Blackwell Science.

Strauss, A. and Corbin, J. (1990) *Basics of Qualitative Research, Grounded Theory Procedures and Techniques*. London: Sage Publications Ltd.

Strauss, A. and Corbin, J. (1998) *Basics of Qualitative Research*. Thousand Oaks, CA: Sage Publications Ltd.

Examples taken from:

Timlin-Scalera, R. M., Ponterotto, J. G., Blumberg, F. C. and Jackson, M. A. (2003) A grounded theory study of help-seeking behaviors among white male high school Students. *Journal of Counseling Psychology*, 50(3), 339–50.

Ward, E. (2005) Keeping it real: A grounded theory study of African American clients engaging in counselling at a community mental health agency. *Journal of Counseling Psychology*, 52(4), 471–81.

21

WRITING UP YOUR QUALITATIVE METHODOLOGY

Objectives

On reading this chapter you should:

- understand the importance of concise and precise detail for writing up your qualitative methodology;
- be aware of the various subsections that make up the method section; and
- be able to write up your methodology subsections with enough detail for transparency of your work.

Overview

Section 21.1 deals with writing up your methodology section of your project. The division of the method into the six possible subsections (theoretical background, setting, participants, measures and apparatus, procedure, and analytical strategy) is dealt with in the following sections using some examples from the literature. Section 21.2 describes the theoretical background for your study subsection and deals with the philosophical correlates of your research paradigm (e.g. grounded theory). Section 21.3 deals with the second subsection of your methodology, the setting. Section 21.4 describes the importance of a comprehensive participants subsection, while Section 21.5 details the materials subsection and describes the information that should be reported for measures and for any apparatus used in your study. Section 21.6 deals with the last subsection, the procedure, and Section 21.7 deals with the analytical strategy used for your qualitative data analysis. Finally Section 21.8 presents a checklist for writing up your qualitative methodology.

21.1 Writing up the Methodology

It is advisable that you write up your methodology section of your project while you are carrying it out. However, due to time constraints this is not always possible for students to do. If you kept a diary or notes during the planning, designing and carrying out of your project, you will be able to refer to those when writing up this section. It is not a good idea to try and write this section from your memory.

The method, in the form of its various subsections, gives a detailed account of the practical aspects of conducting your project. It is also imperative for you to realise that a detailed and precise methodology allows your reader and marker to make an informed decision as to whether you used an appropriate design to answer your research question, and whether the methodology you employed was appropriate. Like quantitative research, it is customary to divide your methodology into subsections; however, there is no universal agreement as to what these subsections are. For example, Silverman (2003) and Langdridge (2004) propose a popular approach, which divides the methodology chapter into three main subsections: the participants, the theoretical background and the analytical strategy.

On analysing the content of qualitative journal articles, a number of patterns emerged in how authors were organising their methodology, as seen in Figure 21.1. It is important to note that not all qualitative projects will utilise all of these subsections; the key is to use the subsections that pertain to your type of study. It is also advisable to refer to your university's guidelines for presenting qualitative projects, as these may vary from university to university, again illustrating the diversity of the qualitative method of inquiry.

21.2 Theoretical Background

It is important that you describe the philosophical correlates of your research paradigm (e.g. grounded theory), cite authors who have defined your research paradigm, and explain the assumptions of your research paradigm. Ideally you should also describe what you intend to accomplish through this research (e.g. expanding a knowledge base, developing a grounded theory). Example 21.1 illustrates how a published article presented the theoretical rationale.

Example 21.1   From Timlin-Scalera et al. (2003)

Given the lack of research examining the help-seeking behaviors of this particular population, as well as the need for fuller, more descriptive and comprehensive data in this area, and the sensitive nature of the topic, a qualitative design was incorporated in the present study. Grounded theory (Glaser & Strauss, 1967) represents one of the more validated and tested methods (Ponterrotto, 2002) and is being used increasingly by counseling researchers (e.g., Pope-Davis et al., 2002; Richie et al., 1997). Lincoln and McGorry

---

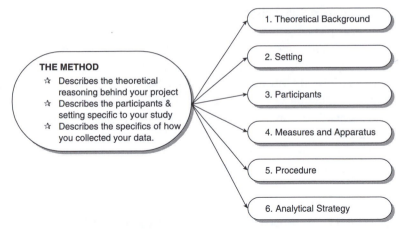

Figure 21.1   Six common subsections of the qualitative methodology section

---

(Continued)

(1995) noted that a first step in developing a help-seeking model is to speak directly to those seeking and providing help. Therefore, the primary data for this study came from semi-structured interviews with male students. Furthermore, to provide triangulation of informant sources (see Creswell, 1998), a small sample of parents, female students, and staff were also interviewed.

21.3   Setting Subsection

In qualitative research it is very important to include information regarding the setting, in order for the reader to understand what types of generalisations can be made from the data later. Example 21.2 demonstrates how the setting subsection can be written up – it is apparent that the aims of the research dictate how much detail is needed here.

Example 21.2   From Timlin-Scalera et al. (2003)

Setting

The public high school where the data were collected was set in an almost entirely White, upper-income suburb in New England. Exact current demographics are not provided to preserve the anonymity of the school and its community. However, as of 1990, the town population was approximately 18,000, and approximately 17,000 of those residents were White. The majority of the residents were of European American descent, and the predominant ancestries were reported as English, German and Irish. As of 1989, the majority of household incomes exceeded $150,000, and the median household income was approximately $90,000. The town had a nearly equal number of males and females (U.S. Department of Commerce, 1990).

21.4   Participants Subsection

Students often skim over this section, failing to realise the importance of a comprehensive participants section. The APA Manual warns that 'conclusions and interpretations should not go beyond what the sample would warrant' (2001) (p. 18). Qualitative research recognises this point, in that each study is specific in its generalisations. A comprehensive participants section is of paramount importance, as it provides a more complete picture of the sample, which has implications for the replication of your study. Example 21.3 below shows the detail needed in writing up the participants section.

Example 21.3   From Timlin-Scalera et al. (2003)

Participants
Thirty-five interviewees participated in this study, including a select sample of 22 White male high school students from middle- to upper-income backgrounds, as well as four female high school students, five guidance department staff members, and four parents from the same community. To provide as much diversity as possible among the student sample, males were chosen from all four academic years, and they represented a variety of different social groups, school activities, and academic ranks. The male student participants ranged in age from 14 to 18 years. All of the males were White, and 21 of them identified their ethnic background as European American. One male identified his ethnic background as Russian Jewish. The four female students interviewed were all White 18-year-old seniors in high school who identified their ethnic background as European American. Two mothers and two fathers were interviewed, and each was a parent of a different male participant.

21.5   Measures and Apparatus Subsection

There is considerable debate as to whether this subsection should be included in a qualitative study. If it is appropriate to use this subsection for your study, then you need to describe any instruments, for example any demographic questionnaires or an interview protocol that you used. The following example describes a brief demographic questionnaire that was developed, and describes how the interviews, as a way of obtaining participants' responses and narratives, followed the grounded theory approach.

Example 21.4   From Ward (2005, p. 473)

Instruments
Brief demographic questionnaire: A brief demographic questionnaire was used to obtain background information. Questions included age, level of education, income, socio-economic

---

(Continued)

status, and racial heritage. Participants completed the questions at the end of the interview, which took 5–10 minutes to complete.

Interviews: In keeping with the tenets of grounded theory, the initial question was designed to allow participants to define the counselling experience the way they perceived it and in their own words. Thus participants were asked, 'tell me about your experiences in counseling'. As the interviews proceeded, the interview questions became more focused on perceived critical dimensions and issues across interviews, with the goal of discovering the potential emerging theory (Bowers, 1990; Charmaz, 2000; Glaser & Strauss, 1967). The following are some of the interview questions asked later in the interviews; 'How do you feel about working with a counselor who is from a different culture than yours?', 'How did you decide to come to counselling?', 'Was your counseling mandated by the court?', and 'What about the counselor made you feel uncomfortable? Participants' responses to these questions then guided formation of other questions during the interview.

It may also be useful to include information regarding the type of recording equipment that you used in your study.

21.6 Procedure Subsection

The procedure section is just as important as any other subsection in the methodology. Yet students often fail to outline in enough detail how they conducted their study. Do not take anything for granted, no matter how obvious the details of how you carried out your study are from the other subsections, you must still explicitly state what you did in sufficient detail. Therefore, you must explain what the participants did, or what was done to them during your investigation. It is also useful to include an account of verbal instructions given to the participants.

For example, if you used the interview to collect your data, you need to describe the interview process. This involves describing the transcription of your data, who did the transcription, in what detail were the transcriptions made, and how many pages of transcript were produced, etc. For grounded theory, you should systematically describe your sampling strategies, for example theoretical sampling, how theoretical saturation was achieved and how you utilised memos. It is also good practice to include a reflective piece to assist the reader in determining the reliability and validity of your interpretations that will follow in your findings and discussion section of your project.

21.7 Analytical Strategy

As already noted, data collection and data analysis occur simultaneously in grounded theory, and indeed in most qualitative research approaches. In this subsection, you should systematically detail how you carried out your analysis, for example for grounded theory you should describe how you carried out open, axial and selective coding as seen in the examples in the previous chapter. You should also state what type of computer-assisted qualitative data analysis package you used, if any, for example NVivo.

21.8   Checklist

- Did you identify a theoretical perspective for your qualitative approach, for example grounded theory?
- Did you explicitly state your research questions and aims?
- Was the selection of your participants well-reasoned?
- Was sampling carried out until theoretical saturation of data was reached?
- Did you outline your role as the researcher in sufficient detail?
- Have you comprehensively described your data collection strategies – enough to support rich descriptions?
- Have you thoroughly described the process of transforming data into themes and codes?

Summary

Analysis of the literature indicated six common subsections that can make up the methodology section of your project: theoretical background, setting, participants, measures and apparatus, procedure and analytical strategy. There is no current agreement on the composition of the methodology section due to the diversity of the field.

Further Reading

Langdridge, D. (2004) *Introduction to Research Methods and Data Analysis in Psychology*. Glasgow: Pearson Education Limited.

Miles, M. B. and Huberman, A. M. (1994) *Qualitative Data Analysis* (2nd edn). Thousand Oaks, CA: Sage Publications Ltd.

Silverman, D. (2004) *Interpreting Qualitative Data: Methods for Analysing Talk, Text and Interaction*. London: Sage Publications Ltd.

Silverman, D. (2003) *Doing Qualitative Research: A Practical Handbook*. London: Sage Publications Ltd.

Examples taken from:

Timlin-Scalera, R. M., Ponterotto, J. G. Blumberg F. C., and Jackson M. A. (2003) A grounded theory study of help-seeking behaviors among white male high school students. *Journal of Counseling Psychology*, 50(3), 339–50.

Ward, E. (2005) Keeping it real: A grounded theory study of African American clients engaging in counselling at a community mental health agency. *Journal of Counseling Psychology*, 52(4), 471–81.

22

WRITING UP YOUR QUALITATIVE FINDINGS/DISCUSSION

Objectives

On reading this chapter you should:

- understand what the qualitative results/discussion contains; and
- understand the importance of using quotes to illustrate your meaning making and interpretation.

Overview

The results/discussion holds much weight regarding the quality of your project, and therefore warrants as much consideration as the introduction and other sections. Section 22.1 deals with the qualitative findings/discussion, and explains how this section can vary depending on the type of analysis you carried out. Qualitative data analysis involves detailed scrutiny of a set of texts and the generation of themes or categories which help describe, understand and explain the data. This chapter deals with writing up the analysis for a grounded theory approach. Section 22.2 deals with the format of the results/findings section. Section 22.3 deals with the writing style appropriate for qualitative research, and finally Section 22.4 presents a checklist for writing up a good qualitative findings/discussion.

22.1 Qualitative Findings/Discussion Section

For qualitative projects, the results are often referred to as findings and this section along with the discussion are generally merged together. This is because the analysis of data includes interpretation and discussion of meaning (Langdridge, 2004). Qualitative data analysis usually involves detailed scrutiny of a set of texts and the generation of themes or categories which help describe, understand and explain the data. The popular approach discussed in Chapter 20 was grounded theory (e.g. Glaser & Strauss, 1967). This chapter, therefore, will use examples from grounded theory research. The qualitative findings/discussion section should also be carefully organised, and this organisation must be clear to the reader. For example, once you have effectively developed major trends or themes, they can serve as an organisational framework for your qualitative findings. You should also include quotations (from open-ended questions or transcripts) to illustrate these themes.

22.2   What to Include?

You should begin this section by restating the aim of your study, and the research question. You should then follow on with a summary of how this section is structured. It is useful to use the core category as your structure, as demonstrated in Example 22.1.

Example 22.1   From Timlin-Scalera (2003)

The core category of the need to fit in, consists of the multiple way males feel pressure to fit in to their environments, the impact of the town culture on intensifying those needs, and special issues for at-risk males. These areas are discussed below as well as the five major related subcategories that emerged during the selective coding process, which subsumes the underlying 15 axial and 48 open categories that add dimensions and properties to delineate and explain the different factors contributing to this story line.

The body of this section can then deal with the major themes that relate to the core category, as demonstrated in Example 22.1.

Example 22.2   From Timlin-Scalera et al. (2003)

The findings of the present study showed that males ... endured enormous amounts of pressure to fit in and be successful in all areas of their lives and to maintain strong and 'manly' independent images while they do so. Specifically, the town culture, which imposed a tremendous amount of pressure on these males to fit in, meaning to be successful across athletic, academic and social domains, created an atmosphere in which male adolescents felt they could not seek help in dealing with their problems, as this would be viewed as a distinct sign of weakness and failure by themselves, their families, and their community.

Use of quotes

As already mentioned, the nature of qualitative data is that it is rich in description, therefore it is useful to include illustrative quotations to convey the meaning of your data, and your understanding of it. Reporting grounded theory typically includes extensive quotations from participants, presumably to demonstrate the grounding of theory in participants' experiences and to highlight their unique perspective and voice. Examples should be short and relevant to the point that you are making, as demonstrated in Example 22.3. It is important that your do not repeat quotes, but feel free to make more than one reference to a particular quote.

Example 22.3   From Timlin-Scalera et al. (2003, p. 344)

Social Pressure

As delineated in the core category, an intense need for males to live up to and maintain a strong, macho image, and fit socially in a competitive, small, conservative, and affluent town culture emerged as the most significant and consistent types of problem faced by males in this community. Without exception, every person interviewed noted as part of fitting in socially, an extreme pressure on males to succeed academically and athletically while maintaining a macho image was a major problem. The following quotes, taken directly from the interview transcripts, illustrate the pressure to fit in. As one male noted:

> For guys, image is probably the biggest thing … your appearance as a guy or how you fit in, in terms of athletics or whatever, what group you're part of, probably good athletics, pretty much kind of smart kid, you know, well liked by people … It's kind of the untouched, unspoken pressure.

A staff participant described the pressure to belong to a group, preferably athletic, that many males face:

> There's a great push for, I don't know if it's just this school, probably many schools, but for males to be part of athletic groups, and for those students who are not athletic, if they don't find some other group to be a part of such as the artistic group or the musicians or something, that disconnectedness becomes a real problem.

Discuss findings in relation to previous research and theory

Qualitative analysis may take you into areas that you would not have anticipated before starting the research and which might be strange for the reader to find in the introduction. As long as the rationale is clear, you can draw on many different areas of past research in order to explicate what your findings mean as seen in Example 22.4 below.

Example 22.4   From Timlin-Scalera et al. (2003, p. 348)

Bussey and Bandura's (1999) discussion of gender-linked social sanctions [is] consistent with this theory, being male and living in a community that emphasizes males' strength, prestige, and success seemed to exacerbate the need to project a strong, autonomous image and made it even more difficult for males to ask for help. This is testimony to the independent, strong male that Pollack (1995) referred to, who has difficulty relying on others for help and rather must be the 'hero' himself.

Methodological flaws

In order to thoroughly assess what your results really mean, you must assess the quality of your piece of research. Example 22.5 demonstrates this.

Example 22.5   From Ward (2005, p. 480)

Grounded theory principles emphasise that it is important to gather data from a more diverse sample an effort to fully explore and discover core dimensions of what is involved in the phenomenon being studied (Schatzman, 1991). Although a sample size of 13 clients was large enough for saturation of the theory, the study might have been strengthened by having a more diverse group of participants.

In assessing the quality of your study, it is important that you strike a balance between its strengths and weaknesses. Remember that if you really rip your study to shreds, and list flaws upon methodological flaws, the question arises as to whether you put sufficient thought and energy into the design of your study. Not only that but it raises the ethical issue of conducting good science. Also, if you have too many methodological flaws, this will undermine the conclusions that you can draw from your findings.

Practical implications

As you already know from your methodology and theory courses in psychology, there is nothing as practical as a good theory (Lewin, 1936). You should therefore consider the practical applications of your findings, as demonstrated in Example 22.6

Example 22.6   From Ward (2005, p. 479)

This study may be one of the first studies to conduct a qualitative investigation of counseling processes and perceptions of counseling specific to African American clients within a community mental health agency. The data from this study generated a model that was helpful in understanding the counseling experiences of these clients.

The most interesting finding is the continuum of self-disclosing. This continuum illuminates how these clients actively monitor and manage their degree of self-disclosing as well as the conditions that influence disclosing.

Directions for future research

The next step is to propose additional research that could be done on the problem under investigation. Students can often find this aspect of the discussion difficult; however, there are some very useful strategies that can be used here. For example, any unanswered questions, or areas that remain unresolved, can become directions for future research. However, it is important again that you do not merely list directions for future research. It is important that they are logical and have a rationale. For any suggestions that you make, it is advisable that you elaborate on why the research would be worth doing, and what results might ensue, as demonstrated in Example 22.7.

Example 22.7   From Timlin-Scalera et al. (2003, p. 349)

As these findings were clearly unique to this select group of White male adolescents from a particular type of affluent community, future qualitative research should be conducted that considers similar areas of inquiry with males from other communities, including those from urban, low SES, and other ethnic backgrounds. Additionally, the males in this study were all attending a public high school with no intentions of dropping out. Future exploratory research should consider the help-seeking behaviors of male adolescents who are not enrolled in public high school. This may include male adolescents in private, night, boarding, parochial, vocational, or military schools, or those who have dropped out of high school. Furthermore, a comprehensive model of the help-seeking behaviors of female adolescents also does not exist. ... Additionally, based on the suggestions of participants in this study, orientations or mandatory mental health programs could be implemented in schools. Researchers could then conduct pretest and postest assessments of students' awareness, perceptions, and feelings about mental health services to see whether this type of outreach is effective.

Reflexive analysis

It is good practice to include a reflective section where you consider how your presence in the research process affected data collection and analysis. As already noted, this helps the reader to determine the reliability and validity of your interpretation.

Conclusion

It is very important that you present the strongest and most important statement that arises from your findings and interpretations as your conclusion. You should aim to end your project as strongly as you begin it. This also lessens the chance of the reader finishing your project and thinking, 'Well, so what?' You need to ensure that there is no ambiguity as to the importance of your study. You should also write an up-beat concluding paragraph where you reiterate the most positive aspects of your research and leave the reader with the impression that your project was worthwhile. The following example from Ward (2005) demonstrates these points very well.

Example 22.8   From Ward (2005, p. 480)

Conclusion

The findings from this study emphasize the importance of understanding African American clients' experiences in counselling. From this study we now know more about the dimensions that influences these participants' experiences in counselling from their own perspective ... More important, the findings from this study emphasize the importance of hearing and honoring the voices of clients we serve, as clients perceptions of counselling determine to a large extent the effectiveness of therapy (Barak & LaCrosse, 1975; Constantine, 2002; Paulson et al., 1999).

Giving a conclusion also ties up your findings, and facilitates a logical and obvious flow throughout your study to the end of your research project.

22.3   A Note on Style

In qualitative research, it is considered appropriate to use the first person, 'I', as opposed to the third person as in quantitative research. The reason for this is because *you* have acted as the research tool. Your findings have been produced from the material that you have produced, for example, the transcripts developed from an interview, and you have used your own creativity to develop meanings and relationships between the categories that emerged.

Remember that it is not appropriate to describe your study as an experiment as you have not manipulated any variables; instead refer to it as a study. Also, avoid using the term hypothesis, as it is important that you stick to using the term research question.

22.4   Checklist

- Does you project contribute to our understanding of the problem under investigation?
- Are your findings consistent with and reflective of your data?
- Are the conclusions persuasive and appropriately drawn from your data?
- Have you used sufficient quotes from your raw data?
- Have you discussed your findings in relation to previous research and theory?

Summary

The results/discussion section holds much weight regarding the quality of your project, and therefore warrants as much consideration as the introduction and other sections. The format of this section will vary depending on the type of analysis you carried out. Qualitative data analysis involves detailed scrutiny of a set of texts and the generation of themes or categories which help describe, understand and explain the data.

Further Reading

Miles, M. B. and Huberman, A. M. (1994) *Qualitative Data Analysis* (2nd edn). Thousand Oaks, CA: Sage Publications Ltd.

Silverman, D. (2004) *Interpreting Qualitative Data: Methods for Analysing Talk, Text and Interaction*. London: Sage Publications Ltd.

Silverman, D. (2003) *Doing Qualitative Research: A Practical Handbook*. London: Sage Publications Ltd.

Examples taken from:

Timlin-Scalera, R. M., Ponterotto, J. G., Blumberg, F. C. and Jackson, M. A. (2003) A grounded theory study of help-seeking behaviors among white male high school students. *Journal of Counseling Psychology*, 50(3), 339–50.

Ward, E. (2005) Keeping it real: A grounded theory study of African American clients engaging in counselling at a community mental health agency. *Journal of Counseling Psychology*, 52(4), 471–81.

UNIT 4

THE FINAL TOUCHES

Introduction

Although this section deals with the write-up of your undergraduate psychology project, it is important to realise that this should not be viewed as a distinct and separate phase of the research process. It is important that you start to write early in the research process and continue to write throughout the process. In this way, you can steadily build up a body of work, so that you do not have to rush the write-up of your project into the final two weeks before your project is due for submission.

If you have not intentionally been writing from the beginning, do not worry. You have probably been writing without realising it. For example, you have written a research proposal including a project outline, and your research design, and you have probably kept records of what you have done. This information goes a long way in aiding your write up.

One of the most important considerations when writing and editing your project is that your project does in fact have a thesis or argument. It is crucial that your main argument is very clear, and acts as the running theme throughout your project. To lose sight of your thesis can have detrimental effects on how your project is perceived during its grading. If the reader is confused because your thesis or argument was not made explicit in every section of your project, then you have not adequately met the requirements of your project, regardless of how much designing and planning you put into it. I always remind students that the reader of your project can only grade what is on paper in front of them; if you have lost your focus, or failed to get your aims across clearly, no exceptions will be made for this. It is therefore *vital* that you give yourself enough time to reread and edit your project, to ensure that you have said exactly what you wanted to say, and that you have done all your hard work justice by presenting it appropriately and accurately.

Chapter 23, *Title and Abstract*, deals with the critical role played by the title and abstract of your project. Together they provide a précis of the study: the title describes the relationship under investigation, while the abstract summarises the report. When combined they allow the reader to determine whether the study is of any relevance to them. The title is the medium for expressing the essential meaning of your project to the reader. Your abstract should be a powerful statement about your project, which will draw the reader in and give a concise road map of your project.

Chapter 24, entitled *References*, deals with the reference section, which appears in the back matter of your project. The importance of an accurate and complete reference section is explained. There are four main types of references which are described: a journal article, a book, a conference presentation and a technical report, using examples throughout. Citing references in the body of your project and using quotations in the text are also dealt with. Chapter 23 also details the APA guidelines for referencing electronic media, and gives some tips for keeping track of your references.

The final chapter in this section, Chapter 25, is entitled *The Final Write-Up*. Although it is expected that, as a final-year psychology student, you will have mastered the intricacies of research design and methodology, it is not as likely that you will have mastered the appropriate style for writing your research project. The chapter deals with the general guidelines laid down in the 5th edition of the *Publication Manual of the American Psychological Association* (APA, 2001)

23

TITLE AND ABSTRACT

Objectives

On reading this chapter you should:

- understand the important roles played by the title and abstract of your psychology project;
- be aware of the different types of titles, and understand the differences between them, and when each should be used;
- be able to develop a good title for you project based on the guidelines presented; and
- be able to write a good abstract following the guidelines given, and be fully aware of exactly what goes into the abstract.

Overview

Section 23.1 deals with the importance of the title and abstract for your research project. The title and abstract provide a précis of your study: the title describes your study, while the abstract summarises it. Section 23.2 portrays the title as the medium for expressing the essential meaning of your project to the reader and to the broader scientific community. Eight different types of title are described and exemplified. Section 23.3 outlines five guidelines for developing a good title for your project. Section 23.4 focuses on the abstract. It is noted that every research project, regardless of whether it is qualitative or quantitative in nature, requires an abstract, which is essentially a brief summary of each aspect of the study. Section 23.5 gives a note on the qualitative abstract, and demonstrates that it adheres to the same logic of the quantitative or experimental abstract. Writing a good abstract can be a very challenging task; therefore Section 23.7 presents some guidelines for writing a good abstract. The structured abstract is dealt with in Section 23.6, which uses pre-specified content headings as opposed to the traditional paragraph format. Writing a good abstract can be a very challenging task; therefore Section 23.7 presents some guidelines for writing the abstract. Finally Section 23.8 presents some common pitfalls in writing the abstract that should be avoided.

23.1   Purpose of the Title and Abstract

The title and abstract provide a précis of the study: the title describes your study, while the abstract summarises it. When combined they give the reader a snapshot of your study. In the scientific community, the title and abstract are also reproduced in electronic databases such as Psychological Abstracts and Social Science Citation Index. Typically, the title and abstract must therefore be able to stand alone, containing no abbreviations or uncommon terms, and more importantly it should communicate the essential meaning of the project. As a novice researcher, you are expected to apply the same stand-alone principle to your project, even though it will not be referenced in a bibliographic database.

> ### Tip: The first shall be last
>
> Although the title and abstract are generally the first sections of the project to be read, and in some cases the only sections read, they are generally written when the project has been completed. As will become apparent, this is to facilitate students' ability to stand back from their projects and abstract the relevant information, and to devise a title that clearly describes their work.

23.2   The Title

The title page represents the first page of your project, and consequently is the part that is most likely to be read. The title acts as the medium for expressing the essential meaning of the project to the reader and to the broader scientific community. Therefore the role of the title is to be simple, direct, accurate, honest and informative. Despite the critical role of the title, students often do not give adequate time and attention to composing a clear and accurate title.

The wording of the title should be as concise and precise as possible, helping the reader to know what the contents of your project are. The following quote, taken from the APA Publication Manual (2001), clearly illustrates the vital role of the title:

> A title should summarise the main idea of the paper and, if possible, with style. It should be a concise statement of the main topic and should identify the actual variables or theoretical issues under investigation and the relationships between them. Titles are commonly indexed and compiled in numerous reference works. Therefore, avoid words that serve no useful purpose; they increase length and can mislead indexers. For example, the words method and results do not normally appear in a title, nor should such redundancies as ... 'An Experimental Investigation of ...' begin a title. (p. 7)

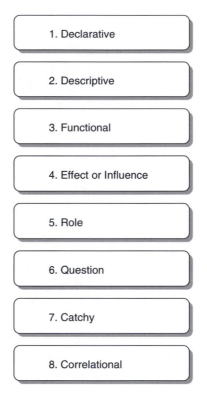

Figure 23.1   Eight title types

1.   Declarative title

There are various effective ways of constructing the title of your project. The first approach can be used by both qualitative and quantitative projects. In this method, the title makes use of a declarative sentence that summarises the main result of your project. It is very important that when a declarative title is used, it should be a true reflection of your results. The declarative title is effective at communicating the key results to the reader in a very direct and simple manner. It is advisable to always choose terms that are specific; never use abbreviations or terms that need to be defined, as illustrated below.

Example
Motivated self-stereotyping: Heightened assimilation and differential needs result in increased levels of positive and negative self-stereotyping.

Pickett, C., Bonner, B., and Coleman, J. (2002) *Journal of Personality and Social Psychology*, 82(4), 543–62.

2. Descriptive title

Descriptive titles are very popular in qualitative research. The aim is to clearly describe the focus of your study. This type of title is very similar to the declarative title, but without the focus on the results of a study. The descriptive title is useful for presenting rich descriptions of a study, as seen in the example below.

Example
Unbearable incidents: Failure to endure the experience of illness.

Dewar, A. L. and Morse, J. M. (1995) *Journal of Advanced Nursing*, 22(5), 957–64.

3. Functional title

The third and fourth approaches to constructing the title are generally used for experimental projects, where causal relationships are being proposed. Here, the title contains the dependent variable (D.V.) as a function of the independent variable (I.V.), for example 'Helping Behaviour as a Function of Self-Esteem'. It is apparent from the title that a causal relationship has been hypothesised; the term 'function' implies that an experiment was conducted, and that changes in the independent variable (helping behaviour) caused changes in the dependent variable (self-esteem). The functional title is very effective at portraying the key variables in a study, and at indicating the experimental nature of your project.

Example
Older people's well-being as a function of employment, retirement, environmental characteristics and role performance.

Warr, P., Butcher, V., Robertson, I. and Callinan, M. (2004) *British Journal of Psychology*, 95, 297–326.

4. Title of effect or influence

This title begins with the phrase 'Effect of' or 'Influence of', for example 'Effect/influence of alcohol consumption on concentration'; here the word 'effect' or 'influence' is causal, implying that an experiment was conducted and that changes in the independent variable (amount of alcohol consumed) caused a change in the dependent variable (level of concentration). This type of title is similar to the functional title, in that it indicates the key variables and the experimental nature of your project.

Example
The influence of grammatical, local, and organizational redundancy on implicit learning: An analysis using information theory.

Jamieson, R. and Mewhort, D. (2005) *Journal of Experimental Psychology: Learning, Memory, and Cognition*, 31(1), 9–23.

Example
The effects of hippocampal lesions on response, and place learning in rats.

Stringer, K., Martin, G. and Skinner, D. (2005) *Behavioral Neuroscience*, 119(4), 946–52.

5. Role title

Role titles are gaining in popularity. In most cases the word role means as a function of, as in the example provided below. Therefore, the role title has similar objectives to both the functional title and the title of effect or influence.

Example
The role of temporal shifts in turnover processes: It's about time.

Kammeyer-Mueller, J., Wanberg, C., Glomb, T. and Ahlburg, D. (2005) *Journal of Applied Psychology*, 90(4), 644–58.

6. Question title

The title of your study can also be posed as a question. It is important to include the main variables under investigation in the title. As in the example below, the independent variable (feedback), and the dependent variable (learning of words) have been included. The question title is a useful tool for eliciting curiosity in the reader.

Example
When does feedback facilitate learning of words?

Pashler, H., Cepeda, N., Wixted, J. and Rohrer, D. (2005) *Journal of Experimental Psychology: Learning*, Memory, and Cognition, 31(1), 3–8.

7. Catchy title

Catchy titles are also becoming increasingly popular. If there is some catchy title that you want to include, make that title a subtitle. Use a colon to append that subtitle to a more straightforward title, as in the example given. Be careful to avoid catchy newspaper headlines; remember that this is not an exercise in journalism. Catchy titles are useful for grabbing attention.

Example
What you see is what you set: sustained inattentional blindness and the capture of awareness.

Most, S., Scholl, B.,Clifford, E. and Simons, D. (2005) *Psychological Review*, 112(1), 217–42.

8. Correlational title

With qualitative, and correlational research, include the main variables of interest in the title. It is very important in these cases, that the title does not imply causality. Such a mistake may suggest that you did not understand the goals of the scientific method, and more specifically the logic of causality. Clearly this is a serious mistake that should be avoided. Correlational titles are effective for communicating the key relationships under investigation.

Example
The relationship between perceptions of politics and depressed mood at work: unique moderators across three levels.

Byrne, Z., Kacmar, C., Stoner, J. and Hochwarter, W. (2005) *Journal of Occupational Health Psychology*, 10(4), 330–43.

23.3   Guidelines for Devising a Good Title

1. *Keywords* – Include all necessary key words to accurately and fully convey your project's content and preview the variables being investigated.
2. *Participants* – It is useful to include information regarding the sample of participants used. Although this may not be common protocol amongst published studies, it serves a number of purposes in the undergraduate project. It illustrates that the student understands the logic of generalisability and external validity, as undergraduate projects usually focus on one type of cohort, and it also fulfils the important goal of precision.
3. *Order* – Order the words to reflect precisely and accurately the meaning that you intend to convey.
4. *Essential Meaning* – Omit all words that are redundant or do not contribute to the essential meaning of your project.
5. *Every word counts* – Try and keep your title as concise as possible. A 12-word maximum is often advised; however, if a few extra words are needed for clarity, it is better to go over. Remember it is better to have a clear 16-word title, than a vague 12-word one.

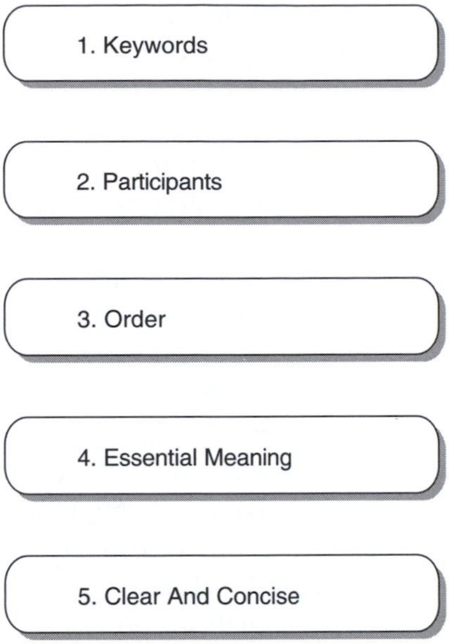

Figure 23.2   Five essentials for a good title

23.4   The Abstract

Every research project, regardless of whether it is qualitative or quantitative in nature, requires an abstract, which is essentially a brief summary of each aspect of the study. As already noted, the abstract is reproduced in computerised databases. Within the scientific community, this is often the section that is read first and in some cases it may be the only section read. Therefore, applying the stand-alone principle, your abstract needs to be a powerful statement about your project, that will draw the reader in and provide a concise road map.

The importance of the abstract is well illustrated in the APA (2001) Manual:

> Most people will have their first contact with an article by seeing just the abstract, usually on a computer screen with several other abstracts, as they are doing a literature search through an electronic abstract-retrieval system. Readers frequently decide, on the basis of the abstract, whether to read the entire article; this is true whether the reader is at a computer or is thumbing through a journal. The abstract needs to be dense with information but also readable, well organised, brief, and self-contained. Also, embedding many key words in your abstract will enhance the user's ability to find it. (p.12)

An abstract in a project means to extract the relevant or pertinent information from your study and present it in a condensed fashion. Considering its importance, the accuracy of the information provided by the abstract is critical.

A good-quality abstract should accurately reflect the purpose and content of your project. The abstract should summarise, using a sentence, each section of the study, as illustrated in Example 23.1. It is very important to note that an abstract should never contain information that is not included in the body of your project itself. Therefore, the abstract must be consistent with the body of your project, highlighting the importance of internal consistency throughout your psychology project.

You should write a draft abstract early, in order to keep you focused. Then, as you approach the end stages of your project, you can critically review your abstract. The end stages of your project are the ideal time to work towards a strong abstract because the material is fresh in your mind. As your project has evolved, the focus may have shifted; this is natural and part of the evolution of a project. Now you must step back, reconsider and condense down all of the major concepts to create a concise abbreviation of your project.

Some researchers use citations in their abstracts. Traditionally, a citation would not have been acceptable in the abstract, but they are becoming common among many qualitative researchers in describing the paradigm that their research follows. If you are planning to use citations in your abstract be sure to check with your supervisor and university policies.

Format

Some APA journals specify a word limit of 175–180 words for the abstract, while theoretical abstracts are usually between 75–100 words. For the undergraduate student, the abstract should be no longer than 180 words, but ideally should be between 100–120 words. The abstract should be presented using a separate page, and takes roman numerals. It is very important to note that the abstract is always single spaced, as it is distinct from the body of your report. Editing and formatting issues are dealt with in more detail in Chapter 25.

Example 23.1   Experimental abstract

The aim of the current experiment was to test for right ear advantage using a dichotic listening task. A dependent groups design was utilised. The 16 participants, 5 male and 11 female, took part in both the right and left ear condition. The mean age was 20, and the age range was 19–26. The dichotic listening task involved the constant-vowel procedure. Participants were presented with a series of computer-generated non-sense syllables via earphones to both ears. A dependent t-test was carried out to test the hypothesis that words would be recalled more accurately in the right ear than the left ear, due to language dominance in the left hemisphere ($t = 3.316$; $df = 15$; $P < 0.05$). Results are discussed with regard to methodological flaws and their practical and future implications.

23.5 A Note on the Qualitative Abstract

The qualitative abstract follows the same logic of the quantitative abstract; therefore you should include information regarding the objectives of your study, and your research question. You should include information regarding your theoretical rationale, for example grounded theory. You should include information about your participants and their selection, and the setting. You can then combine information about your data collection and interpretation of your data. It is also important to include some conclusions regarding the implications of your findings.

23.6 A Note on the Structured Abstract

Writing an abstract using the structured format involves using pre-specified content headings rather than the paragraph format. The pre-specified sub-headings are as follows; background, aim(s), method(s), results, and conclusions. The use of the structured format arose of the Ad Hoc Working Group for the Critical Appraisal of the Medical Literature in 1987, as a suggestion for improving the clarity of abstracts within the medical field. This trend is beginning to creep into psychology. In January 1997, the British Psychological Society (BPS) introduced structured abstracts into four of their eight journals (Hartley, 2003). Also, from 2000 onwards, the BPS has required authors to send conference submissions in this structured format, examples of which can be viewed in the conference proceedings. This change in practice may inevitably cause confusion for the undergraduate psychology student when deciding which format to use – the paragraph or the structured format. It is therefore of critical importance that you check with your university's policies and requirements in this regard.

23.7 Guidelines for Writing a Good Abstract

- Writing a good abstract can be very challenging. It is advised that you write a draft abstract during the early stages of your project. This acts as a tool to keep you focused as it presents an overview of your project. Towards the end of your project, you should rewrite the draft. You should write it last, after you have written the report; this way you should be able to abstract, or paraphrase, your report more effectively. You will be able to make any changes necessary due to the evolution of your project. This also helps students to write up the abstract in the past tense, which is the required tense for the abstract.
- The aim of the current investigation should be described in the first sentence, and should (ideally) be one sentence in length.

- The participants should be described clearly, specifying significant characteristics of the population under investigation.
- The research method used in the study should be described, including details such as the design, apparatus, data-gathering techniques, etc.
- The findings should also be described, including the statistical levels.
- The conclusions, the theoretical and practical implications, and directions for future research should also be described. This is generally the last sentence of the abstract.

23.8   Common Pitfalls in Writing the Abstract

1. Omission of relevant information.
2. Inconsistency between the abstract and the body of your project.
3. Incorrect reporting of results.
4. The ommission of your independent and dependent variables.
5. The ommission of your overall design.

Summary

The title and abstract provide a précis of the study; the title describes the study, while the abstract summarises the project. The title and abstract must be able to stand alone, containing no abbreviations or uncommon terms, and more importantly they need to communicate the essential meaning of the project. There are eight popular types of titles used for psychological research: declarative, descriptive, functional, effect or influence, role, question, catchy and correlational. It is very important that you choose a title that reflects the aim of your project. Your abstract needs to be a powerful statement about your project, which will draw the reader in and provide a concise road map of your study.

Further Reading

American Psychological Association (2001) *Publication Manual of the American Psychological Association* (5th edn). Washington, DC: American Psychological Association.

Field, A. and Hole, G. (2004) *How to Design and Report Experiments*. London: Sage Publications.

Harris, P. (2002) *Designing and Reporting Experiments in Psychology*. Buckingham: Open University Press.

Silverman, D. (2003) *Doing Qualitative Research: A Practical Handbook*. London: Sage Publications.

24

REFERENCING

Objectives

On reading this chapter you should:

* understand what the reference section of your project entails;
* be aware of the seven main types of references;
* be able to cite references in your text correctly and accurately;
* be able to use quotations in your project; and
* understand the importance of a complete reference section.

Overview

Section 24.1 deals with the reference section, which appears in the back matter of your project. The importance of an accurate and complete reference section is explained. There are seven main types of references which are described: a journal article, a book, a conference presentation, a technical report, a secondary reference, a web-based reference, and software and apparatus, using examples throughout. Section 24.2 goes on to deal with citing references in the body or text of your project. Using quotations in the text is then dealt with in Section 24.3, and is illustrated with examples. Finally Section 24.4 gives some tips for keeping track of your references.

24.1 The Reference Section

The hallmark of scientific research is that experiments and research projects build on previous research and ideas. The reference list documents the scientific literature cited and provides the necessary information for the reader to identify and retrieve each source. It is imperative that each reference is relevant, and that only sources that were utilised are included. APA Manual

(2001) states: 'just as data in the paper support interpretations and conclusions, so reference citations document statements about the literature' (p. 28). The APA guidelines espouse the use of reference lists as opposed to bibliographies.

The reference list provides the reader with the information needed to seek out the original source of information. Each item has its first lines indented, as in a paragraph indent, known as a hanging indent. Each study that you discuss in your project should be listed in alphabetical order by the last name of the author(s). Works by the same author should be arranged chronologically according to publication date.

1. Journal article

The most common reference is to an article in a research journal. The format for such a reference is to list: (1) the author(s), last name first; (2) the year the paper was published listed in parentheses; (3) the title of the article; (4) the journal title; (5) the volume number of the journal; and (6) the pages of the article. The journal title and the volume number are in italics. It is important to note that the references are single spaced, with hanging indents.

Example of a reference for a journal article:
Adams, J. S. (1968) Effects of overpayment: Two comments on Lawlor's paper. *Journal of Personality and Social Psychology, 10,* 315–16.

2. Book

Again, list: (1) the author(s); (2) the year the book was published in parentheses; (3) the title of the book, which should be in italics; (4) the city in which the book was published; and (5) the publisher.

Example of a reference for a book:
Alderfer, C. P. (1972) *Existence, Relatedness and Growth: Human Needs in Organisational Settings.* New York: The Free Press.

Example of chapter from a book:
Aditya, R. N., House R. J. and Kerr, S. (2000) Theory and practice of leadership: Into the new millennium. In C. Cooper, and E.A. Locke (eds) *Industrial and Organisational Psychology.* Oxford: Blackwell Publishers Ltd. Oxford: Blackwell Business, pp. 130–65.

3. Conference presentation

Science as a scientific community relies greatly on communication. Presentations at conferences are increasingly popular ways of getting new research into the public arena quickly. The format for referencing a conference presentation is to list: (1) the author(s); (2) the date (including month) of the

Figure 24.1   Seven types of references

conference presentation; (3) the title of the presentation; and (4) the conference and the location of the conference.

Example of a reference of a conference presentation:
Murphy, J. (2001, May) The importance of reporting effect sizes and confidence intervals when using the null hypothesis significance test procedure. Paper presented at the Psychological Society of Ireland Convention, Dublin.

4. Technical report

Some sources of information are not published in the sense that they are made widely available, but they are written as technical reports, which may be available through universities or from the author.

Example of a reference of a technical report: from a university:
Yukl, G. (2000) Preliminary results from validation research on the extended version of the Influence Behaviour Questionnaire. Technical Report, State University of New York Albany.

5. Secondary source

The APA states that a secondary reference should be cited in the text as follows: 'French and Raven (1959, cited in Yukl, 2002)' and that the primary reference should be cited in the reference list, without citing the secondary reference in the reference list. However, some researchers *do* suggest including the secondary reference as follows:

French, J. and Raven, B. H. (1959) The bases of social power. Cited in G. Yukl
   (2002) *Leadership in Organizations* (5th edn). New Jersey: Prentice-Hall.

The logic behind this is that the reader can easily source the secondary reference without having to refer to the secondary source for the reference:

6. Web-based

When referencing sources from the internet it is important that you adhere to the following guidelines from the APA (2001). It is suggested that a reference of an internet source should provide the following information:

*   A document title or description.
*   A date which should either be the date of publication or an update of retrieval.
*   An address known as a uniform resource locator, or URL.

Whenever possible, you should also identify the authors of a document .

   The URL is the most critical element – if it doesn't work, readers will not be able to find the cited material, and the credibility of your argument will suffer. It is important to note that a website may disappear, and it may have been updated or changed completely. It is therefore advisable that you test the URLs in your references regularly. References to the web are usually less satisfactory than journal articles. The importance of evaluating information from the web was dealt with in Chapter 7. It is important that you check your institution's rules on citing websites. My advice is to be cautious, and don't overuse such citations. In particular, don't use a web citation where you could reasonably use a 'hard' citation.

   Check out the APA Electronic Reference Formats at http://www.apa. org/journals/webref.html for an extensive list.

Example of an electronic copy of a journal article retrieved from full-text journal article database:

Judge, T. A., Jackson, C. L. and Shaw, J. C. (2007). Self-efficacy and work-
   related performance: The integral role of individual differences. *Journal of
   Applied Psychology*, 92(2), 107–127. Retrieved 10 April, 2007, from
   PsycARTICLES database.

Example of an article in an internet-only journal:
Clark, A. (2007, Fall). Changing classroom practice to include the project approach. *Early Childhood Research & Practice (ECRP)*, *8 (2)*. Retrieved 10 April 2007, from http://ecrp.uiuc.edu/v8n2/clark.html

Example of a daily newspaper article, electronic version available by search 2001:
Reid, M. (30 April 2007). 'Think before you drive the boy racers off the road' *London Times*. Retrieved 30 April 2007, from http://www.timesonline.co.uk

6. Software and apparatus

Reference entries are not necessary for standard off-the-shelf software and programming languages such as Microsoft Word and Excel. In the text, give the proper name of the software, along with the version number. It is very important to provide a reference for specialised software or computer programs with limited distribution. Some computer analysis packages such as SPSS are often considered so common that they do not require a reference. It is advisable to check your university's regulations on this issue.

Example of software reference: (APA, 2001).
Miller, M. E. (1993) *The Interactive Tester* (Version 4.1) [Computer software]. Westminster, CA: Psytek Services.

Example of apparatus reference:
Mirror Tracer Model 31010. Lafayette Instrument Company (2002), 3700 Sagamore Parkway North, IN 47903 USA.

24.2 Citing References in the Text

Citing a single work by one author

There are two standard approaches for citing a single study in the text. The first is to list the citation after a statement based on the paperarticle.

> Murphy (2006) argued that the evidence for predetermined genetic influences in schizophrenia is overwhelming.

The second is to list the authors in the text, with the year of publication listed immediately after the author list.

> The evidence for predetermined genetic influences in schizophrenia is overwhelming (Murphy, 2006).

Citing a single work by more than one author

When an author list is integrated into the text, the word 'and' is used between the last two authors. When an author list is included in parentheses, the word 'and' is replaced by the ampersand symbol (&). APA uses a serial comma in author lists, which means that there is a comma just before the 'and' or ampersand in the list.

> Barlow, Murphy, and Roberts (2000) argue that incorporating research methodology into clinical practice will dramatically improve services.
>
> Incorporating research methodology into clinical practice will dramatically improve services (Barlow, Murphy, & Roberts, 2000).

When there are two to five authors on a single study, all authors are listed the first time the study is cited. For subsequent citations to the same study, only the first author is listed followed by the phrase 'et al.'. If there are six or more authors, the et al. notation is used even for the first reference to the paper. If there might be some confusion about what paper was being referenced because the senior author published several papers cited in your study in the same year, you should list as many authors as necessary to make the citation unambiguous.

Citing multiple studies

Often there is more than one study that supports a given statement, so multiple investigations are cited. This is done at the end of the sentence. The studies are ordered by the last name of the senior author and if necessary by the last names of junior authors. Studies are separated by semi-colons as shown below. Although such lists of studies occur most often at the end of a sentence, multiple lists can occur in a single sentence, with each list supporting the statement that immediately precedes it.

> MRIs allowed researchers to look at the structure of the brain of patients with schizophrenia and compare it with the structure of the brains of controls (e.g. Murphy, 2000; Lawlor, Fines, O'Reillt Jones & Hogan, 2003).

24.3   Quotations in the Text

A quotation is any section of verbatim material taken from another source and included in your paper experiment. Such material must be identified as a quotation, with the source of the quoted material noted. Failure to do so is considered plagiarism. Short quotations (less than 40 words) are incorporated into the text material and surrounded by quotation marks. Longer quotations are typed as a paragraph, where all lines of the quotation are indented five spaces from the left margin. Such long quotations are not placed in quotation marks. The quotation should be an accurate representation of the original material. If there is an error, such as a misspelled or incorrect word in the original, it should be reproduced as originally written, but the word *sic* should be places in brackets and underlined immediately after the error. If any material is inserted to help clarify the meaning of quotation, it should be placed in square brackets to indicate that it was not a part of the original. If any material is omitted, three periods (...) should be inserted to indicate that material was omitted. Block quotes should be indented five spaces from the left hand margin and omit quotation marks.

The source of any quotation, regardless of its length, should be indicated. If the source is obvious from the flow of the paper, the page number source should be included immediately afterward. If the source is not obvious, the reference to the source and the page numbers should appear in parentheses immediately afterward. Listed below are two such examples taken from Graziano and Raulin (1997).

> Graziano and Raulin (1997) note that certain characteristics of scientists 'are equally well developed in poets, sculptors, painters, composers, philosophers, writers, and others.' (p. 5)
> 'The essence of science is its systematic, disciplined way of thinking' (Graziano & Raulin, 1997, p. 5).

24.4   Tips on Keeping Track of your References

On completion of your project, it is vital to check the citations in the body of your project against the list in the reference section. First of all, make sure that every source mentioned in the text is given a listing in the reference section. Then make sure that every reference listed in the reference section is cited in the text. This cross-checking strategy will help ensure that you have included all your references.

Summary

The reference list documents the scientific literature cited and provides the necessary information for the reader to identify and retrieve each source. The six main types of reference are from a journal article, a book, a conference presentation, a technical report, the web, and software and apparatus. It is very important that you cite all your references very carefully and accurately, and that you use quotations in the text appropriately.

Further Reading

American Psychological Association (2001) *Publication Manual of the American Psychological Association* (5th edn). Washington, DC: American Psychological Association.

Amato, C. J. (2002) *The World's Easiest Guide to Using the APA: A User-friendly Manual for Formatting Research Papers According to the American Psychological Association Style Guide* (3rd edn). Corona, CA: Stargazer Publishing.

25

FINAL WRITE-UP

Objectives

On reading this chapter you should:

*   know how to format your project;
*   know what to include in the body of your project, and the front and back matter; and
*   understand the importance of leaving enough time to edit and review your project properly.

Overview

Section 25.1 describes the general format of your project, which is something that students often neglect, and hence lose precious marks. The general layout and format of your project should follow the same issues of precision as your writing. Section 25.2 details the components of the front matter of your project, which comprises the front cover, title page, declaration, acknowledgement, abstract and table of contents. Section 25.3 reiterates the body of your project, which consists of the introduction, methodology, results and discussion. Section 25.4 deals with the back matter, consisting of the references and the appendices. Finally, Section 25.5 deals with editing and reviewing your project.

25.1 General Format

Paper

Your project should be printed on standard-sized, A4 paper of 8½ × 11 in or 22 × 28 cm. You should use good-quality white bond paper of at least 90gsm weight. All pages of your project must be of the same size.

Table 25.1   Four format issues

1.	Paper
2.	Typeface
3.	Margins and line spacing
4.	Submission

Typeface

The preferred typefaces for your project are 12-pt Times Roman or 12-pt Courier, although students sometimes use 12-pt Arial, which is usually acceptable. A serif typeface is preferred for text because it improves the readability and reduces eye fatigue. A sans-serif type is used in figures to provide a clean and simple line that enhances the visual presentation.

Margins and line spacing

It is very important that you leave uniform margins of at least 1 in (2.54 cm) at the top, bottom, left and right of every page. Most word processing packages have these margins set as default. Your right margin should be left ragged, so you should not right justify the lines. For any copies of your project that are to be bound, remember to create a left margin of 1½ inches, i.e. an extra half an inch to accommodate binding.

Project submission

Students are generally required to submit a hard copy and two soft copies of their project to their university or college. The hard copy might eventually end up in the university library, while the two soft copies usually go to the supervisor and a second reader. Although this is the norm, it can differ among universities, so it is imperative that you check your university's policy on this regard.

25.2   The Front Matter

The front matter can vary from university to university, so again check with your supervisor to make sure that you follow the requirements of your college or university. In general, the front matter consists of the front cover, title page, copyright notice, declaration, acknowledgements, abstract and the table of contents, as illustrated in Figure 25.1. The title page is numbered but the number is not seen, and the remaining front matter is numbered with lower-case roman numerals (i, ii, iii, iv, v, etc.).

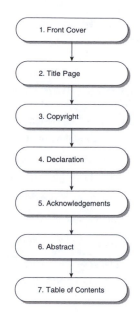

Figure 25.1   Components of the front matter of your project

1. Front cover

The hard copy of your project must be bound in the specified colour, for example navy blue or black, and normally has the following information on the front cover in GOLD lettering:

- The title of the project in at least 24-point (80mm) type.
- Your name.
- The award for which the project is submitted, e.g. BA (Hons), and the year of submission.

The same information, excluding the title, should be printed in the same order in at least 24-point type along the spine of the cover in such a way as to be easily legible when the copy is lying flat with the front cover uppermost. You need to ensure that you leave sufficient time for a hard-bound version of your thesis to be prepared by a printing company. Make enquiries as soon as possible.

2. Title page

The title page should contain the following information:

- The full title of the project and subtitle (if any).
- The qualification for which the thesis is presented.
- Your name.

- The name of the university and supervisor.
- The month and year of submission.

Example 25.1   From Barry (2004)

The Effects of Spatial Ability on the Learning of Complex Scientific
Instructional Material

Project submitted in part fulfilment of the requirements for the degree of
Bachelor of Arts in Psychology

[Your Name] Shane Barry

Department of Psychology

American College Dublin

[Supervisor's Name]

May 2006

---

3. Copyright notice

Some institutions require that you include a copyright notice. The Copyright Act of 1976 provides for statutory copyright protection of a work from the moment it is tangibly fixed. To secure this protection, a copyright notice should be affixed on a separate page immediately following the title page; it should include the Copyright symbol ©, year in which copyright is established and the full legal name of the author.

4. Declaration

A declaration is also included, on the page following the title page, which you should sign and date. Check the wording required by your institution, and whether there is a standard form.

Example 25.2

I hereby certify that this material which I now submit for assessment on the programme of study leading to the award of BA ——————— is entirely my own work and has not been taken from the work of others save to the extent that such work has been cited and acknowledged within the text of my work.

Signed——————————— Date———————————

---

5. Acknowledgements

You may wish to include an acknowledgement page, which is optional. This page usually contains an acknowledgement of the support and advice given by your supervisor, any additional help from other faculty members, and any permission given to use tests and measures by other researchers. Students also like to extend thanks to those friends and family members who have provided personal support throughout their projects.

6. Abstract

As already noted, the abstract is a single-spaced continuous paragraph, positioned before the table of contents page. The abstract is numbered with roman numerals.

7. Table of contents

The table of contents should list the major chapters of your psychology project. If some chapters have subsections, it is appropriate to include those also as illustrated in example 25.3.

25.3　Body of the Project

The body of your project consists of the introduction, methodology, results and discussion sections with their coinciding subsections, as illustrated in Figure 25.2.

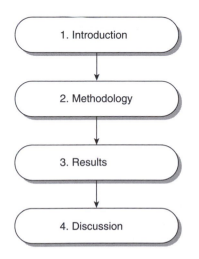

Figure 25.2　Components of the body of your project

Example 25.3   From Barry (2004)

TABLE OF CONTENTS

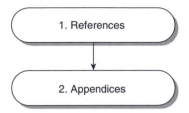

Figure 25.3   Components of the back matter of your project

25.4   Back Matter

The back matter of your project consists of the references and appendices. The references have been dealt with in the previous chapter. The purpose of the appendices is to expand on information that you only referred to in the text. If there is material that should be in the project but which would break up the flow or bore the reader include it as an appendix. Some things which are typically included in appendices are: important and original computer programs; data files that are too large to be represented simply in the results chapters; and pictures or diagrams of results which are not important enough to keep in the main text.

25.5   Editing and Reviewing your Project

The quality of research is evaluated by the quality of the written document. Once you have a first draft of your project on your computer, the really hard part is over. Now you can focus on refining your work, improving what you have said as opposed to worrying about what to say.

You should invest time in editing for content, style and organisation. Check that you have said everything that you wanted to say. It is crucial that you check if all the sections of your project are consistent with each other, and consistent with your abstract and outline. As already noted, your main argument and thesis must be very clear, and should act as a running theme throughout your project.

Proof-reading is also very important. You need to give your project and ideas the credit they deserve by presenting a polished paper, free of inaccurate spelling, typing errors and incorrect formatting. The number of drafts necessary for a really good piece of writing depends on your individual ability and experience. At undergraduate level, you should realistically write at least two or three drafts. However, students rarely leave enough time for drafts. It is always evident to the reader, whether the student has spent time preparing drafts. The quality and the argument of the project are on another level to a student who has not invested time into preparing drafts and thinking critically about what they have said.

Summary

There are a number of general format issues, for example the type of paper used, the typeface, the use of specified margins and line spacing. The front matter of your project consists of the front cover, title page, copyright notice, declaration, acknowledgements, abstract and table of contents. The body of your project consists of the introduction, methodology, results/findings and the discussion. Finally, the back matter consists of the references and the appendices. You should invest time in editing for content, style and organisation. Check that you have said everything that you wanted to say. It is crucial that you check if all the sections of your project are consistent with each other, and consistent with your abstract and outline. As already noted, your main argument must be very clear, and should act as a running theme throughout your project.

Further Reading

American Psychological Association (2001) *Publication Manual of the American Psychological Association* (5th edn). Washington, DC: American Psychological Association.

Amato, C. J. (2002) *The World's Easiest Guide to Using the APA: A User-friendly Manual for Formatting Research Papers According to the American Psychological Association Style Guide* (3rd edn). Corona, CA: Stargazer Publishing.

APPENDIX A
STUDENTS' PERSONAL EXPERIENCES OF THEIR PSYCHOLOGY PROJECT

- I think it is important to plan every aspect of the research project from the introduction right down to the reference section so that it doesn't all pile up at the end.
- It is good to remember that even if your results don't work out as you first anticipated, this in itself adds to the learning experience, is a key part of the research project and discussion, and it is how you interpret and analyse your results that counts.
- Before doing research, a broad investigation should be carried out which may involve consulting a variety of books, journal articles, friends and supervisors. In forming the research question, try to be as explicit as possible about the experimental design and operationalisation. Sometimes it can be very hard to come up with an appropriate method, in which case brainstorming can help. In considering all the alternatives and options, try to be creative and critical in weighing the pros and cons of each possible option. Sufficient planning is of extreme importance to an experiment, yet not everything of an experiment.
- During research, be prepared for the unexpected, which may be that procedures might go wrong, participants may not be as helpful as expected, or results may turn out completely opposite. Conducting a few pilot studies and test runs will greatly help in these situations. Also be prepared for anything novel in the results, which is actually quite worth noticing.
- The discussion of the results is just as important as all the previous planning, as it summarises the whole experiment and further suggests valuable advice for future research.
- One should always bear in mind that there is a vast discrepancy between theory and practice. Theoretically, anything is possible and feasible since human creativity and imagination is unlimited. However, in reality, there is always limitation as to the time and resources that are required, leaving aside the unexpected. Research, in a large part, is about putting theory into practice or testing theory in practice in order to refine the theory. A comprehensive, well-planned experiment procedure that is adaptive (only to a certain degree) to the unexpected will speed up the research process efficiently.
- Embarking on a research project is always a daunting task – it can feel like there's a whole world of topics to choose from, yet somehow you still have no idea which

topic to choose. Even when you do eventually pick a topic, hearing what others have opted for can often leave you doubting your choice, as if you've gotten it 'wrong' because everyone else is doing something different.

- Don't be afraid to be creative, or to choose a topic that's a bit different. Remember, examiners read many projects every year and they can get bored. So make them sit up and take notice. A fresh idea or new approach can really make your project stand out.

- Chose a topic you are interested in. Do not under-estimate how important this is. You will spend a large amount of time working on your project and, no matter how fascinating it is, there will probably be times when you'll want to rip up your notes, throw your laptop out the window and never hear another word on the topic. Of course, these moments are likely to be a lot more frequent if you've chosen a topic because you think it's 'worthy or 'impressive', rather than because it's an area you actually want to explore. Having a genuine interest in the area you're studying will help pull you through the tough times, and with any luck your enthusiasm for what you're learning will shine through in your project too.

- However, no matter how enthusiastic you are about your topic, make sure you think it through fully before committing to it. Consider all the problem areas you may encounter and decide how you will tackle these issues. Think about issues such as availability of samples, tools you require and how you will analyse your data. If you do realise your first choice of subject will prove impossible to pursue in the set amount of time, remember it's better to suffer a little disappointment now than to hit a brick wall three months down the line!

- Set a realistic timeline for your project. Every section of the project is of importance, so try to allocate your time evenly. A very impressive introduction and methodology can be let down by a hastily written discussion.

- Listen to your supervisors' advice. They are genuinely there to help you, and they want to see you do well. This may be your first research project, but they've probably been through this process with dozens of students over the years. Take advantage of their experience – they understand what examiners are looking for, and they want you to understand too.

- Most importantly, remember: this is an opportunity to put into practice the theoretical and practical knowledge that you have gained over the last three years. Make the most of it … and show off!

- Don't procrastinate – start early. Putting things on the long finger is one of the worst things a researcher can do. At the outset, you may feel that you have plenty of time to complete the project. However, the reality is that every single day counts when carrying out a research project, and most researchers (myself included) rue the fact that they didn't start their project earlier. Thus, it is useful to start thinking about potential research topics in advance so that you can begin the literature review early.

- Starting the literature review early is very important, as it is a very time-consuming process. Bear in mind, for example, that some books or journals required for your literature review may need to be ordered in from other libraries, and these can take some time to arrive.

- Most literature searches are now carried out on the internet, so it is important to ensure that you only use articles that are empirically sound. I found that Google Scholar was a good starting point for accessing articles, but not all articles from this search engine are from authoritative sources. Thus, it is better to stick to more reputable search engines such as Pro-Quest, which allows you to refine your search to only display peer-reviewed articles.

- When carrying out the literature review, I found it useful to compile the references section as I went along. Compiling the references section takes longer than one may think, and leaving it until the end can be a nightmare as there are so many other things to worry about at that stage of the project.

- Manage your time effectively. Carrying out a research project is almost as much a test of your time-management skills as it is of your research skills. I found it very useful to construct a timetable at the outset of the project; A timetable not only ensures that you don't spend too much time on one aspect of the project; it also helps to focus the mind when you have a deadline to work towards. Finally, when constructing a timetable, bear in mind that you will need to leave plenty of time at the end for house-keeping issues such as formatting, proof-reading, printing and binding.

- It is important to develop and maintain a good working relationship with your project supervisor, and ensure that you arrange to meet each other as often as possible. These meetings are invaluable for keeping your research project on the right track, as well as for ironing out any difficulties that you might have. Supervisors have 'been there, done that', and will often have encountered similar problems or difficulties that your project may encounter. In order to maximise the benefit of supervisor meetings, it is useful to prepare a list of questions that you have – it can be a waste of time for both of you if you do not have anything prepared before the meeting.

- Finally, back up, back up and back up again! I cannot emphasise enough the importance of backing up your files on a daily basis. It is the greatest fear of all researchers that they will sit down at their computer only to find all their work has disappeared! To avoid this nightmare, try and get into a routine of backing up your work at the end of every day, and keep the back-up files of your work in a safe place. An easy way of backing up your work is to email it to yourself every week – this means that if your laptop or PC breaks down, your work can still be accessed through your email account.

Students that participated included: Danielle Lyons, Jiaying Zhao, Shane Barry, Sinead O'Loughlin, Nereko Lekuona, John O'Donoghue and Joanna Elomari, who completed their psychology projects at the American College Dublin.

APPENDIX B
CARRYING OUT COMMON STATISTICAL ANALYSES USING SPSS V14

Comparisons Between Groups

Running an independent t-test using SPSS V14

Main Menu → Analyse → Compare means → Independent samples t-test

→ Transfer your dependent variable into the **Test Variable** box.
→ Independent variable into the **Grouping Variable** box.
→ **Define Groups,** enter the values for your two groups.
→ Click into **Options,** and check that your confidence interval is set at 95%.
→ **OK.**

Running a one-way non-repeated ANOVA using SPSS V14

Main Menu → Analyse → General Linear Model → Univariate

→ Transfer your DV into the **Dependent Variable** box.
→ Transfer you IV into the **Fixed Factor(s)** box.
→ Click into **Post Hoc** to reveal the **Univariate: Post Hoc Multiple Comparisons for Observed Means** dialog box.
→ Transfer IV grouping variable to the **Post Hoc Tests** box and click **Tukey.**
→ **Continue.**
→ Back on the **Univariate** diolog box, click into the **Options** button. Tick **Descriptives, Estimates of Effect Size,** and **Homogeneity tests,** and click **Continue.**
→ Back on the **Univariate diolog** box, click into the **Plots** button, to reveal the **Univariate: Profile Plots** dialog box. Transfer your IV to the **Horizontal Axis,** and click on the activated **Add** button to transfer the name of IV to the **Plots** box below.

→ Continue.
→ OK to run the analysis.

Running a Mann-Whitney U using SPSS V14

Main Menu → Analyse → Nonparametric Tests → Independent Samples

→ Two-Independent-Samples dialog box.
→ Transfer the DV to the Test Variable List, and the IV to the Grouping Variable List. Click Define Groups, and enter the values for your two groups.
→ Under Test Type tick Mann-Whitney U.
→ Click the Exact button-to reveal the Exact Tests dialog box, and tick Exact.
→ Continue.
→ OK.

Running a Kruskal Wallis one-way ANOVA using SPSS V14

Main Menu → Analyse → Nonparametric Tests → K Independent Samples

→ Transfer the DV to the Test Variable List, and the IV to the Grouping Variable List. Click Define Groups, and enter the values for your two groups.
→ Under Test Type tick Kruskal-Wallis H. Click either Exact tests which can take some time to run, or leave at the default asymptotic p-value.
→ OK.

Running a χ^2 using SPSS V14

Main Menu → Analyse → Nonparametric Tests → Chi-Square Test

→ Transfer DV into the Test Variable List.
→ Click into Exact… to open the Exact Test dialog box, and choose Exact.
→ Click Continue.
→ OK.

Comparisons within Groups

Running a dependent t-test using SPSS V14

Main Menu → Analyse → Compare Means → Paired-Samples T Test

→ Transfer faired Variables box.
→ Click into Options, and check that your confidence interval is set at 95%.
→ OK.

Running a repeated one-way ANOVA using SPSS V14

Main Menu → Analyse → General Linear Model → Repeated Measures

→ **Repeated Measures Define Factor(s)** dialog box.
→ Replace **factor1** from the **Within-Subject Factor Name**, and add the name of your first factor.
→ Add the number of levels into the **Number of Levels** box.
→ Click the highlighted **Add** button below, to enter the factor name and the number of levels into the box. To add additional factors repeat the procedure.
→ Add the name of your DV into the **Measure Name** box and press **Add**.
→ Click **Define** to return to the **Repeated Measures ANOVA** dialog box.
→ **Continue.**
→ **OK.**

Running a Wilcoxon paired signed ranks test using SPSS V14

Main Menu → Analyse → Nonparametric Tests → Related Samples

→ **Two-Related-Samples Tests.**
→ Transfer the variable names to the **Test Pair(s) List** box.
→ Under **Test Type** tick **Wilcoxon.**
→ Click the **Exact** button at the end of the dialog box, to open up the dialogue box, and tick the **Exact** button.
→ Click the **Options** button, to reveal the **Two-Related-Samples Tests: Options** dialogue box, and tick **Descriptive.**
→ **Continue.**
→ **OK.**

Running a Friedman's ANOVA using SPSS V14

Main Menu → Analyse → Nonparametric Tests → K Related Samples

→ **Tests for Several Related Samples.**
→ Transfer over the relevant variables to the **Test Variables** box.
→ Under **Test Type** tick **Friedman.**
→ Click the **Exact** button at the end of the dialog box, to open up the dialogue box, and tick the **Exact** button.
→ **Continue.**
→ **OK.**

Relationsships Between Variables

Running a simple correlation using SPSS V14

Main Menu → Analyse → Correlate → Bivariate

→ Transfer over the two variables into the **Variables** box.
→ Under **Correlation Coefficients** tick **Pearson**.
→ Under **Tests of Significance** tick **Two-tailed.**
→ Tick **Flag significant correlations**.
→ Click into the **Options** button, to reveal the **Bivariate Correlations: Options**, to calculate means and standard deviations.
→ Tick **Means and Standard Deviations**.
→ **Continue**.
→ **OK**.

Running a Kendall's tau and Spearman's rho using SPSS V14

Main Menu → Analyse → Correlate → Bivariate

→ Under **Correlation Coefficients**, **Pearson** is set at default, click off **Pearson**.
→ Tick **Kendall's tau-b** and **Spearman**.
→ Transfer over the two variables into the **Variables** box.
→ Under **Tests of Significance** tick **Two-tailed**.
→ Tick **Flag significant correlations**.
→ **Continue**.
→ **OK**.

(Note: These two statistics are based on different theoretical foundations hence different r values. Kendall's tau statistic τ gives a lower correlation value than spearmans rho.)

Running Phi and Cramér's V using SPSS V14

Main Menu → Analyse → Descriptive Statistics → Crosstabs

→ Transfer variable for rows into **Row(s)**, and variable for columns into **Column(s)**.
→ Click into **Statistics**, to reveal the Crosstabs: Statistics dialog box.
→ Under **Chi-square** tick **Phi and Cramér's V**.
→ Click into **Cells** to reveal the **Crosstabs: Cell Display**. Under **Counts** tick **Observed** and **Expected**.

→ Continue.
→ OK.

(Note: it is better to report Cramérs V than phi.)

Running simple linear regression using SPSS V14

Main Menu → **Analyse** → **Regression** → **Linear**

→ To reveal the **Linear Regression** dialog box.
→ Transfer the DV into the **Dependent** box.
→ Transfer the IV into the **Independent(s)** list.
→ Click into **Statistics**, to reveal the **Linear Regression: Statistics** dialog box. Under **Regression Coefficients** tick **Estimates**. Select **Model fit**, and **Descriptives**. Under **Residuals** tick **Casewise diagnostics**.
→ Click into **Plots** to reveal the **Linear Regression: Plots**. Transfer standardised predicted residuals i.e. **ZRESID** to **Y** box, and the standardised predicted scores, i.e. **ZPRED** to the **X** box.
→ Continue.
→ OK.

Running multiple regression using SPSS V14

Main Menu → **Analyse** → **Regression** → **Linear**

→ To reveal the **Linear Regression** dialog box.
→ Transfer the DV into the **Dependent** box.
→ Transfer the IVs into the **Independent(s)** list.
→ Click into **Statistics**, to reveal the **Linear Regression: Statistics** dialog box. Under **Regression Coefficients** tick **Estimates**. Select **Model fit**, and **Descriptives**. Under **Residuals** tick **Casewise diagnostics**.
→ Click into **Plots** to reveal the **Linear Regression: Plots**. Transfer standardised predicted residuals, i.e. **ZRESID** to **Y** box, and the standardised predicted scores, i.e. **ZPRED** to the **X** box.
→ Continue.
→ OK.

(Note: the procedure for the simple and multiple linear regression is the same, except that for simple linear regression only one IV is brought over, whereas two or more IVs are brought over for multiple regression.)

REFERENCES

Abelson, R. P. (1995) *Statistics as Principled Argument*. Hillsdale, NJ: Lawrence Erlbaum Associates Inc.

Ad Hoc Working Group for Critical Appraisal of the Medical Literature (1987) A proposal for more informative abstracts of clinical articles. *Ann. Intern. Med., 106*, 598–604.

Adler, P. A. and Adler, P. (1987) *Membership Roles in Field Research*. Newbury Park, CA: Sage Publications Ltd.

APA (American Psychological Association) (2002) Ethical principles of psychologists and code of conduct. *American Psychologist, 57*, 1060–73.

APA (American Psychological Association) (2001) *Publication Manual of the American Psychological Association* (5th edn). Washington, DC: American Psychological Association.

Anastasi, A. and Urbina, S. (1997) *Psychological Testing* (7th edn). Upper Saddle River, New Jersey: Prentice Hall.

Atkinson, J. W. (1964) *An Introduction to Motivation*. New York: D. Van Nostrand Company.

Auberbach, C. F. and Silverstein, L. B. (2003) *Qualitative Data: An Introduction to Coding and Analysis*. New York: New York University Press.

Bandura, A. (1988) Self-regulation of motivation and action through goal systems. In V. Hamilton, G. H. Bower and N. H. Fryda (eds) *Cognitive Perspectives on Emotion and Motivation*. Dordrecht, The Netherlands: Martinus Nijhoff. pp. 37–61.

Barry, (2004) 'the Effects of Spatial Ability on the Learning of Complex Scientific Instructional Material'.

Bazeley, P. and Richards, L. (2003). *The NVivo® Qualitative Project Book*. London; Sage Publications Ltd.

Berg, B. (1989) *Qualitative Research Methods for the Social Sciences*. Boston: Allyn & Bacon.

Bishop, C. M. (1994) Neural networks and their applications. *Review of Scientific Instruments, 65(6)*, 1803–32.

Blanck, P. D., Bellack, A. S., Rosnow, R. L., Rotheram-Borus, M. J. and Schooler, N. R. (1992) Scientific rewards and conflicts of ethical choices in human subjects research. *American Psychologist, 47*, 959–65.

BPS (British Psychological Society) (1978) *Code of Conduct, Ethical Principles and Guidelines*.

Camic, P., Rhodes, J. and Yardley, L. (eds) (2004) *Qualitative Research in Psychology: Expanding Perspectives in Methodology and Design*. Washington: APA.

Campion, M. A., Palmer, D. K. and Campion, J. E. (1998) Structuring employment interviews to improve the reliability and validity, and user reaction. *Current Directions in Psychological Science, 7(3)*, 77–83.

Cannell, C. F. and Kahn, R. L. (1968) Interviewing. In G. Lindzey and E. Aronson (eds) *The Handbook of Social Psychology, 11* (2nd edn). Reading, MA: Addison-Wesley. pp. 526–95.

Chalmers, A. (1990) *Science and its Fabrication.* Buckingham: Open University Press.

Chambers, J. M. (1983) *Graphical Methods for Data Analysis (Statistics).* Chapman & Hall/CRC: New Ed Edition.

Charmaz, K. (2000) Grounded theory: Objectivist and constructivist methods. In N. K. Denzin and Y. S. Lincoln (eds) *Handbook of Qualitative Research* (2nd edn). Thousand Oaks, CA: Sage Publications Ltd. pp. 509–35.

Clark-Carter, D. (2004) *Quantitative Psychological Research: A Student's Handbook.* Hove and New York: Psychology Press.

Clark-Carter, D. (1997) *Doing Quantitative Psychological Research: From Design to Report.* Hove, East Sussex: Taylor & Francis: Psychology Press.

Cohen, J. (1988) *Statistical Power Analysis for the Behavioral Sciences* (2nd edn). Hillsdale, NJ: Lawrence Erlbaum Associates.

Corbin, J. and Strauss, A. L. (1990) Grounded theory research: Procedures, canons, and evaluative criteria. *Qualitative Sociology, 13(1)*, 3–21.

CPA (Canadian Psychological Association) (2000) Canadian Code of Ethics for Psychologists (3rd edn). Retrieved 10 May 2006, from http://www.cpa.ca/cpasite/userfiles/Documents/Canadian%20Code%20of%20Ethics%20for%20Psycho.pdf

Cronbach, L. J. (1957) The two disciplines of scientific psychology. *American Psychologist, 12*, 671–84.

Cryer, P. (2000) *The Research Student's Guide to Success.* UK: Open University Press.

Cutliffe, J. R. (2000) Metodological issues in grounded theory. *Journal of Advanced Nursing, 31(6)*, 1476–83.

Daft, R. L. (1985) Why I recommend that your manuscript be rejected and what you can do about it. In L. L. Cummings and P. J. Frost (eds), *Publishing in the Organizational Sciences,* Homewood, IL: Irwin. pp. 193–209.

Denzin, N. K. and Lincoln, Y. S. (eds) (1994) Introduction: Entering the field of qualitative research. In *Handbook of Qualitative Research.* Thousand Oaks, CA: Sage Publications Ltd. pp. 1–18.

Denzin, N. (1997) *Interpretative Ethnography: Ethnographic Practices for the 21st Century.* Thousand Oaks, CA: Sage Publications Ltd.

Donaghy, W. C. (1990) The interview, skills and applications. Salem, WI: Sheffield.

Douglas, J. D. (1970) *Understanding Everyday life: Toward the Reconstruction of Sociological Knowledge.* Chicago: Aldine.

Downs, C. W., Smejak, G. P. and Martin, E. (1980) *Professional Interviewing.* New York: Harper & Row.

Eisner, E. W. (1991) *The Enlightened Eye: Qualitative inquiry and the Enhancement of Educational Practice.* New York, NY: Macmillan Publishing Company.

Ericsson, K. A. (2002) Toward a procedure for eliciting verbal expression of non-verbal experience without reactivity: Interpreting the verbal overshadowing effect within the theoretical framework for protocol analysis. *Applied Cognitive Psychology, 16*, 981–7.

European Federation of Psychologists Associations (1995) *Meta-code of Ethics.* Brussels: European Federation of Psychologists Association.

Fassinger, R. E. (2005) Paradigms, praxis, problems, and promise: Grounded theory in counselling psychology research. *Journal of Counselling Psychology, 52(2)*.

Fine, M. (1992) Disruptive Voices: *The Transgressive Possibilities of Feminist Research*. Ann Arbor: University of Michigan Press.

Fisher, C. (2003) *Decoding the Ethics Code: A Practical Guide for Psychologists*. Thousand Oaks, CA: Sage Publications Ltd.

Foster, J. and Parker, I. (1999) *Carrying out Investigations in Psychology: Methods and Statistics*. Leicester: PBS Books.

Gauthier, J. (2003) Toward a universal declaration of ethical principles for psychologists. In J. B. Overmier and J. A. Overmier (eds) *Psychology: IUPsyS Global Resource*, Hove, UK: Psychology Press.

Gibbs, G. R. (2002) *Qualitative Data Analysis: Explorations with NVivo*. Buckingham: Open University Press.

Gilbert, N. (1996) Writing social research. In N. Gilbert (ed.) *Researching Social Life*. London: Sage Publications Ltd. pp. 328–44.

Glaser, B. G. and Strauss, A. L. (1967) *The Discovery of Grounded Theory: Strategies for Qualitative Research* Chicago: Aldine.

Glaser, B. J. (1995) More grounded theory methodology: A reader. Mill Valley, CA: Sociology Press.

Glaser, B. J. (1998) *Doing grounded theory: Issues and discussions*. Mill Valley, CA: sociology Press.

Graziano, A. M. and Raulin, M. L. (1997) *Research Methods: A Process of Inquiry*. New York: Harper Collins.

Hammersley, M. and Atkinson, P. (1995) *Ethnography: Principles in Practice* (2nd edn). London: Routledge.

Harré, R. (1997) Is there a basic ontology for the physical sciences? *Dialectica, 51*, 17–34.

Hartley, J. (2004) Case Study Research. In C. Cassell and G. Symon (eds) *Essential Guide to Qualitative Methods in Organizational Research*. London: Sage Publications Ltd. pp. 323–33.

Hartley, J. (2003) Improving the clarity of journal abstracts in psychology: The case for structure. *Science Communication, 24(3)*, 366–79.

Have, P., ten. (1999) *Doing Conversation Analysis: A Practical Guide*. London: Sage Publications Ltd.

Havercamp, B. E. (2005) Ethical perspectives on qualitative research in applied psychology. *Journal of Counselling Psychology, 52(2)*, 146–55.

Henwood, K. L. and Pidgeon, N. F. (2003) Grounded theory in psychology. In P. M. Camic, J. E. Rhodes and L. Yardley (eds) *Qualitative Research in Psychology: Expanding Perspectives in Methodology and Design*. Washington, DC: American Psychological Association Press. pp. 131–55.

Hilgard, E. R. (1987) *Psychology in America: A Historical Survey*. San Diego, CA: Harcourt Brace Jovanovick.

Hoaglin, D. C., Mosteller, F. and Tukey, J. W. (1991) *Fundamentals of Exploratory Analysis of Variance* (eds) (Wiley Series in Probability and Mathematical Statistics). USA: Wiley-Interscience.

Holloway, I. (1997) *Basic Concepts for Qualitative Research*. Oxford: Blackwell Science.

International Union of Psychological Science (1976) *Statement by the International Union of Psychological Science*. Amnesty International.

Irwin, D. M. (1980) *Observational Strategies for Child Study.* New York: Holt, Rinehart and Winston.

Jonas, H. (1969) Philosophical reflections on experimenting with human subjects, *Daedalus, 98,* 219–47. Cited in W. Mackillop and P. Johnston (1986) Ethical problems in clinical research: The need for empirical studies of the clinical trial process. *Journal of Chronic Diseases, 39,* 177–88.

Jones, E. and Gerard, H. B. (1967) *Foundations in Social Psychology.* New York: Wiley.

Judd, C. M. and McClelland, G. H. (1989) *Data Analysis: A Model-Comparison Approach.* San Diego, CA: Harcourt Brace Jovanovich.

Kanfer, R. (1987) Task-specific motivation: An integrative approach to issues of measurement, mechanisms, processes, and determinants. *Journal of Social & Clinical Psychology, 5,* 237–64.

Kanfer, R. and Ackerman, P. L. (1989) Motivation and cognitive abilities: An integrative/aptitude-treatment interaction approach to skill acquisition. *Journal of Applied Psychology, 74(4),* 657–90.

Kici, G. and Westhoff, K. (2004) Evaluation of requirements for the assessment and construction of interview guides in psychological assessment. *European Journal of Psychological Assessment, 20(2),* 83–98.

King, N. (2004). Using interviews in qualitative research. In C. Cassell and G. Symon (eds) *Essential Guide to Qualitative Methods in Organizational Research.* London: Sage Publications Ltd. pp.11–22.

King, N. (1994) The qualitative research interview. In C. Cassel and G. Simon (eds) *Qualitative Methods in Organizational Research: A Practical Guide.* London: Sage Publications Ltd. pp.14–36.

Kotter, J. P. (1996) *Leading Change.* Boston, MA: Harvard Business School Press.

Kvale, S. (1996) *Interviews: An Introduction to Qualitative Research Interviewing.* London; Thousand Oaks, California: Sage Publications Ltd.

Kvale, S. (1983) The qualitative research interview: A phenomenological and hermeneutic mode of understanding. *Journal of Phenomenological Psychology, 14,* 171–96.

Langdridge, D. (2004) *Introduction to Research Methods and Data Analysis in Psychology.* Glasgow: Pearson Education Limited.

Leonard, D. and Swap, W. (1999) *When Sparks Fly: Igniting Creativity in Groups.* Boston, MA: Harvard Business School Press.

Levine, J. H. (1993) *Exceptions are the Rule: An Inquiry into Methods in the Social Sciences.* Boulder, CO: Westview.

Lewin, K. (1936) *Principles of Topological Psychology.* New York: McGraw-Hill.

Lindsay, G. (1996) Psychology as an ethical discipline and profession. *European Psychologist, 1,* 79–88.

Lipsey, M. W. (1990) *Design Sensitivity.* London: Sage Publications Ltd.

Locke, E. and Henne, D. (1986) Work motivation theories. In C. L. Cooper and I. Robertson (eds) *International Review of Industrial & Organizational Psychology.* Chichester, England: Wiley. pp.1–35.

Locke, E. and Latham, G. (2004) What should we do about motivation theory? Six recommendations for the twenty-first century. *Academy of Management Review, 29(3),* 388–403.

Locke, E. and Latham, G. (1990) *A Theory of Goal Setting and Task Performance.* Englewood Cliffs, NJ: Prentice-Hall.

Lofland, J. and Lofland, L. (1984) *Analyzing Social Settings.* Belmont, CA: Wadsworth.

Maslow, A. H. (1943). A theory of human motivation. *Psychological Review, 50,* 370–396.

Maxwell, J. A. (1992) Understanding and validity in qualitative research. In A. M. Huberman and M.B. Miles (eds) *The qualitative researcher's companion.* Thousand Oaks, CA: Sage Publications Ltd. pp. 37–64. (Reprinted from *Harvard Educational Review* (1992) *62(3),* 279–300.)

McGrath, J. E. (1982). Dilemmatics: The study of research choices and dilemmas. In J. E. McGrath and R. A. Kuhla (eds) *Judgement Calls in Research.* Beverly Hills, CA: Sage Publications Ltd pp. 69–102

Meltzoff, J. (1999) *Critical Thinking about Research: Psychology and Related Fields.* Washington, DC: APA.

Micceri, T. (1989) The unicorn, the normal curve, and other improbable creatures. *Psychological Bulletin, 105,* 156–66.

Miles, M. B. and Huberman, A. M. (1994) *Qualitative Data Analysis* (2nd edn). Thousand Oaks, CA: Sage Publications Ltd.

Morrow, S. L. and Smith, M. L. (2005). Qualitative research for counseling psychology. In S. D. Brown and R. W. Lents (eds) *Handbook of Counseling Psychology* (3rd edn). New York: Wiley. pp. 199–230.

Morrow, S. L. (2005) Quality and trustworthiness in qualitative research in counseling psychology. *Journal of Counseling Psychology, 52,* 250–60.

Morse, J. M. (2000) Determining sample size. *Qualitative Health Research, 10(1),* 3–5.

Morse, J. M. (1994a) Designing funded qualitative research . In N. Denzin and Y. Lincoln (eds) *Handbook of Qualitative Research,* Thousand Oaks, CA: Sage Publications Ltd. pp. 220–35.

Morse, J. M. (1994b) Emerging from the data: the cognitive processes of analysis in qualitative inquiry. In J. M. Morse (ed.) *Critical Issues in Qualitative Research Methods.* Thousand Oaks, CA: Sage Publications Ltd.

Morse, J. M. (ed.) (1989) *Qualitative Nursing Research: A Contemporary Dialogue.* Newbury Park, CA: Sage Publications Ltd.

New Zealand Psychological Society (2002) *Code of Ethics.* Aukland: Author.

O'Loughlin, (2005) The Influence of Unilateral Forced Nostril Breathing on Performance of Lateralised Cognitive Tests in Trained and Untrained Participants.

Oppenheim, A. N. (1992) *Questionnaire Design, Interviewing and Attitude Measurement.* London: Printer.

Orr, J. M., Sackett, P. R. and DuBois, C. L. Z. (1991) Outlier detection and treatment in I/O psychology: A survey of researcher beliefs and an empirical illustration. *Personnel Psychology, 44, 473–86.*

Pack-Brown, S. and Williams, C. (2003) *Ethics in a Multicultural Context.* Thousand Oaks, CA: Sage Publications Ltd.

Pendersen, P. (1995) Culture-centred ethical guidelines for counsellors. In J. Ponteratto, J. Caca, L. Suzuki and C. Alexander, *A Handbook of Multicultural Conselling.* Thousand Oaks, CA: Sage Publications Ltd. pp. 34–49.

Pettifor, J. (2004) Professional ethics across national boundaries. *European Psychologist, 9(4),* 264–72.

Pettifor, J. (1996) Ethics: Virtue and politics in the science and practice of psychology. *Canadian Psychology, 37,* 1–12.

Pomerantz, A. and Fehr, B. J. (1997) Conversation analysis: An approach to the study of social action as sense making practices. In T. A. van Dijk (ed.) *Discourse As A Social Interaction*. London: Sage Publications Ltd.

Popper, K. (1959) *The Logic of Scientific Discovery*. New York: Basic Books, Inc.

Potter, J (1996) *Representing Reality: Discourse, Rhetoric and Social Construction*. Thousand Oaks, CA: Sage Publications Ltd.

Potter, J. and Wetherell, M. (1987) *Discourse and Social Psychology*. London: Sage Publications Ltd.

Psychological Society of Ireland (PSI) (1998) *Code of Professional Ethics and List of Registered Psychologists 1998*. Dublin: Author.

PSI (2003). Code of Professional Ethics of the Psychological Society of Ireland. Dublin: Author.

Punch, K. F. (2005) *Introduction to Social Research: Quantitative & Qualitative Approaches*. London: Sage Publications Ltd.

Punch, K. F. (2001) *Developing Effective Research Proposals*. London: Sage Publications Ltd.

Reissman, C. (1993). *Narrative Analysis: Qualitative Research Methods Series 30*. Newbury Park, CA: Sage Publications Ltd.

Rennie, D. L. (1995). On the rheotorics of Social Science: Let's not conflate natural science and human science. *The Humanistic Psychologist, 23*, 321–332.

Rosenthal, R. (1994) Science and ethics in conducting, analysing, and reporting psychological research. *Psychological Science, 5*, 127–34.

Rosnow, R. L. and Rosenthal, R (1997) *People Studying People: Artifacts and Ethics in Behavioral Research*. New York: W. H. Freeman & Company.

Sartorius, N. (1999). The declaration of Madrid and current psychiatric practice: Users' and advocates' views -Introduction. *Current Opinion in Psychiatry, 12(1)*, 1–2.

Schuman, H. and Kalton, G. (1985) Survey methods. In G. Lindzey and E. Aronson (eds) *The Handbook of Social Psychology*. New York: Random House. pp. 635–98.

Seale, C. (2003) Quality in qualitative research. In Y. S. Lincoln and N. K. Denzin (eds) *Turning Points in Qualitative Research*. Walnut Creek, CA: AltaMira Press. pp. 169–84.

Seidman, I. (1998) *Interviewing as Qualitative Research: A Guide for Researchers in Education and the Social Science* (2nd edn). New York: Teachers College Press.

Shaugnessy, J. J., Zechmeister, E. B. and Zechmeister, J. S. (2003) *Research Methods in Psychology* (6th edn). New York: Mc Graw Hill Inc.

Shweder, R. A. (1996) Quanta and qualia: What is the 'object' of ethnographic research? In R. Jessor, A. Colby and R. A. Shweder (eds) *Ethnography and Human Development: Context and Meaning in Social Inquiry*. Chicago: University Press. pp. 175–182.

Silverman, D. (2004) *Interpreting Qualitative Data: Methods for Analysing Talk, Text and Interaction*. London: Sage Publications Ltd.

Silverman, D. (2003) *Doing Qualitative Research: A Practical Handbook*. London: Sage Publications Ltd.

Sinclair, C., Poizner, S., Gilmour-Barrett, K. and Randall, D. (1987) The development of a code of ethics for Canadian psychologists. *Canadian Psychology, 28*, 1–8.

Smith, J. A. (1996) Evolving issues for qualitative research. In J. Richardson (ed.) *Handbook of Qualitative Research Methods*. Leicester: BPS. pp. 189–202.

Smith, J. A. (ed.) (2003) *Qualitative Psychology: A Practical Guide to Research Methods*. London: Sage Publications Ltd.

Smith, J. A. and Osborn, M. (2003) Interpretative phenomenological analysis. In J. A. Smith (ed.) *Qualitative Psychology: A Practical Guide to Research Methods*. London: Sage Publications Ltd. pp. 51–80.

Smith, S. and Richardson, D. (1983). Amelioration of deception and harm in psychological research: The important role of debriefing. *Journal of Personality and Social Psychology, 44*, 1075–1082.

Stacey, J. (1991) *Brave New Families*. New York: Basic Books.

Staddon, J. E. R. and Bueno, J. L. O. (1991) On models, behaviourism, and the neural basis of learning. *Psychological Science, 2*, 3–11.

Stark, C. (1998) Ethics in the research context: Misinterpretations and misplaced misgivings. *Canadian Psychology, 39(3)*, 202–11.

Sternberg, R. J. (2003) *The Psychologist's Companion: A Guide to Scientific Writing for Students and Researchers* (4th edn). New York: Cambridge University Press.

Strauss, A. and Corbin, J. (1998) *Basics of Qualitative Research*. Thousand Oaks, CA: Sage Publications Ltd.

Strauss, A. and Corbin, J. (1990) *Basics of Qualitative Research, Grounded Theory Procedures and Techniques*. London: Sage Publications Ltd.

Thorne, S. (1997) The art (and science) of critiquing qualitative research. In J. M. Morse (ed.) *Completing a Qualitative Project: Details and Dialogue*. Thousand Oaks, CA: Sage. pp. 117–32.

Todd, Z., Nerlich, B., McKeown, S. and Clarke, D. (eds) (2003) *Mixing Methods in Psychology*. Hove and New York: Taylor & Francis: Psychology Press.

Tukey, J. W. (1977) *Exploratory Data Analysis*. Reading, MA: Addison-Wesley.

Underwood, B. J. (1957) An orientation for research on thinking. *Psychological Review, 59*, 209–20.

Vicari, S. and Troilo, G. (2000) Organizational creativity: a new perspective. In G. von Krogh, et al. (eds) *Knowledge Creation: A Source of Value*. New York: St. Martins Press.

Wetherell, M., Taylor, S. and Yates, S. (eds) (2001) *Discourse as Data: A Guide for Analysis*. London: Sage Publications Ltd.

Whetten, D. A. (1989). What constitutes a theoretical contribution? *Academy of Management, 14(4)*, 490–495.

Wolcott, H. F. (1990) *Writing up Qualitative Research*. Newbury Park, CA: Sage Publications Ltd.

Woods, (2004) 'Mood Dependent Memory in Eyewitness Testimony: The Effects if Negative Mood Regulation at Recall on the Accuracy of Report'.

York University Task Force on Ethical Issues in Research (1992) *Interim Report*. North York, Ont: York University Task Force on Ethical Issues in Research.

Yukl, G. (2002) *Leadership in Organisations* (5th edn). London: Prentice-Hall International Publishing.

INDEX